PUBLIC FINANCE

Selected Readings

PUBLIC FINANCE

SELECTED READINGS

Helen A. Cameron
OHIO STATE UNIVERSITY

William Henderson
DENISON UNIVERSITY

Random House | New York

Library of Congress Catalog Card Number: 65–23333
MANUFACTURED IN THE UNITED STATES OF AMERICA BY
H. Wolff Book Manufacturing Co., New York

Design by Tere LoPrete

❦ *Contents*

SECTION IV

Criteria for Evaluating Government Financing 155

SECTION V

Local Government Finances 277

PUBLIC FINANCE

Selected Readings

SECTION I

❧ *Budgeting*

The federal budget is a plan for the management and control of the government's fiscal activities, and thus a document which must serve as a unique source of accounting and economic data. For the fiscal theorist this means that information relating to economic consequences of government resource use—the potential effects of federal activities upon resource allocation, income distribution, employment, and growth—must be readily available. Yet, its ultimate usefulness depends on budget format, procedure, and contents.

At present, changes in budget format are of concern because the presentation of expenditure data is generally incompatible with the primary functions of budget use. Problems involved in evaluating the economy's performance with present budget data are analyzed by Roy Moor in the first article, "The Budget Doesn't Tell Us Enough." Moor uncovers the weaknesses in current procedures and assesses the budget's ability to provide information on the probable effects of projected government policies. Improvements in budget reporting are also considered.

The attainment of the "optimum" level of government expenditure is not only a function of budget procedure, but rests on the administration's overall budget policy as well. Levels of expenditure for various governmental functions are established by the executive branch of the federal government in preparing the budget document—this is the first stage in the budget "cycle." In the second stage, Congress reviews the requests for expenditures in extensive committee hearings, thus providing for legislative control over executive decisions. The level of expenditures finally arrived at during this period of bargaining between the executive and legislative branches of government reflects a consensus as to the level of social wants to be satisfied through government actions. Richard Musgrave, in the article "Principles of Budget Determination," presents a series of guidelines for achieving optimal budget policy based on an evaluation of social wants and the alternative ways and means of providing for all human wants.

THE BUDGET DOESN'T
TELL US ENOUGH

Roy E. Moor

In an average day, the federal government withdraws about $400 million from the national economy and injects a comparable amount into it. The best source of information on these cash inflows and outflows is the federal budget, a document assembled annually by the Bureau of the Budget in cooperation with the various agencies of the federal government. The primary focus of the budget, which is presented to Congress each January by the President, is on the appropriations requested by the agencies for functions to be undertaken during the forthcoming fiscal year.

Since the government's economic policies influence all of us —and the money used to implement these policies belongs to all of us—we should know how effective the federal budget is as an instrument for providing information on the nature and significance of government financial policies. Precisely what in-

Reprinted from *Challenge, The Magazine of Economic Affairs* (May, 1962), pp. 16-19, by permission of the publisher. Published by the Institute of Economic Affairs, New York University. This article is based on Roy E. Moor's longer study, "The Federal Budget as an Economic Document."

formation should the budget contain if citizens are to understand the financial operations of the federal government? How well does the present budget reflect the influence of the government on the economy? How can the structure of the budget be revised to more clearly reflect that influence?

I shall attempt to answer these questions one by one later on. First, however, it is important to understand the decision-making process by which the level and composition of federal receipts and expenditures, as estimated in the budget, are finally determined.

On the revenue side, tax bills originate in the House of Representatives. They go first to the House Ways and Means Committee and later to the Senate Finance Committee. Also, of course, many tax decisions are made within the Internal Revenue Service and in the federal courts.

On the expenditure side, the process is more complex. Any Congressional committee may initially consider legislation authorizing a specific agency of the government to perform a certain function. (Thus, federal expenditure programs are not weighed by the same committees which consider revenue matters.) If Congress enacts such legislation, the next step is for the government agency involved to request from Congress an appropriation, a request considered first by the Appropriations Committee. If the appropriation is granted, the Bureau of the Budget apportions the specified amount to the agency. Then the agency hires personnel, makes contracts with private firms, or in other ways obligates the government. Finally, payments are made to those rendering the services contracted for by the government.

Decisions made at each of these stages determine the ultimate level and nature of federal receipts and expenditures. Moreover, since the decisions are overt, individuals and business firms can react as each of the decisions is being made. For example, while Congress is considering the closing of a tax loophole, taxpayers who are benefiting from the loophole are placed on notice that more funds may have to be set aside for taxes in the future. Similarly, the effects of a decision to build a new missile will begin to occur long before the government makes the expenditures necessary to pay for the missile. Contractors will be hiring workmen, purchasing capital equipment and actually producing the required items before they receive payment from the government.

The complex process I have just described does not by any means tell the whole story of the full extent of government receipts and expenditures arising from budget decisions. On the revenue side, in addition to individual income taxes, corporate income taxes and excise taxes, the government receives every year substantial funds from customs collections, estate and gift taxes, and Social Security and unemployment insurance taxes. The gross receipts from government enterprises—the Post Office Department, the Commodity Credit Corporation, the Federal National Mortgage Association, etc.—also come to several billions of dollars.

Then there are the miscellaneous receipts from fees, fines, gifts, rents and sales of products. And there are the bank balances in foreign countries created by sales of U.S. government supplies to those countries. Finally, the federal government obtains money by printing it. While most new currency replaces old money being taken out of circulation, it must be recognized that the government *can* print money and thereby increase its bank balances.

On the expenditure side, it must be noted that the federal government spends considerably more than is called for by the items in the conventional budget. In 1960, for example, the government paid out, over and above expenditures for budgeted items, more than $5 billion in refunds on taxes that had been previously collected. Through its Employment Trust Funds, the government also paid out more than $16 billion for retirement benefits and unemployment compensation. In addition, expenditures by government enterprises amounted to several billions, foreign balances were depleted by more than $1 billion, and more than $7 billion worth of old currency was purchased.

The federal budget should ideally provide information on all of these cash flows. However, the budget is concerned primarily with the *future* policies of the government, and the statistics in the budget are based on estimates, projections and guesses. These estimates are for several different types of situations, including:

1. Commitments which exist at the time the projections are made—e.g., expenditures for construction already in process.

2. Programs that remain relatively stable year after year.

3. Projections of changes in the private economy—changes which may affect, for example, the level of unemployment compensation payments.

4. Assumptions about noneconomic variables, such as weather conditions (which influence agricultural subsidies).

5. Programs that have recently been initiated and for which no prior experience is available.

6. Proposals that have not yet been enacted. The 1963 budget, for example, includes a reduction in agricultural expenditures of $500 million on the assumption that Congress will enact new agricultural legislation. However, President Kennedy had not even recommended any legislation on this subject to Congress at the time the budget was presented.

All of these different types of estimates are added together to develop budget totals, and no distinctions are made in the budget between the various types of "guestimates."

Once presented to Congress, the budget goes to the House Appropriations Committee, where it is dismantled, never to be assembled again. Gradually, the House Appropriations Committee releases individual appropriations bills which pass through normal legislative channels. However, Congress never examines the budget as a whole in terms of all government expenditures and receipts. After Congress adjourns, the Bureau of the Budget releases a small pamphlet, "The Mid-Year Budget Review," which revises the budget estimates on the basis of the Congressional actions. This pamphlet receives much less attention than it deserves in view of the fact that it is the only source—aside from the budget itself—for estimates on the amounts which the federal government may be receiving and spending during the forthcoming year.

All these processes have a tremendous impact on the private economy. They affect the use of economic resources, the stability of business conditions, the distribution of private income and the rate of the nation's economic growth. Ideally, the federal budget should provide information on each of these aspects of government influence on the economy. And since the budget is essentially a planning document for the future, the information on each of these matters should be in terms of programs contemplated in the future.

In the area of government influences on economic resources, a number of questions should be answered in the budget: How many new employees will be needed by the government for anticipated activities? How will their salaries compare with those of other government employees and similar occupations in private enterprise? Are the additional employees available? To what extent can employees now holding jobs with the government be shifted to new projects? Similar information should be available about capital goods obtained by the government. For example, what is the cheapest and most efficient way to construct a new office building, and what are the alternatives to constructing it?

Exactly the same type of information should be provided if the government intends to employ men and capital through intermediaries, such as government contractors. There are obvious political questions involved in the decision as to whether goods and services for the government should be produced by the government or by private firms. However, from an economic standpoint, there is little difference between the two alternatives. In both cases, resources are being used to satisfy government wants.

What about the government policies designed to influence economic stability? The budget should provide information about the primary and secondary effects of these policies and the timing of the effects. For example, the President has asked Congress for discretionary power to lower tax rates in a recession. If he is given this power, and decides to exercise it, individuals will have more disposable income. However, this increase in disposable income will have no economic effects until individuals actually begin to demand more goods and services.

Hence, it is important to estimate who will obtain the additional income, how rapidly it will be spent and how the economy will react to these increases in demand. If the economy reacts largely by raising prices, little or no increase in employment will occur. These are the types of estimates that would be useful to have in the budget, if the President expects to exercise his discretionary powers to reduce taxes or take other counter-cyclical actions.

The budget should also estimate the extent to which budget policies are likely to influence the distribution of personal incomes within the economy. For instance, if the government lets a new contract, what percentage of the expenditures will go to wage and salary earners, and what percentage will go to the contractors in the form of additional profits? What per cent of these wages and profits are likely to go to families with incomes below $10,000? If a corporate tax increase is contemplated, how much of the increase may be reflected in higher prices to consumers and how much in reduced profits? Such estimates are essential if an understanding of the government's potential impact on the economy is to be obtained.

Finally, the government contributes in many ways to the economic growth of the nation. It invests in the nation's future by making expenditures for education, highways, dams, harbors and many other items. The budget should provide some estimates of the future benefits that may be expected from such federal investments.

How well does our present federal budget provide information on the effects of contemplated government policies? One answer is that the 1963 budget presented to Congress by President Kennedy in January represents a substantial improvement

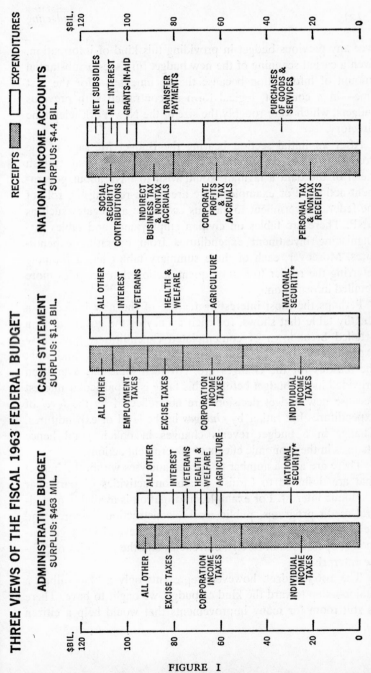

THREE VIEWS OF THE FISCAL 1963 FEDERAL BUDGET

RECEIPTS (shaded) EXPENDITURES (white)

ADMINISTRATIVE BUDGET
SURPLUS: $463 MIL.

Receipts: ALL OTHER, EXCISE TAXES, CORPORATION INCOME TAXES, INDIVIDUAL INCOME TAXES

Expenditures: ALL OTHER, INTEREST, VETERANS, HEALTH & WELFARE, AGRICULTURE, NATIONAL SECURITY*

CASH STATEMENT
SURPLUS: $1.8 BIL.

Receipts: ALL OTHER, EMPLOYMENT TAXES, EXCISE TAXES, CORPORATION INCOME TAXES, INDIVIDUAL INCOME TAXES

Expenditures: ALL OTHER, INTEREST, VETERANS, HEALTH & WELFARE, AGRICULTURE, NATIONAL SECURITY*

NATIONAL INCOME ACCOUNTS
SURPLUS: $4.4 BIL.

Receipts: SOCIAL SECURITY CONTRIBUTIONS, INDIRECT BUSINESS TAX & NONTAX ACCRUALS, CORPORATE PROFITS & TAX ACCRUALS, PERSONAL TAX & NONTAX RECEIPTS

Expenditures: NET SUBSIDIES, NET INTEREST, GRANTS-IN-AID, TRANSFER PAYMENTS, PURCHASES OF GOODS & SERVICES

$BIL. 120 100 80 60 40 20 0

*Includes spending for defense, atom and space development and international affairs

FIGURE I

over any previous budget in providing this kind of information. Even a casual scanning of the new budget furnishes a substantial amount of information because the document is—for the first time—in a compact, logical form as contrasted with previous budgets, which were roughly the size of the New York telephone directory.

After an initial section bearing the Budget Message of the President, there are a series of summary tables that furnish much of the data a layman would wish to have about government actions. For example, there are tables relating the role of the federal government to various economic aggregates such as GNP. There are tables on civilian employment and tables distinguishing investment expenditures from operating expenditures. Moreover, each of these summary tables has a footnote referring the reader to a subsequent section that provides more detailed information.

Perhaps the most interesting feature of the new budget is a lengthy table that shows, for each agency of the government, a detailed breakdown of contemplated expenditures, how these expenditures compare with those of previous years, and what the reasons for the changes are. No such table has ever been provided in the budget before. This table is of particular interest because new budget decisions are not reflected by the *level* of expenditures but rather by *changes* in the level of expenditures. Change in a budget reveals changes in policies and hence changes in the economic effects of government actions.

There are also a number of special analyses within the budget that are designed to furnish details on activities of particular economic interest. For example, information is available on federal credit programs, public works, construction, research and development activities, grants-in-aid to state and local governments, operations in foreign currencies and the activities of public enterprises.

The 1963 budget, however, represents only a first—albeit a major—step toward the kind of budget we ought to have. There is still room for many improvements that would help a citizen understand more fully the economic consequences of his govern-ment's actions. One of these improvements would be to provide more cataloging of the types of estimates contained in the budget. Uncertainties exist in making any estimates about the future, but some projected revenues and expenditures can be es-timated with much greater precision than others, and it would be helpful if the budget reader could understand the differences in types of estimates within the budget.

Another improvement would be to incorporate within the budget much of the information on government policies that is now available only within the various government agencies. The agencies obviously consider their own proposed policies in depth, and some of this detailed analysis would be extremely informative. In addition, much more information should be pro-vided on the nature of government employment—e.g., by pro-fessions, by salary levels, by amount of training, etc.

Further, the budget should provide greater detail on the oper-ations of government enterprises. These enterprises clearly have important economic effects. Yet they are frequently shown in the budget only by a single net figure representing the deficit or surplus of the enterprises. A number of government enterprises, particularly those dealing with financial matters, are not even shown in the budget. Many of these improvements can be made without significantly increasing the size of the budget document, and some of the material could be presented in supplementary analyses.

A major weakness of the present budget is that it does not indicate the timing of the effects of government policies. For example, as I have pointed out earlier, the impact of government contracts is felt by the economy long before federal expenditures related to these contracts are made, and tax changes usually affect the economy only sometime after the changes have oc-curred. Since the budget is based upon estimates in any case, these estimates should be constructed to reflect the best assess-ment of the time when the policies will affect the economy.

Moreover, since economic conditions change rapidly, the

budget estimates should be for quarterly periods and should be revised at the end of each quarter. At present, the budget contains only annual data. Once the budget estimates are presented, no periodic revision of these estimates occurs as conditions change. Only rarely is any explanation available concerning the reasons why final results vary from original estimates.

The present budget furnishes surprisingly little information on the actual cost of operating the government. Moreover, practically no estimates are available on the benefits being obtained from government expenditures. Comparisons of anticipated returns from investments and expected costs of investments are a basic part of any business budget. Such comparisons of costs and benefits should certainly be made by the federal government.

Finally, two general improvements should be considered. First, it would be highly desirable to extend the time horizon of the federal budget. Virtually all federal budget data is related to only a single year. It would be useful, for example, in appraising the significance of a proposed new hydroelectric program, to know the total anticipated cost of such a program, not merely that portion of the cost that will be incurred in the current year. It would also be helpful to have estimates of the total benefits anticipated over the life of the program, or at least for some reasonable period in the future. The budget should also provide more information on alternatives to proposed policies and the advantages and disadvantages of these alternatives.

Only with the aid of such information can the average citizen —and the policy maker—effectively assess the merits of government action. In the operation of a democratic society, the provision of such information would seem to be an essential goal of budgetary reform.

PRINCIPLES OF BUDGET DETERMINATION

Richard A. Musgrave

The people of the United States are generally agreed that the economy is to be organized on the premise of free consumer choice, that production is to be carried on by privately owned and operated firms, and that the market should be relied upon where possible to transmit the desires of the consumer to these firms. This being our basic form of organization, why is it that a substantial part of the economy's output is provided for through the budget? This question must be answered to begin with, if we wish to say something about the "proper" scope or composition of the budget.

The budgetary activity of the Government is needed because the pricing system of the market cannot deal with all the tasks that must be met in order to operate a sound economy and a healthy society. Certain tasks must be performed by government. Some may deplore this fact and dream of a setting where everyone could live in peace without any kind of governmental activity; others may feel that the necessity of social and eco-

Reprinted from 85th Congress, 1st Session, *Federal Expenditure Policy for Economic Growth and Stability* (Washington, D.C.: U.S. Government Printing Office, November, 1957), pp. 108-115.

nomic policy at the governmental level enriches the challenge of social life and makes for a more balanced society. Whatever one's values in this respect, the nature of things is such that budgetary activity is needed. The question then is under what circumstances and why this need arises.

The answer to this question is too complex to permit a simple and uniform solution. In my own thinking I have found it useful to distinguish between three major functions of budget policy, including—

1. The provision for social wants, which requires the Government to impose taxes and make expenditures for goods and services, to be supplied free of direct charge to the consumer;

2. The application of certain corrections to the distribution of income as determined in the market requiring the Government to add to the income of some by transfers while reducing the income of others by taxes; and

3. The use of budget policy for purposes of economic stabilization, rendering it necessary under some conditions to raise the level of demand by a deficit policy and under others to curtail demand by a surplus policy.

I shall comment briefly on the nature of each of these three functions, and on how they are interrelated.

PROVISION FOR SOCIAL WANTS

When I say that the Government must provide for the satisfaction of social wants, it does not follow that the Government itself must carry on the production of the goods and services which are needed to satisfy these wants. This may be necessary in some cases, as for instance with the provision for police protection, which can hardly be left to a private agent, but this is the exception rather than the rule. In most cases there is no such need. If new planes or government buildings are to be provided for, they may be purchased from private firms. The essence of budgetary provision for the satisfaction of social wants, therefore, is not production by government. It is payment for goods and services through budgetary finance, and supply of such services free of direct charge to the consumer.

What, then, are the social wants which must be provided for in this fashion? Some people have argued that they are wants which in a mysterious fashion are experienced by the Nation as a whole, and thus reflect the desires of the collective entity. This makes little sense in our setting. The desire for the satisfaction of social wants is experienced by individuals, no less than that for the satisfaction of private wants. This is not where the difference lies. The basic problem of social wants arises because their satisfaction, by their very nature, requires that the goods and services in question must be consumed in equal amounts by all. Social wants differ in this important respect from private wants, where each consumer may arrange his personal pattern of consumption such as to satisfy his own personal tastes. Thus, I may go to the market and purchase whatever amounts and type of clothing, housing, or food may suit my tastes and resources; but I must be satisfied with the same municipal services as are received by my neighbors, or with the same degree and type of foreign protection as is granted to all other citizens of the United States. This crucial fact, that certain services must be consumed in equal amounts by all, has important consequences.

One consequence is that you cannot apply what I like to refer to as the exclusion principle.[1] Since all people must consume the same amounts, no one can be excluded from the enjoyment of services aimed at the satisfaction of social wants. Everyone benefits, whether he contributes little or heavily to their cost. Now you might say that this is not too difficult a problem. Let the tax collector see to it that everyone pays. Unfortunately this overlooks the real difficulty. The real difficulty is not that people

[1] A second consequence, which has been pointed out by Professor Samuelson, is that there would be no single best solution to the budget problem, applying the usual criterion of economic efficiency, even if the preferences of all individuals were known. This aspect is omitted from the present discussion.

are unwilling to pay unless forced to; it is that of determining just how much various people should be called upon to contribute.

This difficulty does not arise with the satisfaction of private wants in the market. Here the individual consumer is forced to bid against others in order to get what he wants. The pricing mechanism, as it were, is an auctioning device by which things go to those who value them most, as evidenced by what they are willing to pay. People must bid to get what they want, and thereby provide the producer with the necessary signal of what to produce. In the case of social wants this signal is not forthcoming. Consumers know that they cannot be excluded and that their own contribution will weigh very lightly in the total picture. Thus they will not reveal their true preferences on a voluntary basis and offer to pay accordingly. Therefore it is no easy task to determine just what social wants should be recognized and how much each should be called upon to contribute. A further difference is this: For goods supplied in the satisfaction of private wants, competition sets a uniform price in the market. Individual consumers, depending on their personal tastes, can buy different amounts at that price. For goods supplied in the satisfaction of social wants, all must consume the same amount, and those who value public services more highly must pay a higher unit price.

This much is clear, but the question is just what should be supplied and just how much each should pay. The market cannot give the solution and a political process is needed to accomplish this task. By choosing among various budget programs, including various expenditure plans and various tax plans to cover the costs, the voters can express their preferences in the matter. Since they know that the law, once decided upon, will apply to each of them, they will find it in their interest to reveal their preferences and to vote for the plan, or the approximation thereto, which is most appealing to them. Thus preferences are revealed through the political process. While the minority might be dissatisfied, and strategies might be used in voting, an acceptable approximation to the preferences of the individual members of the group is reached.

All this is somewhat of an oversimplification. Individuals do not vote personally on each issue. Rather, they elect representatives who vote for them. Thus, the function of the representative is to crystallize public opinion with regard to such issues, budgetary and other, and to find groups of issues on which their constituents can agree. The Member of Congress is a go-between, whose function it is to work out compromises and solutions which are acceptable to the majority. By saying this I do not mean to slight the educational function of political leadership, nor do I wish to underestimate the importance of the contribution to be rendered by the executive branch and by the civil service. All these are important, but the basic process is one of transforming individual preferences into social wants.

In taking this view of social wants, I am thinking in the framework of what since Adam Smith has been referred to as the benefit principle of taxation. In other words, budget policy should provide for goods and services in response to the social wants of individuals, and to make this possible, individuals should contribute as closely as possible in response to their evaluation of these social wants. The great value of this approach, from the point of view of the economist, is that it requires us to determine public expenditures together with the revenue side of the budget. In this basic sense, there can be no theory of public expenditures without a theory of taxation, and vice versa.

What does the benefit approach mean regarding the distribution of the tax bill between people with different levels of income? I will not attempt to answer this in a categorical form, but I can point to the considerations on which the answer should depend: This is whether the goods and services supplied for the satisfaction of social wants are largely in the nature of necessities or luxuries. If they are largely in the nature of necessities, the answer leads to regression; if they are primarily in the nature of luxuries the answer points to progression. If people wish to spend the same fraction at all levels of income the answer leads to proportional taxation.[2] While a moderate degree of progression would seem the reasonable answer, this is by no means the only consideration entering into the distribution of the total tax bill.

Finally, a word about the matter of budgetary balance. Insofar as the satisfaction of social wants is concerned, the budget must be balanced, in the sense that goods provided for through the budget must be paid for over their useful life. This merely reflects the fact that resources used for the satisfaction of social wants cannot be used for other purposes, and someone must bear the cost. At the same time, we shall see that this is only one among other considerations. It does not follow that the total budget must be balanced.

I need hardly add that this brief discussion of social wants does not cover the entire picture. Not all public services are supplied in response to the individual preferences of the consumers. There may be instances when the majority decides that certain wants of individuals should be satisfied, even though these individuals would prefer to be given the cash and use it for other purposes. Free education or hospital services may be cited to illustrate this case. This type of public service requires a different explanation. However, note that the benefits derived from such services extend beyond the specific beneficiary, and thus approach what I have described as the central type of social wants.

ADJUSTMENTS IN THE DISTRIBUTION OF INCOME

I now turn to the second function of budget policy, which is to provide for adjustments in the distribution of income. We are all agreed that it is the responsibility of society to undertake certain adjustments in the distribution of income, which results from the forces of the market, the laws of inheritance, and differences in

[2] In technical terms, the tax structure will be proportional if the income elasticity of social wants is unity, progressive if it is greater than unity, and regressive if it is smaller than unity.

abilities to acquire income. Babies must be assured adequate food, the sick and the aged must be given proper care, and so forth. Beyond this, some hold to an idea of the good society which requires a fairly extensive degree of income equalization, others would favor a moderate degree of equalization, while still others might oppose any such measure and favor a high degree of inequality. These are matters of social philosophy and value judgment on which we all have our own views. Moreover, consideration must be given to the interrelation between income distribution and the total income which is available for distribution.

My concern here is not with the question as to which is the best set of values. While I happen to feel that progressive taxation is fair, this is not the point. My point is that if society wishes to make distributional adjustments, it is desirable as a matter of economic policy to make them through the tax-transfer mechanism of the budget. This is preferable to distributional adjustments via manipulation of particular prices, be it of products or of factors of production. Certainly, we cannot accept the stricture that the purpose of taxation is to finance public services and nothing else, and that, therefore, they "must not" be used for distributional adjustments. There is no such law in the order of things. Indeed, where distributional adjustments are to be made, this is the logical way in which to make them.

The determination of the desired degree and type of distributional adjustment is again a matter of political process, and I will not discuss it here. Let us suppose that some degree of income equalization is to be accomplished. This calls for taxes on some people with incomes above the average and for transfer payments to some people with incomes below the average. Insofar as distributional adjustments are concerned, the budget must again be balanced. Now you may argue that such a general tax-transfer scheme does not appear in the budget, except perhaps in the social-security programs, and that our budget does not engage in distributional adjustments. This is not the case. The distributional adjustments are implicit in a distribution of the overall tax bill in a way which is more progressive than would be justified on the basis of assigning the cost of social wants on a benefit basis. In other words, the budget as we know it and as it is enacted reflects the net result of various component policies. More about this in a moment.

Just as my discussion of allocating the cost of social wants moved in the context of a benefit approach to taxation, so does the problem of distributional adjustment belong in the sphere of ability to pay and equal sacrifice doctrines. The two approaches are wholly compatible if each is viewed in its own context. The argument that the cost of public services should be allocated in accordance with ability to pay sounds nice, but it gives us no foundation on which to decide what public services should be rendered. This can be done only in relation to individual preferences and implies the spirit of benefit taxation. I can see no other approach that leads to a sensible solution. At the same time, it is non sequitur to argue that progressive taxation is out of order because (assuming this to be the case) benefit taxation requires proportional rates. The element of progression may be called for in order to implement distributional adjustments, which is quite a different matter.

Failure to distinguish between the problem of distributional adjustment and the problem of providing for the satisfaction of social wants leads to confusion on both counts. If the degree of distributional adjustment is tied to the level of the budget, some may favor an increase in the level of public services as a means of extending distributional adjustments, even though they do not support budget expansion on the basis of benefit taxation; and others, who would favor an expansion of the budget on this basis, will oppose it because in practice it is related to an extension of distributional adjustments. Moreover, these relationships change with the level of taxation and the existing tax structure. While there was a time when the marginal taxpayer was the fellow with the large income, we are now in a situation where increased levels of public services largely involve increased tax contributions from (or exclude tax reductions for) people in the middle or middle to lower income groups. Thus the politics of the fiscal problem are changed and essential public services will go begging in the process.

BUDGET POLICY AND STABILIZATION

I now turn to my third function of budget policy, which is the use of tax and expenditure measures as a means of economic stabilization. The great achievement of the fiscal-policy discussion of the last 25 years is the by now fairly general recognition that fiscal policy must play an important role in economic stabilization. The old view that the budget should be balanced is applicable only if we consider our first and second functions of budget policy, and even here some temporary exceptions may arise. Once the stabilization function is introduced, deficit finance is called for under conditions of potential depression, and surplus finance is called for under conditions of potential inflation. The point to be noted here is that the stabilization objective of budget policy can be achieved without contradicting the other requirements of budget policy, namely, efficient provision for social wants and the application of distributional adjustments.

Regarding the proper level of public services, this means that there is no excuse for make-work expenditures during a depression, just as there is no excuse for cutting essential public services during periods of high activity. Precisely the same fallacy is involved in both cases. An increase in public services during the depression is in order, only to the extent that the decline in private expenditures for some purposes (such as investment) frees resources which people may wish to allocate in part to the satisfaction of social wants; and a decrease in public services is in order during the boom only to the extent that people wish to divert resources from public use to meet an increased demand for resources for other uses. This sets the limits of the permissible adjustment: There is no justification for raising the level of public services merely to increase aggregate demand, since this can be done also by lowering taxes; and there is no justification for cutting public services merely to curtail demand since this can be done also by raising taxes.

Moreover, there is no need for permitting considerations of stabilization policy to interfere with desired distributional adjustments. Thus it was argued frequently during the thirties and forties that taxes on lower incomes should be avoided because this would undermine demand and that therefore a more progressive tax structure was needed; and vice versa for the current case of inflation where it is held that progression should be reduced to secure a shift of resources from consumption to investment, thus providing for increased capacity in order to check inflation. The argument makes sense in both cases if we assume that the total level of tax yield is given, but it breaks down if we allow for adjustments in the level of taxation. The level of taxation which is required for purposes of stabilization should depend upon the distribution of the tax bill, and not the other way round.

NET BUDGET AND SEPARATION OF ISSUES

To bring my point into focus, let me exaggerate a little and assume that there are actually 3 different budgets, pursuing respectively my 3 functions of budget policy. First, there is the budget to provide for the satisfaction of social wants, where taxes are allocated in line with a benefit principle of taxation. By its nature, this budget is balanced over the useful life of the services which are supplied. Secondly, there is the budget to provide for distributional adjustments, involving tax and transfer payments. By its nature, this budget is balanced as well. Then there is the budget designed to stabilize the level of demand. By its nature, this budget involves either taxes or transfer payments, proportional to what is considered the proper state of income distribution.

We may think of these budgets as being determined in an interdependent system, where the manager of each of the three branches takes the action of the other branches as given.[3] Having determined the three budgets, the Government may proceed to administer each budget separately. This would involve various sets of taxes and/or transfers for any one person. To simplify matters, it will be desirable to clear the tax and transfer payments against each other, and thus to administer one net budget policy only.

The actual tax and expenditure plan enacted by the Congress in any one year reflects such a net budget. This is of advantage as a matter of administrative convenience, but it blurs the issues. While it may be difficult as a matter of legislative procedure to determine independently each of the three subbudgets noted in my discussion, some lesser steps may be taken in the organization of the budget process, on both the executive and the legislative side, to move the problem into a better perspective. To say the least, an understanding of the three objectives as distinct issues is prerequisite to efficient budget planning.

The preceding discussion will suffice to show that it is exceedingly difficult to establish a simple set of principles by which to

[3] To illustrate, let me assume that there are two taxpayers only, X and Z. Assume further that the full employment income equals $100, and that X's earnings are divided such that X receives $70 while Z receives $30. Now suppose that the Distribution Branch imposes taxes of $10 on X and pays $10 of transfers to Z, the desired distribution being such that X is to receive 60 percent and Z is to receive 40 percent.

Next, let me suppose that with an income of $100, distributed in this fashion, private expenditure on consumption equals $60 and that expenditures on investment equal $30. Moreover, the manager of the Stabilization Branch is informed that expenditures for the satisfaction of social wants equal $22. This means that total expenditures equal $112 and are $12 above the full employment level. To simplify matters, let us hold investment constant. In order to lower consumption by $12 the Stabilization Branch will impose taxes of $20, it being assumed that the ratio of consumption to income is constant at 60 percent. In order not to interfere with the distributional adjustment, $12 will be paid by X and $8 by Z.

The income of X now equals $70 − $10 − $12 = $48, while that of Z equals $30 + $10 − $8 = $32. Now suppose that both wish to spend 27.5 percent of their income on the satisfaction of social wants. Thus for the satisfaction of social wants taxes equal $13.20 for X and $8.80 for secure an efficient determination of public expenditures. This task involves the determination of the total budget plan, including the revenue as well as the expenditure side, and it comprises quite distinct sets of objectives or functions of budget policy. The issues involved are the more difficult as they cannot be solved, or be solved in part only, by the ordinary tools of eco-

Z, with total expenditures for the satisfaction of social wants equal to $22.

The three subbudgets involve the following transactions:

	X	Z	Total
Satisfaction of social wants:			
Goods and service expenditures			22.0
Taxes	13.2	8.8	22.0
Balance			00.0
Distributional adjustment:			
Taxes	10.0		10.0
Transfers		10.0	10.0
Balance			00.0
Stabilization adjustment:			
Taxes	12.0	8.0	20.0
Transfers			
Balance			20.0
Net budget:			
Taxes	35.2	6.8	42.0
Transfers			
Goods and service expenditure			22.0
Balance			20.0

Instead of collecting 3 separate taxes from X it will be more convenient to collect the total of $35.20; and instead of collecting 2 taxes from Z and paying 1 transfer, it will be more convenient to collect net taxes of $6.80. We thus have net tax receipts of $42 which after allowing for goods and service expenditures of $22 leave us with a surplus of $20, equal to the surplus in the stabilization operation. A similar illustration might be given where the stabilization operation involves a deficit, in which case there appears a corresponding deficit in the net budget. Finally note that the distribution of the tax bill in the net budget is more progressive than that for carrying the cost of social wants, but less progressive than that involved in the distributional adjustment only.

nomic analysis. The political process of decision-making becomes an inherent part of the problem.

At the same time, the complexity of the problem establishes no presumption that the use of resources for the satisfaction of social wants is less efficient than its use for the satisfaction of private wants. This must be kept in mind if we are to see the problem of social-want satisfaction in its proper perspective. While it is obvious that any expenditure objective, once decided upon, should be accomplished at minimum cost, the objective of efficiency in public expenditure planning must not be confused with minimizing the level of such expenditures. By the very nature of the budget as an allocation problem, the danger of inefficiency arises with insufficient as well as with excessive outlays.

SECTION II

✖ Fiscal Policy

Fiscal policy affords a means by which the Government can alleviate structural imbalance in the private sector of the economy. Since fiscal policy may provide for a variety of federal goods and services, as well as stabilization and growth programs, the design and composition of the budget represents a way of meeting selected economic objectives. Inasmuch as the budget helps to determine the level of national income, revenues from taxation and expenditures are subject to evaluation as to their effects upon allocation and distribution.

In modern economic analysis, taxes, as a part of fiscal policy, are employed as tools to influence the levels of consumption and investment and thus the level of national income. Although taxation or tax structures may be evaluated from the viewpoint of constitutionality or problems of justice and administration, the economic effects of a given tax structure are more important in the analysis of fiscal policy. Taxation or the rate structure of federal taxes may be designed to eliminate bottlenecks to growth and full employment. But tax rate changes must be coordinated with expenditure decisions if the changes are to be beneficial.

Tax programs, expenditure programs and the state of the

economy will determine the size of budget surpluses and deficits. Thus a well coordinated budget program will fix tax rates at levels which will yield optimum results. Expenditures as well as surpluses or deficits will vary with the level of the economy's performance. This approach to fiscal policy represents a new design for federal budget programs. The significance of this comprehensive design rests with the fact that budget policy requires complete coordination of tax policy, expenditure policy and debt policy for the attainment of aggregative economic goals.

The first reading in this section, "Budget Policy, 1958-1963," presents an example of the modern fiscal emphasis on the attainment of a balanced budget at full employment. The reading summarizes the extent to which total fiscal policy coordination is required to achieve full employment and a balanced budget. The basic arguments by The Council of Economic Advisers for the 1964 tax reform were predicated upon the ideas advanced in this selection.

The persuasive arguments used by the Advisers in advocating 1964 tax changes have been spelled out repeatedly for several years. An eloquent summary of guidelines to modern income tax policy was made by Professor Neil Jacoby in his testimony before the Committee on Ways and Means in 1959, and is included here. Dr. Jacoby's statements of the objectives sought in income tax reform emphasize the modern concern with the cyclical flexibility of taxation and tax effects upon employment and economic growth. Dr. Jacoby suggests that the fundamental guideline for income tax reform during the decade of the 1960's is growth of output.

"You may think the Corporate Profit Tax is 'Bad,' But . . ." illustrates a special case in the area of structural changes in income taxation. Mr. Burck's evaluation of the corporate income tax points to a series of tax features that inhibit the American corporation in attempts to increase profits, investment and output, and concludes that most of the features of a "bad" tax are to be found in the federal corporation income tax.

BUDGET POLICY, 1958-1963

ECONOMIC REPORT OF THE

PRESIDENT, 1962

The Federal budget has influenced economic activity in recent years in two ways: through the workings of the built-in stabilizers, and through discretionary changes in the budget program. It is not easy to separate these two influences. In order to do so, it is necessary, first, to view Federal fiscal transactions in the same accounting framework used to describe the whole economy. The *national income accounts budget* is a way of measuring and classifying Federal transactions which accords with the national income and product accounts for the economy. Second, it is convenient to have a numerical measure of the expansionary or restrictive impact of a budget program on the economy. The *full employment surplus* is such a measure. This section discusses these two somewhat unfamiliar but highly useful tools and then applies them in an analysis of recent and prospective budget policies.

Reprinted from the *Economic Report of the President, 1962* (Washington, D.C.: U.S. Government Printing Office, January, 1962), pp. 77-84.

THE NATIONAL INCOME ACCOUNTS BUDGET

The effects of Federal receipts and expenditures on the income stream are most accurately represented when the budget is viewed in the framework of the national income accounts. These accounts present a consistent record and classification of the major flows of output and income for the entire economy, including the transactions of the Federal Government. There are three major differences between the Federal budget as it is conventionally presented (the so-called "administrative budget") and the accounts of the Federal sector as they appear in the national income. The major differences between these two budgets, and between both of them and the consolidated cash budget, are schematically summarized in Table I. There are other, less significant differences among the budgets, such as the treatment of intragovernmental transactions.

First, the national income accounts budget, like the consolidated cash budget, includes the transactions of the trust funds, which amount currently to about $25 billion per year and have a significant impact on the economy. Highway grants-in-aid, unemployment compensation payments, and social security benefits are examples of trust fund transactions. Because the traditional budget—or administrative budget—is primarily an

TABLE I—*Major differences among three concepts of the Federal budget*

Item	Budget concept		
	Adminis-trative	Consolidated cash	National income accounts
Timing of receipts	Collections	Collections	Accruals
Treatment of net loans and other credit transactions	Included	Included	Excluded
Treatment of trust fund transactions	Excluded	Included	Included

Source: Council of Economic Advisers.

instrument of management and control of those Federal activities which operate through regular congressional appropriations, it excludes the trust funds, which have their own legal sources of revenue.

Second, transactions between government and business are, so far as possible, recorded in the national income accounts budget when liabilities are incurred rather than when cash changes hands. This adjustment in timing affects both government purchases and taxes, shifting them to the point in time at which they are likely to have their principal impact on private spending decisions. The choice of an accrual, rather than a cash, basis for timing is particularly important for the highly volatile corporate income tax. Since these taxes are normally paid more than six months after the liabilities are incurred, payments of corporate income taxes, as recorded in the administrative budget, run substantially below accruals in a period of rising economic activity. For fiscal year 1962, this difference is estimated at about $3 billion.

Finally, unlike the administrative budget, the national income accounts budget omits government transactions in financial assets and already existing assets. The largest omission is the volume of loans extended by the Federal Government. This volume is estimated at $4 billion net of repayments in fiscal year 1962. While these loans have important effects on economic activity, they are properly viewed as an aspect, not of fiscal policy, but of monetary and credit policy, and are so discussed later in this chapter. Borrowers from the Federal Government, like borrowers from private financial institutions, acquire cash by incurring debts. They add thereby to their liquidity, but not directly to their incomes.

THE FULL EMPLOYMENT SURPLUS

As pointed out earlier in this chapter, the magnitude of the surplus or deficit in the budget depends both on the budget program and on the state of the economy. The budget program fixes both tax rates and expenditure programs. The revenues actually yielded by most taxes, and the actual expenditures under certain programs like unemployment compensation, vary automatically with economic activity. To interpret the economic significance of a given budget it is, therefore, essential to distinguish the *automatic* changes in revenues and expenditures from the *discretionary* changes which occur when the Government varies tax rates or changes expenditure programs. The discussion that follows runs in terms of the national income accounts budget.

In Figure 1 this twofold aspect of fiscal policy is portrayed for the fiscal years 1960 and 1962. Since tax revenues and some expenditures depend on the level of economic activity, there is a whole range of possible surpluses and deficits associated with a given budget program. The particular surplus or deficit in fact realized will depend on the level of economic activity. On the horizontal scale, Figure 1 shows the ratio of actual GNP to the economy's potential, labeled the "utilization rate." On the vertical scale, the chart shows the Federal budget surplus or deficit as a percentage of potential GNP.

The line labeled "fiscal 1960 program" represents a calculation of the budget surplus or deficit which would have occurred at various levels of economic activity, given the Federal expenditure programs and the tax rates of that year. For the reasons explained earlier, the same budget program may yield a high surplus at full employment and a low surplus or a deficit at low levels of economic activity. The actual budget position in fiscal year 1960, a surplus of $2.2 billion or 0.4 percent of potential GNP, is shown at point A; this accompanied a level of GNP 5 percent below potential. Had full employment been achieved that year, however, the same basic budget program would have yielded a surplus of about $10 billion, or nearly 2 percent of gross national product (point F in Figure 1). The line labeled "1962 program" similarly shows the relationship between economic activity and the surplus or deficit, for the budget program of 1962; the expected deficit is shown at point B, and the full employment surplus at point G.

EFFECT OF LEVEL OF ECONOMIC ACTIVITY
ON FEDERAL SURPLUS OR DEFICIT

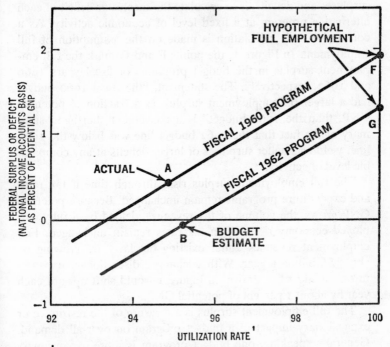

' ACTUAL GNP AS PERCENT OF POTENTIAL GNP.
SOURCE: COUNCIL OF ECONOMIC ADVISERS.

FIGURE I

It is the height of the line in Figure 1 which reflects the basic budget program; the actual surplus or deficit depends both on the height of the program line and the level of economic activity. In other words, discretionary fiscal policy, by changing the level of Government expenditures or tax rates shifts the whole program line up or down. The automatic stabilizing effects of a given budget program are reflected in the chart by movements along a given line, accompanying changes in economic activity. One convenient method of comparing alternative budget programs, which separates automatic from discretionary changes in surpluses and deficits, is to calculate the surplus or deficit of each alternative program at a fixed level of economic activity. As a convention, this calculation is made on the assumption of full employment. In Figure 1, the points F and G mark the full employment surplus in the budget programs of fiscal years 1960 and 1962, respectively. The statement, "the fiscal 1960 budget had a larger full employment surplus, as a fraction of potential GNP, than the 1962 budget" is a convenient shorthand summary of the fact that the 1962 budget line was below the 1960 line, yielding smaller surpluses or larger deficits at any comparable level of activity.

The full employment surplus rises through time if tax rates and expenditure programs remain unchanged. Because potential GNP grows, the volume of tax revenues yielded by a fully employed economy rises, when tax rates remain unchanged. Full employment revenues under existing tax laws are growing by about $6 billion a year. With unchanged discretionary expenditures, a budget line drawn on Figure 1 would shift upward each year by about 1 percent of potential GNP.

The full employment surplus is a measure of the restrictive or expansionary impact of a budget program on over-all demand. Generally speaking, one budget program is more expansionary than another if it has a smaller full employment surplus. One budget program might have the smaller full employment surplus because it embodies great Federal purchases of goods and services, in relation to potential GNP. By the same token, it leaves a smaller share of full employment output for private purchase. This means that full employment is easier to maintain under the budget program with the smaller surplus, because less private demand is required. It also means that inflation is more difficult to avoid, because there are fewer goods and services to meet private demand should it prove strong. Alternatively, one budget program might have a smaller full employment surplus than a second because it involves either lower tax rates or larger transfer payment programs. In that event, private after-tax incomes are larger at full employment for the first budget program than for the second. As a result, private demand would be stronger under the first program.

If the full employment surplus is too large, relative to the strength of private demand, economic activity falls short of potential. Correspondingly, the budget surplus actually realized falls short of the full employment surplus; indeed, a deficit may occur. If the full employment surplus is too small, total demand exceeds the capacity of economy and causes inflation.

But whether a given full employment surplus is too large or too small depends on other government policies, as well as on economic circumstances affecting the general strength of private demand. If the full employment surplus is too large, more expansionary monetary and credit policies may strengthen private demand sufficiently to permit full employment to be realized. Changes in tax structure, stimulating demand while leaving the yield of the tax system unchanged, might have the same effect. Similarly, restrictive changes in other government policies can offset the expansionary influence of a low full employment surplus.

A mixture of policies involving (1) a budget program with a relatively high full employment surplus and (2) monetary ease and tax incentives stimulating enough private investment to maintain full employment, has favorable consequences for economic growth.

THE BUDGET IN 1958-60

The analysis of the budget program in terms of the full employment surplus points to a probable major cause of the incomplete and short-lived nature of the 1958-60 expansion. The most restrictive fiscal program of recent years was the program of 1960. Its full employment surplus exceeded any from 1956 to date. Estimates of the full employment surplus by half years are

shown in Figure 2. The full employment surplus declined
sharply as a result of higher expenditures during the 1957-58
recession until it reached an estimated $3 billion in the second
half of 1958. Thereafter, it rose gradually through most of 1959
but then increased sharply to about $12½ billion in 1960.
Thus, whereas the Federal budget contributed to stability during
the contraction phase of the cycle and during the first year of the

FEDERAL SURPLUS OR DEFICIT:
ACTUAL AND FULL EMPLOYMENT ESTIMATE
(NATIONAL INCOME ACCOUNTS BASIS)

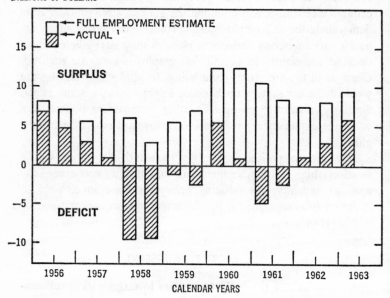

BILLIONS OF DOLLARS`*

*. SEASONALLY ADJUSTED ANNUAL RATES; DATA ARE FOR HALF-YEARS.
[1] ESTIMATED BEGINNING SECOND HALF 1961.
SOURCES: DEPARTMENT OF COMMERCE, BUREAU OF THE BUDGET,
         AND COUNCIL OF ECONOMIC ADVISERS.

FIGURE 2

expansion, it was altered abruptly in the direction of restraint late in 1959 at a time when high employment had not yet been achieved.

FEDERAL FISCAL ACTIVITY IN 1961-62

Immediately upon taking office, the new Administration moved vigorously to use the fiscal powers of the Federal Government to help bring about economic recovery. Federal procurement was accelerated by Presidential directive early in February, and tax refunds were also expedited. A listing of Administration stabilization policies during 1961 is provided in the Appendix to this chapter. Changes in transfer programs added about $2 billion to the combined total of transfer payments for fiscal years 1961 and 1962. The Veterans Administration advanced the payment of $150 million of veterans' life insurance dividends into the first quarter of calendar year 1961, and then made an extra dividend payment of $218 million at midyear. The Congress promptly adopted a number of measures requested by the President. A Temporary Extended Unemployment Compensation Act was adopted, providing for extension of exhausted benefits and giving the Administration time to develop a comprehensive program for permanent improvement in unemployment compensation. Social security benefits were increased effective in August, and aid was extended to children dependent on unemployed persons. Transfer payments represent a major element of flexibility in Federal expenditures. While transfer programs—like any Federal outlays—ought to stand on their merits, the precise timing of worthwhile new programs properly depends on economic conditions. The objectives of economic stabilization in 1961 argued strongly for speeding the introduction of programs like improvements in social security, scheduled to be adopted later.

Other Federal outlays increased in 1961 to meet specific national needs. Federal grants to States and localities for urban renewal, area redevelopment, highways, and public assistance increased. Direct payments to farmers were increased as a result of participation in the feed grains program. The largest increases in expenditures came in the areas of defense and space exploration. These programs were expanded for reasons of national security, not for economic stabilization. However, stabilization objectives ruled against any increases in tax rates to finance these new expenditures.

During 1961, the estimated full employment surplus declined significantly, from an annual rate of $12½ billion in the second half of 1960 to $8½ billion in the second half of 1961. As shown in Figure 2, the actual surplus or deficit has been substantially different from its full employment counterpart. Since private incomes declined during late 1960 and into 1961, the actual budget position shifted from a surplus of $1 billion in the second half of 1960 to a deficit of $5 billion in the first half of 1961. Then as the economy began to recover, the deficit, in the national income accounts, shrank to $2 billion in the second half of the year. The rising deficit in the early part of 1961 was due both to a shift downward in its budget program line (as discretionary budget outlays were increased) and to a movement to the left along the new line (as private incomes and Federal tax receipts declined).

The Federal national income accounts budget appropriately showed its largest deficit early in 1961, when the economy was near the trough of recession. Since then, the deficit has been steadily declining in spite of rising expenditures, and a surplus is expected in the first half of 1962. The administrative and cash deficits show a different time pattern, with deficits rising in the 1962 fiscal year, primarily because tax collections lag behind tax liabilities.

The fiscal actions taken during the past year reflect the Administration's philosophy that the budget is a positive instrument for economic stabilization. According to the original January 1961 budget estimates, expenditures on national income-and-product account were expected to reach a level of $98 billion in fiscal year 1962. Present estimates, which incorporate all of the changes made by executive and legislative action, indicate that these expenditures will amount to more than $106 billion. This increase in expenditures is itself responsible for a rise in the gross national product that can be estimated conservatively at $15 billion.

BUDGET POLICY FOR FISCAL 1963

The balanced administrative budget proposed for fiscal year 1963 projects an increase over the current fiscal year of nearly $6 billion in Federal outlays on income-and-product account. Because of the $2 billion a year increase in social insurance taxes effective January 1, 1963, the full employment surplus rises in the first half of 1963. But it remains considerably below the level of 1960 (Figure 2). Fiscal policy will be less restrictive than it was in the late stages of the last recovery. The budgetary program, yielding a surplus on income-and-product account of $4.4 billion reflects the reasonable expectation that 4 percent unemployment will be reached by the end of the 1963 fiscal year. Obviously, the strength of private demand over the next 18 months cannot now be assessed with precision. Any plans covering the uncertain future are necessarily risky. A less expansionary budget with a larger full employment surplus would provide added assurance of price stability but only at the cost of increased dangers of an incomplete recovery. A more expansionary budget would, on the other hand, improve the outlook for maximum production and employment but increase the risks of rising prices.

The risks of an incomplete recovery, on the one hand, or of rising prices on the other, are fortunately reduced by the automatic stabilizing characteristics of the budget. If private demand proves excessively buoyant, the added revenues can be expected to enlarge the surplus in the budget, thereby moderating inflationary pressures. Conversely, any shortfall in private demand will likewise be partially countered by a shortfall in tax revenues. In addition, discretionary policy will remain flexible. First, monetary policy can be used flexibly. The Federal Reserve can attune its policies to the pattern of output, employment, and prices as it unfolds during the months ahead. Second, as the experience of 1961 demonstrated, the budget itself is a flexible tool which can be adjusted during the course of a fiscal year by varying the timing of outlays and by legislative action. Finally, the President's stabilization proposals described earlier in this chapter, would, if adopted, significantly strengthen the government's ability to act swiftly and energetically in meeting unforeseen economic developments.

GUIDELINES OF INCOME TAX REFORM FOR THE 1960 TAX REVISION COMPENDIUM

Neil H. Jacoby

It is an honor to be invited by this committee to express views about American income tax reform, a subject of paramount importance to the future of our country.

My assignment is to state the economic objectives to be sought in any reform of the structure of American income tax laws. Others deal with particular aspects of those laws. Of course, the two tasks cannot be separated sharply. Conclusions about the appropriate goals of income taxation necessarily imply the desirable directions of tax reform. Without going into details, I shall later point out the major implications of those goals which appear to be dominant in framing the future income tax structure.

My discussion will embrace both personal and corporate taxes on net income; and it will encompass State and local as well as Federal levies. Manifestly, taxes on personal and corpo-

Reprinted from Ways and Means Committee, *Tax Revision Compendium,* Vol. 1 (Washington, D.C.: U.S. Government Printing Office, November 16, 1959).

rate incomes constitute a single integrated system for the purpose of this inquiry. The objectives of personal income taxes cannot be studied fruitfully in isolation from those on corporate incomes because individual partnership and corporate forms of conducting economic activity are interchangeable over wide areas.

It is equally clear that the economic objectives of Federal income tax reform are also applicable to those of State and municipal governments. Historically, Federal income taxes have so dominated the national scene that the rising burdens of State and local levies on net income are often overlooked. Yet during 1958 almost two-thirds of the States collected more than $2.5 billions of personal and corporate income taxes, and many municipalities also imposed them. An accurate, current, integrated statistical map of all levies on net income on all parts of the United States is needed.

I propose to take the decade of the 1960's as the horizon of my discussions. The particular objectives that should guide structural reforms of income taxes and the priorities to be assigned each of them are not timeless and immutable. They are relative to the political and economic environment and tasks of the nation in each era. An income tax structure appropriate to wartime is not well adapted to the goals of peacetime. One framed to meet the needs of an undeveloped economy will not well serve an advanced economy. One structured for a society of highly concentrated wealth and income will not be applicable to a more egalitarian society. One designed to stimulate consumption will not foster saving. We must predicate our selection and weighting of the goals of American income tax reform in 1959 upon our vision of the years ahead. A decade is a suitable planning period, because structural changes in taxes should not be made too frequently and 10 years is about as far ahead as one may look with any confidence. By 1970 this committee probably will find it necessary again to review the suitability of the income tax structure.

Let us begin with the classical guidelines of taxation, contrast them with subsequent views, and show how each involved economic goals appropriate to their times. Then we shall set forth hypotheses about the world environment and tasks of the U.S. economy during the 1960's. On a basis of these assumptions we shall identify the dominant consideration in income tax reform and shall suggest the lines of reform that will serve this goal.

CLASSICAL CANONS OF TAXATION

From the beginnings of systematic economic thought, men have sought to identify the primary qualities of a good tax. Adam Smith, the founder of classical British economics and himself a one-time collector of customs, put forth four "maxims" applicable to taxes in general:[1] First, taxes on individuals should be "in proportion to their respective abilities; that is, in proportion to the revenue which they respectively enjoy under the protection of the State." Secondly, "the tax each individual should pay should be certain, not arbitrary." Thirdly, "every tax should be levied at a time, or in the manner, in which it is most likely to be convenient for the contributor to pay it." Fourth, "every tax should be so contrived as both to take out and to keep out of the pockets of the people as little as possible over and above what it brings into the public treasury of the State." This last maxim Smith interpreted to mean that a tax (1) should be capable of economical administration, (2) should not "obstruct the industry of the people," (3) should not offer undue opportunities for evasion, and (4) should not impose "unnecessary trouble, vexation, and oppression" upon the public.

Evidently, Adam Smith proposed to judge the excellence of a tax by the criteria of equity, simplicity, convenience, administrative cost, susceptibility to evasion, and expense to the taxpayers. This remains an admirable list of criteria, although modern tax theorists would add some new factors and will weigh those enumerated by Smith differently than Smith would have weighed them.

[1] See *The Wealth of Nations,* book V, ch. II, pt. II.

When Smith wrote, around 1775, the British revenue system consisted almost entirely of customs duties, excises, and real property taxes and was highly regressive in its incidence. It expressed the Mercantilist objective of a protected home market. Smith's demand that taxes on individuals should be "proportional" to the revenues they enjoyed was quite radical for its time. It represented a protest against the heavy taxation of landless workers and tenant farmers to finance public expenditures made primarily for the benefit of the landed gentry. Of course, we have long since abandoned the view that flat proportionality in personal income taxation is equitable. Contemporary tax theory universally accepts some degree of progression in tax rates upon incomes, inheritances, and estates as consistent with the "ability to pay" doctrine. At the same time, contemporary tax theory gives a place for application of the "benefit" principle in connection with such taxes as those on real estate or motor fuel.

THE 19TH CENTURY EMPHASIS ON MITIGATION OF PERSONAL INEQUALITIES

During the 19th and early 20th centuries economic thought about the appropriate guidelines of taxation became increasingly preoccupied with the problem of equity in the distribution of the tax burden among individuals. The gradual development of free markets, strong governmental administration, and business accounting records had caused the older problems of tax enforcement, smuggling, and arbitrary action by tax officials to sink into relative unimportance. Meanwhile, the rapid industrialization of Western Europe and America under laissez-faire policies was creating great fortunes for a few, while the masses of workers had not yet acquired much property. The problem of chronic unemployment had not yet emerged in acute form.

MODERN VIEWS OF TAX OBJECTIVES

During the 1st half of the 20th century there gradually emerged in the United States a public consciousness of the problem of business cycles and large-scale involuntary unemployment. This interest reached an acute form with the economic collapse following 1929 and the incomplete recovery of the early 1930's. A consensus gradually emerged—finally expressed in the Employment Act of 1946—that government could not leave the level of employment to chance, and that it had a positive responsibility to use all its powers, including taxation, to regulate aggregate demand so as to prevent both booms and recessions.

Because of these changes during the present century, economic thought about tax objectives shifted from its earlier preoccupation with theories of progression. A concern emerged for new criteria of taxes such as the adequacy of revenues, their cyclical flexibility and their effects upon employment and economic growth. In the light of these fundamental shifts in the nature and environment of the U.S. economy up to the end of World War II, it is illuminating to consider the list of qualifications for postwar taxes drawn up in 1945 by Prof. Harold M. Groves in a study undertaken for the Committee for Economic Development.[2] This list has special interest because it reflected expert opinion on the proper guidelines of Federal taxation 15 years ago, when basic problems of income tax structure were last considered by Congress and the public.

Professor Groves' list may be summarized as follows:

(1) Taxes should be fair, and not arbitrary.

(2) Taxes should reduce inequalities in wealth, income, and power.

(3) Taxes should conserve human resources.

[2] See Harold M. Groves, *Postwar Taxation and Economic Progress* (New York: McGraw-Hill Book Co., Inc., 1946), pp. 373, 374.

(4) Taxes should preserve a wide market; they should not aggravate oversaving.

(5) Taxes should preserve incentives.

(6) Taxes should be as direct as feasible.

(7) Direct taxes should be widely shared.

(8) Taxes should be adequate.

(9) Tax reductions and increases should be administered to reduce business instability.

The major conclusions drawn by Professor Groves were:

> These considerations sustain the view that the main source of support for postwar government should be a direct personal income tax with a broad base, an adequate standard rate, substantial graduation, no loopholes, and much stronger administration.

Viewed in the perspective of 14 years, Professor Groves' guidelines of tax reform continue to possess much merit. To the qualities of a good tax cited by Adam Smith, he added directness, breadth of base, incentive, stimulation of consumption, adequacy, and cyclical flexibility. While none of these factors is irrelevant, his listing does not reveal the appropriate weights to be given each factor in making tax policy. Thus, it does not resolve such knotty problems as the appropriate degree of progression in personal income tax rates. To find more specific guidelines for contemporary tax policy, we must consider what changes have occurred since World War II, and what changes impend during the 1960's, in the nature of the U.S. economy and its environment.

When Groves wrote near the close of World War II Americans were deeply concerned with the reemployment of millions of men and women about to be demobilized from the Armed Forces. With the bitter memories of chronic mass unemployment during the Thirties fresh in mind, most people saw adequacy of demand for goods and services and full employment as the primary postwar economic problem. Hence, they put great emphasis upon taxation which would encourage consumption expenditures and prevent oversaving.

Instead, the postwar years have witnessed a generally high level of employment, and recurrent periods of excessive demand which have placed the U.S. economy under inflationary pressures. The reason for this has been that forces initiated by World War II have profoundly changed the nature of our economy. These basic new forces include an explosion of population, a revolutionary diffusion of income and wealth, and a new age of scientific and technological advancement. The pervasive problem of our times has been to find investment funds for the myriad of new opportunities opened up by scientific research and development, while meeting the great demands for consumer goods emanating from increasing millions of households.

Fifteen years ago the Soviet Union was an ally of the United States, apparently devoid of imperialistic ambitions, devastated by war and requiring a generation for resuscitation. Now, the U.S.S.R. has emerged as a powerful and belligerent antagonist in a world divided into two ideological camps. Because of the insistent demands of a multitude of new and undeveloped nations for rapid economic progress, and the competition of the Western and Soviet nations for their political affiliation, world political conditions have become tense and unstable.

Fifteen years ago the United States monopolized nuclear weapons and their means of delivery, thus possessing undisputed military power over the world. Today, there is no monopoly; and the time is rapidly approaching when many nations will possess the awful destructive power of nuclear weapons. Meanwhile, the most advanced countries have entered an era of missile development, rocketry, and the exploration of outer space—which appears to be the new frontier of both military power and civilian scientific progress.

These radical changes in the environment and nature of the U.S. economy surely establish new guidelines of income tax reform.

THE ENVIRONMENT AND CHARACTER OF THE U.S. ECONOMY IN THE SIXTIES

In recent testimony to the Joint Economic Committee of Congress, I suggested that the following salient economic tasks confront the United States as we enter the 1960's:[3]

(1) Economic provision for national security.

(2) Increasing efficiency and economic growth.

(3) Fostering economic growth throughout the free areas of the world.

(4) Strengthening the U.S. position in foreign trade.

(5) Defending the purchasing power of the dollar.

(6) Invigorating competition.

(7) Adapting to rapid population increase.

(8) Increasing the geographic and occupational mobility of people.

(9) Improving education of all kinds and at all levels.

These tasks were identified as the crucial tasks of the next decade upon a basis of certain assumptions about the world environment and the nature of the U.S. economy during the 1960's. We may postulate the following developments during this decade as being the most probable among the alternatives.

(1) U.S. population will continue to grow rapidly, reaching about 210 million by 1970. Additional family formations will amount to about 10 million during the decade, giving rise to vast markets for housing, home appliances, automobiles, and consumer equipment, and banishing the specter of market saturation for consumer goods.

(2) Governmental and private expenditures on scientific research and development, which mounted from $1 billion in 1940 to about $10 billion in 1958, will continue to expand relative to the gross national product and may reach $20 bil-

[3] *Employment, Growth, and Price Levels,* hearings before the Joint Economic Committee, pt. I, p. 56 ff., 86th Cong., 1st sess. (Washington, D.C.: U.S. Government Printing Office, 1959.)

lion a year by 1970. This will accelerate the rate of obsolescence of the existing stock of capital goods while magnifying the demand for new types of plant and equipment, thus creating a sustained strong demand for producer durable goods and nonresidential construction.

(3) Startling advances in science and industrial technology will both require a much higher level of formal education and technical training by the work force, and will reduce the demand for relatively unskilled manual and clerical personnel as a result of the automation of repetitive processes. U.S. expenditures on education will increase rapidly as a percentage of the GNP. This growth in educational opportunities, accompanied by a further decline in racial discrimination and barriers to personal mobility, will tend to further reduce inequalities in individual productivity and income. At the same time, it will produce serious problems of structural unemployment to which increasing attention will be given.

(4) The explosive growth of world population will continue, as death rates fall while birth rates remain high. This will add about 30 percent to world population in the sixties, and produce a world with about 3½ billion human beings by 1970.

(5) The existing stalemate among the big world powers in nuclear weapons and missiles will continue. It will deter any of them from precipitating World War III. However, the rising nationalism and ambition for economic improvement among the Latin American, African, and Asian nations, combined with rapid population growth that will defeat efforts to raise per capita incomes quickly, will create much political instability in the world. International tensions will continue to be high, and local wars will continue to require the United States to maintain strong, mobile military forces throughout the world, as well as to compete with the U.S.S.R. for supremacy in the command of outer space. Hence, national security expenditures will continue to expand during the sixties, probably at a rate approximating the growth in GNP.

(6) By 1970 the Common Market and other steps toward the economic integration of Western Europe will be well advanced. This region, as well as Canada, Japan, and other prosperous and politically stable nations, will be the destination of much private American investment. Concurrently, world political considerations will have maintained the level of U.S. Government gifts, grants, loans, and technical assistance to the underdeveloped countries. Private capital outflow (including reinvested earnings) which was about $2.8 billion during 1958, may be running at an annual rate of $5 billion or more in 1970; foreign economic aid and investment by Government, which was about $3.5 billion during 1958, will be well maintained.

All of these probable oncoming developments form guidelines for reform of the American income tax to meet the needs of the next decade. They emphasize the need for an income tax structure that fosters more saving and risk-taking investment, larger capital formation, and thus rapid and better-sustained growth of the U.S. economy.

The United States needs a more rapid average annual rate of growth in its real national output during the 1960's than the approximately 3 percent realized since World War II for these reasons:

To supply millions of new families with homes and a complement of durable and nondurable goods and services.

To obliterate the remaining pockets of substandard living in our land.

To support massive scientific research and development efforts and a huge enlargement of educational activities.

To provide our industries with the most efficient equipment that will make it capable of meeting intense competition from abroad. (A 1958 McGraw-Hill survey disclosed that it would then cost $95 billion to replace outmoded equipment. *Business Week,* September 27, 1958.)

To supply the new capital goods that will take advantage of the burgeoning body of scientific knowledge.

To enlarge the outflow of American investment abroad.

To reduce the danger of inflation.

To provide an example to the world of a dynamic economy based on open markets and private enterprise.

TAX REFORM FOR RAPID ECONOMIC GROWTH

If our vision of the coming decade is reasonably accurate, and strong emphasis should be placed on the objective of rapid and sustained economic growth, what structural changes in income taxes will contribute to this goal?

In the writer's opinion at least six lines of reform are indicated:[4]

(1) Reduction in the progressivity of the personal income tax.

(2) Elimination of many exclusions, deductions, and exemptions from taxable income.

(3) Averaging of personal incomes for determining tax liability.

(4) Scaling the tax rate on capital gains to the holding period of assets.

(5) Reduction in the tax on corporate income and ultimate integration with the personal income tax.

(6) Liberalization of depreciation allowances on business assets.

Taken together, these reforms contemplate a broader based, simpler income tax system, so structured as to encourage productive effort, saving, and risk-bearing investment more strongly than does the present system. While fostering economic growth, it would also eliminate many inequities in the present system. We shall briefly comment on each line of reform.

(1) *Reduction in the progressivity of the personal income tax.*—The degree of progressivity in current Federal income tax rates is extravagantly high, whether measured by impact on production or on Federal revenues or when compared with income

[4] Most of these recommendations were advanced by the writer in *Can Prosperity Be Sustained?* (New York: Henry Holt & Co., 1956), ch. 1.

tax rates in progressive nations of the world. Comparatively little income is really taxed at the maximum rate of 91 percent, because persons able to enter this bracket either choose not to earn ordinary income; or they donate income-producing assets to tax-exempt or low-taxed trusts; or they enter the business of oil or gas production; or they purchase tax-exempt securities; or they transform ordinary income into capital gains. The upper-bracket rates have thus become largely "phantom" rates, paid by few while deterring productive effort and distorting investment.

The progressivity of personal income tax rates should be reduced not only in the top brackets of income over $100,000 per annum, but also in income brackets in the $10,000 to $100,000 range where a relatively high percentage of personal savings occurs.[5] While persons in these brackets have much "ability to pay" taxes, they also have much capacity to save and are more likely than persons in low-income brackets to save a large fraction of any reduction in their tax liabilities. If real economic growth without inflation is our prior economic objective, less graduation in personal income tax rates is a logical implication of this choice.

True, the U. S. economy has grown, the rate of net capital formation has not fallen, and new businesses have continued to be formed in the face of highly progressive tax rates maintained since World War II. But this is not enough. The U. S. economy has not been growing fast enough to perform its gigantic tasks in the world of the sixties. It has been said that present graduated rates above the first bracket provide only 14 percent of individual income tax liability and therefore cannot have an important impact. Yet this is clearly an inadequate test of the impact of progression, because a disproportionately large part of the Na-

[5] See Irwin Friend and Stanley Shor, "Who Saves?" *Review of Economics and Statistics,* vol. XLI, No. 2 (May 1959). According to BLS-Wharton estimates, urban families with annual incomes of $10,000 or more in 1950 saved 31 percent of their after-tax incomes and accounted for 58.7 percent of personal savings, while forming but 4 percent of the population.

tion's personal savings occurs in these higher brackets of income, and the figures do not show the amount of taxable income not earned and reported because of the deterrent effect of excessive progression. It is also argued that progression is really not excessive because (to take the extreme case) individuals with adjusted gross income over $1 million paid an average effective tax rate of 54.4 percent on their 1957 incomes. Clearly, however, it is the marginal rather than the average rate that influences capital formation.

(2) *Elimination of many exclusions, deductions, and exemptions.*—A potent reason for scaling down current excessive progression in tax rates is that it will make it easier to reduce the differentiation, exclusions, credits, exemptions, and special features which unduly complicate the present laws and which are necessary to make the current rate structure at all tolerable. We should put a stop to the process that Henry C. Simons so aptly described as "dipping deeply with a sieve."

Exclusions, deductions, and exemptions from taxpayers' net incomes have been carried so far that in 1957 taxable income was less than 40 percent of personal income. The occasions for such special treatment have been the desire to encourage activities deemed socially desirable or to grant selective relief from taxation. The consequences have been to introduce great administrative complexities into the law, costly both to the Internal Revenue Service and the public, to create opportunities for evasion, and to encourage demands upon Congress by other groups for favored treatment. The desirable line of reform, consistent with both the Government's needs for continued large revenues and with democratic requirements of a broad tax base, is to reduce drastically such differentiation. While it would not per se affect economic growth, broadening the base of the personal income tax would make it possible to reduce rates without sacrifice of revenue or, indeed, of true equity.

(3) *Averaging of personal incomes.*—At present the person whose income fluctuates widely from year to year pays higher taxes than the person whose income is stable from one year to

the next, even though their total incomes over a period of years are the same. Because persons with widely fluctuating annual incomes are likely to be self-employed persons operating their own enterprises or taking the risks of economic development, the present tax system discriminates against them. It should, at least, place them on an equal footing with those with stable incomes, usually derived from salaried employment. It can do this by permitting taxpayers to average their annual incomes in computing their tax liabilities.

(4) *Scaling down the rate on realized capital gains.*—The treatment of capital gains poses one of the most difficult and controversial issues of income tax structure. Plausible theoretical arguments can be made for either one of two extreme positions: treating them the same as ordinary income—as the United States once did—because they add to the economic power of the recipient; or regarding them as being something different from taxable income, as is true today in the United Kingdom and the Commonwealth countries.[6] Current U.S. practice represents a compromise, which attempts to take into account revenue yield to the Treasury and effects upon financial markets, investment, and capital formation, as well as individual equities. It is obvious that a personal income tax with progressive rates up to 91 percent would almost paralyze risk-taking investment, unless realized capital gains bore a lower maximum rate.

If economic growth really should be a dominant consideration in tax policy, as we have argued, then the conflicting considerations in the treatment of capital gains should be resolved in favor of a system which offers individuals strong incentives to capital formation and risk assumption. The current treatment of capital gains does tend to "freeze" capital assets in the hands of investors who are reluctant to sell appreciated assets and pay up to 25 percent of their gain to the Federal Government. Thus, it

---

[6] See Lawrence H. Seltzer, *The Nature and Treatment of Capital Gains* (New York: National Bureau of Economic Research, Inc., 1951), especially ch. 11.

does in some measure impede the mobility of investment funds, with adverse consequences for the productivity of capital. In addition, the capital gains tax rate, while relatively favorable to capital gains versus ordinary income, continues to be high enough to deter some risky investment that would otherwise occur. The forces of economic growth would be strengthened by scaling down the maximum rate from 25 percent through a series of steps to (say) 5 percent, according to the number of years assets are held.

For example, the maximum rate of 25 percent might apply to long-term capital gains on assets held more than 6 months but not more than 1 year, and this maximum rate might be reduced by 2 percent for each additional year an asset was held before sale. This would tend to encourage risk-assumption on investments that promised to bear fruit far in the future. It would encourage realization of large gains on assets already held for a number of years, and reinvestment of the proceeds in assets having better potentialities of appreciation.

(5) *Reduction in the tax on corporate income.*—The present tax on corporate net income (30 percent on the first $25,000 and 52 percent on all in excess) lays too heavy a burden on business profits for the welfare of a vigorous, private enterprise economy. The incidence of the corporate profits tax is a complex issue and depends on circumstances, but the consensus of economic theory is that the stockholder bears most of the burden in most instances. A 52-percent tax rate makes the Federal Government, in effect, the majority stockholders of every business corporation of appreciable size. It favors wage and price inflation and other inefficiencies by enabling corporate managements, in effect, to charge the bulk of costs to the Government. It diminishes both the incentive to make, and the means of financing, new investment in the most modern and efficient equipment, and thus retards the growth of production.

For an income tax system structured primarily to foster economic growth, as well as to distribute the tax burden equitably by eliminating haphazard double taxation of dividend income, the ultimate goal should be integration of the tax on corporate net income with the tax on personal income. This implies that the Federal Government should return to the policy followed during the early years of U.S. income tax history, and treat the corporate tax as a withholding levy (levied at the first-bracket personal rate) in respect to earnings distributed to stockholders, and as an advance payment of taxes with respect to retained earnings.[7] Fiscal considerations obviously dictate a gradual approach to this goal, through a series of stepdowns in corporate tax rates so timed as to exercise a stabilizing effect on business cycles.

(6) *Liberalization of depreciation allowances.*—A tax system structured to foster economic growth should give businessmen wide latitude in determining the amounts of depreciation allowed each year against their fixed assets. This is so for two reasons: First, liberal depreciation reduces tax liability and thus increases the cash available for purchase of new assets; secondly, liberal depreciation allowances permit the firm to recover the costs of new assets more quickly and thus act as an incentive to modernize and add to its assets.[8] In a society with an accelerating pace of technological change, allowable depreciation charges should be increased to reflect the rising rate of functional obsolescence of assets which become outmoded. Headway was made in this direction in the Tax Revision Acts of 1954 and 1958. However, the rules of the Internal Revenue Service in regard to depreciation allowances continue to be illiberal, in comparison both with the facts of U.S. industrial obsolescence and with the income tax practices of other industrially advanced countries. At the minimum, this present discrimination against business investment inherent in our income tax laws should be removed, even if we do not go further, and permit accelerated depreciation as an incentive for business investment.

[7] See Harold S. Groves, *op. cit.*, pp. 72-78.
[8] Cf., Evsey D. Domar, "The Case for Accelerated Depreciation," *Quarterly Journal of Economics,* LXVII (November 1953), pp. 493-519.

CONCLUSION

The formulation of American income tax policy has always been complicated by the presence of conflicting criteria, none of which could properly be ignored, and each of which has been accorded a weighting dependent upon the particular economic tasks of the times. The considerations that now impel our country to seek a more rapid and steady growth of real production during the 1960's are powerful. Hence, growth of output, within the framework of a reasonably stable price level, should be the dominant guideline of reform of the income tax structure for the proximate future.

YOU MAY THINK THE CORPORATE PROFIT TAX IS "BAD," BUT . . . IT'S A WHOLE LOT WORSE THAN YOU THINK

Gilbert Burck

The most predictable thing about the Administration's tax program was that it paid so little attention to the real defects of the corporate income tax, and the most deplorable thing about this neglect is that it was hardly remarked on by those who should have been having at it with volleys of disapproval. Both lapses are explained alike. The corporate income tax, like many long-standing public evils, has assumed the status of a public good mainly because it is politically sacrosanct. Since nearly all voters are densely ignorant of how this levy really hurts them, they are presumed to be hot for it; therefore no politician is supposed to run counter to the tax, and therefore those few experts who know it well would be impractical and idealistic to take up arms against it.

Yet the tax is a hoax on us all. Although nobody knows how it works or who really pays it, the tax distorts grossly the country's economic behavior. Every bright tax lawyer and accountant, on the rare occasions when he takes enough time from the intricacies of his highly rewarding craft to reflect on the tax it-

Reprinted from *Fortune*, LXVII, 40 (April, 1963), 86-89, and 229-230, by permission of the publisher. Copyright © 1963 Time, Inc.

self, is struck by the way it perverts economics to expediency. Although most businessmen have learned to live with the tax, and many "realists" among them feel it is too thoroughly entrenched to be abandoned or radically modified, most are well enough aware of its egregious discriminations and distortions. As for the nation's economists, those professional caretakers of capitalism's Ark of the Covenant, they surely are not happy about it. A small minority is partial to the tax because "it produces $21 billion with a minimum of effort," or because it is "our second-best tax," or because "any *old* tax is a *good* tax," or even because "it is a means of controlling monopoly power." But the great majority of economists would argue that the tax is execrable in principle; provided its elimination were accompanied by certain reforms in the capital-gains and personal income taxes, most would get on their legs for its abolition. Professor William Vickrey of Columbia University did just that last year at a convention of the Tax Institute, when he flatly asserted that the combination of corporate property and income taxes made the U.S. the most anti-capitalist nation in the free world, and described the corporate income tax as "this incubus we have fastened around our necks."

The anti-tax case has never been stated more eloquently than in the closing days of World War II, when many organizations, economists, and business leaders, looking ahead to the promises of a new and reformed postwar world, argued persuasively for its abolition. And no one put the case with more relevance and cogency than Henry Calvert Simons, associate professor of law and economics at the University of Chicago until his death in 1946. More than perhaps any market economist of our time, Simons understood the practical value of principles; he argued that capitalism's disregard of the rules of the game had got it into the mess of the 1930's and that the New Deal's remedies, by all but abrogating capitalism's basic principles, were bound to make the mess worse. Simons consequently argued that free enterprise (a term he disliked because so many free enterprisers were interested in freedom only for their own enterprises) would flourish only under what he called an "elegant" tax structure—a simple, adequate, fair, enforceable, coherent layout that sticks to basic principles.

These principles, Simons reasoned, demanded that the great bulk of federal taxes be levied *directly*—i.e., on personal incomes. He characterized business income and other concealed taxes as appropriate for insecure governments, backward countries, and factions aspiring to permanent and irresponsible power, but as degrading and costly for a great republic of free men and brave. Hidden taxes allowed politicians to buy votes without paying the price in taxpayer reactions, developed the something-for-nothing delusion about public spending, and resulted in a vast misuse of the nation's resources. An elegant as distinguished from an ugly tax structure, Simons insisted, must not tax business as business and must not discriminate against innovating and long-odds enterprise. Business decisions should and could be rid of tax considerations, *given proper rules of the game*. If the corporate income tax were retained, Simons predicted, its discriminations would be constantly aggravated, and attempts to mend the defects would render those defects all the worse.

Simons' analysis, after nineteen years, is astonishingly apposite and exigent. Like a problem child that has grown up to be a problem adult, the tax's capacity for economic mischief has flowered with age. All taxes distort economics with expediency and opportunism, but this tax distorts and inhibits economic decisions in company executive offices, precisely where most of the creative decisions are made. It is impartial only in its propensity to discriminate, and even its discrimination is coy and whimsical. It fortifies and augments large aggregations of capital and is biased against equity investment and particularly against risky and long-odds enterprise; yet it is biased against efficient companies and those financed by paid-in stock. It results in a pervasive misuse of national resources, measurable and unmeasurable, including a large part of the gross national brain product accounted for by thousands of tax lawyers, accountants, economists, and financial specialists. One could draw up an arresting thesis to the effect that the corporate income tax costs the nation much of the $21 billion or so it fetches in annual revenues; but such a study would merely waste additional resources by ferreting out the obvious. The corporate tax testifies plainly and powerfully that it is better economics to adhere to principle than to bend principle.

A METAPHYSICAL TAX

To understand why the tax is so bad, one must first understand its elusiveness. If tax concealment were the only measure of a nation's immaturity, the corporate income tax would put the U.S. even below Indonesia. The tax is so hidden that legions of Ph.D.'s, after thirty years of producing exquisitely wiredrawn ratiocination, cannot agree who pays it or how or when. Is the tax passed on in the form of higher prices or lower wages or both, or is it really a tax on equity capital? The problem is almost metaphysical in its gluey complexities, and examining the learned speculations of the academicians, the untutored layman finds himself recalling Macaulay's comment on the medieval schoolmen who "showed so much acuteness and force of mind arguing on their wretched data, that one is perpetually at a loss to comprehend how such minds came by such data."

Yet the subject is a compelling one, well worth a look. "If we ever found out who actually bears the tax," says Professor E. Cary Brown of M.I.T., one of the nation's leading tax authorities, "all hell would break loose." Indeed it might. If the tax is *not* shifted, or perhaps if it is shifted only over the long run, then it plainly has all kinds of complex and sinister effects on profits and investment. If, however, the tax is shifted to the consumer in the form of higher prices or shifted to labor in the form of lower wages, or both, then the complaints about double taxation of dividends have no basis, and labor's antiquated and fiercely beloved notion that the tax is borne by corporate capital is a hollow joke; the tax becomes a discriminatory, capricious excise or payroll tax that elevates prices, reduces wages, and inhibits trade. But there is a joker here. As we shall see presently, these alternatives are far from being mutually exclusive.

The recent trend in academic analysis runs toward the notion that the tax *is* passed on. Only last month Professors Richard A. Musgrave of Princeton and Marian Krzyzaniak of Wayne University committed to the printer a pioneering study that uses samples of industry and company records to show that manufacturing companies as a group shift the tax enough *over the short term* "to prevent decline in the net rate of return, and that those adjustments are maintained subsequently."

Common sense and business habits tend to reinforce the supposition that the tax is shifted, partly or wholly, sooner or later, by some if not all companies. Regulated utilities are allowed to treat the tax as an expense in rate making, and usually do pass it on. Others try hard without benefit of regulation. Perhaps not one in five hundred executives could give, offhand, a thoroughly clear account of how he compensates for the tax. But for all of them, getting around it is as routine as coming to work every morning. As Beardsley Ruml remarked to a *Fortune* editor just before he died, "Businessmen don't tell economists about how they pass the tax on and they don't tell Uncle Sam." And they probably don't even tell themselves; they just adapt to the tax, and the luckier and more skillful of them doubtless adapt better than the others.

THE MAJORITY PARTNER

This phenomenon is supremely important, for it suggests why so much of the argument about the incidence of the tax is academic. Since every corporate manager must regard the government as a majority partner with a 52 percent lien on every dollar he makes, he must behave as if he had to pass the tax on, for he must earn more than twice as much as he would without the tax. As Henry Simons kept insisting, what counts is the tax's point of impact. Thus one clean-cut fact arises from the molasses barrel of contention about the tax: whatever its incidence and timing, its effects on the economy are malefactory. For business inexorably finds the tax bending and confounding its cost, price, and investment decisions. Specifically what happens is this: (1) The tax tends to penalize efficient companies and to favor inefficient ones. (2) The tax discriminates against equity capital and favors debt capital. (3) The tax discriminates against corporations and favors unincorporated business. (4) The tax inhibits vital creative capital spending. (5) The tax discriminates against small, long-odds enterprise and favors large, established companies. (6) The tax distorts corporate spending patterns and fosters an enormous professional gimmickry. (7) The tax is virtually useless as a means of curbing monopoly.

The bias of the corporate income tax against efficiency is easy to grasp. Simply imagine two competing companies with comparable sales, one of which is efficient enough to make twice as much money as the other. The former pays twice as much tax. To the extent that it absorbs the tax, its capital is penalized severely, and to the extent that it tucks the tax into prices, it is unable to pass its efficiency along to the consumer. Although some economists argue the tax does not *prevent* a company from turning in a superior performance, superior performance is punished. And there is no doubt that the high income taxes paid by U.S. firms put them at a disadvantage against less heavily taxed foreign corporations.

Now look at the discrimination against equity capital, which is all the worse if (or to the extent that) the tax is not shifted. The tax misses completely any return on borrowed capital, as distinguished from stock or equity capital. Ideally, almost everyone still agrees, risky enterprise should be financed largely by equity. Too much debt in any company renders it vulnerable to temporary adversity, and too much corporate debt in the economy, by forcing companies to rate liquidity too high, can theoretically turn mild recession into severe deflation. Since interest on debt is tax deductible, however, corporations today are powerfully influenced to finance with debt, and investors are driven to find "tax shelters" in mortgageable real estate. The record over the postwar years does not suggest that debt financing other than real estate has increased alarmingly, but the pressure is there; corporate treasurers can supply many examples of how the tax has impelled firms to resort to debt. Kaiser Industries, which has grown large and profitable by the skillful use of cheap debt, is an example. But today even a Kaiser cannot start from scratch on debt. And because a strong, established company can safely support a higher level of debt than the small and struggling company, cheap debt ironically discriminates against the small and struggling company.

The corporate income tax by definition also misses completely the return on capital employed by individuals and partnerships. Professor Arnold Harberger of the University of Chicago, who regards the tax as falling primarily on capital, argues that this omission tends to raise prices of "equity intensive" commodities or those made by equity-financed corporations, and to lower prices in other industries. For example, real-estate prices, which have very little corporation tax in them, are lower than they otherwise would be; but chemical prices, which contain a large amount of corporation tax, are higher than they would otherwise be. Thus the economy is encouraged to spend more on real estate and less on chemicals than it would if there were no tax. As a result of such pressures, Harberger estimates, Americans adopted a consumption pattern in 1953-54 that cost the economy about $500 million more than it would have if the tax had been neutral, or if there had been no tax. At today's levels of production, the figure might be much higher.

Since corporate industry must earn twice as much on the same investment as non-incorporated industry. Harberger goes on, the tax has encouraged investment in enterprise whose yields are relatively low and discouraged investment in enterprise whose yields are high, to the obvious detriment of the whole economy. In 1953-55, Harberger shows, virtually no corporate tax was paid in agriculture and real estate (where few corporations exist), while the corporate tax took more than 60 percent of the aggregate return to capital in many industries like rubber products, electrical machinery, and transportation equipment. Harberger estimates that if the return to all industries had been taxed equally, say at about 30 percent, the improvements in efficiency could have gained the economy as much as $1.5 billion; and at today's production levels, again, the figure might be much higher. Without the corporation tax, of course, such a misuse of resources could not occur.

THE DYNAMIC BRAKE

But the cost of misusing existing resources is probably trivial compared to the cost of repressed and distorted economic growth. Corporations account for more than two-thirds of all U.S. private capital investment; and every corporation, when it weighs buying new capital goods, is acutely aware it must earn $2.08 for every dollar it can keep. As well he might, George Terborgh of the Machinery and Allied Products Institute demonstrates indefatigably how the corporate income tax automatically excludes a whole range of investment proposals that would be eligible without it. Outlays for replacements that would otherwise occur now are postponed several years, and costs and prices that would otherwise go down stay up. Existing plant and equipment, protected against new competition, are allowed to grow much older and less efficient than they should before being replaced. Industry is less likely to invest in "optional" equipment and improvements. Thus an untold number of man-hours and machine-hours are lost forever, employed in tasks that could have been discharged with a smaller outlay of resources. Because productivity has not risen as fast as it could have, in other words, national economic growth has been retarded.

This tax brake on the corporate propensity to invest has a related serious consequence. It looks as if many existing industries, making their usual products, could not absorb the unemployed and new employables even if they were operating at much higher rates. What the country needs is not merely more investment but more investment in new products, new processes, new companies—investment that will create new jobs while rising productivity is enabling established industries to do their usual jobs with steadily fewer people per unit of output. The corporate tax, however, inhibits risky new capital expansion even more than it inhibits capital replacement. The total cost in reduced efficiency and insufficient employment might be reckoned only in billions.

Certain questions often arise. If the corporate income tax inhibits capital spending, why did U.S. industry pile up so much excess capacity in the years 1955-57? Wasn't this excess capacity the reason private capital investment remained sluggish during the past few years? And don't corporations right now have plenty of money for investment? Such questions, some argue, only strengthen the case against the corporate tax. Much useful capacity may be obsolete, as companies with plenty of useful capacity will spend for new equipment—if it promises to pay for itself. On the other hand, companies with modern capacity will spend to innovate or to introduce new products—if the investment promises a satisfactory return. And companies with plenty of money will spend it for new capital goods—if those goods promise to pay off. Because the tax more than doubles the prospective return needed to justify the investment, the urge to invest is reined at its source.

So most American economic thinking agrees that investment has been lagging, and the government in turn has been trying to do something about it. The tax code of 1954 allowed business to write off proportionately more of the cost of capital goods in the early years of their life, and in effect gave all companies a tax-free loan, and growing companies a permanent tax-free loan. Last year, after much pressure by the advocates of depreciation "reform," the government liberalized depreciation schedules, so that industry can write off capital goods over shorter periods. Also Congress allowed a 7 percent tax credit for capital spending (which really amounts to 3.36 percent, since the depreciable basis of the asset is reduced by 7 percent), and now the Administration proposes to cut the tax itself a little. But not even all these expedients offset the tax's tendency to repress economic investment. What is more, the tax actually encourages uneconomic investment. For in trying with partial success to offset one of the many faults of the tax, the government has made another and very different defect all the worse.

That defect is the apparently incurable tendency of the corporate income tax to overfortify established and well-heeled business as distinguished from risky, small, long-odds enterprise. The tax is naturally rough on the latter. As we have already noted, the ability of the large and well-established company to assume cheap debt safely puts the little or struggling company at a disadvantage. Many large, protectively diversified companies can pass on the corporate tax, but this is just what small, struggling companies with single lines of goods often cannot do. Big, diversified companies can write off development expenses for a given product against other income, but the new firm must first survive long enough to earn something. Small companies usually have little or no access to an equity-capital market, and when they do the price comes high. Because they usually must rely mainly or wholly on retained earnings for new equity capital, the tax hamstrings their ability to grow. As for the risky would-be company, Professor Merton Miller of the University of Chicago remarks, "The entrepreneurs you can't ask about the impact of the tax are those who couldn't get the capital to go into business because the return was inadequate for the risks."

THE UNHOLY TRINITY

The present tax system, moreover, encourages the well-established business to generate more and more of its capital internally. About two-thirds of all U.S. corporate investment is coming from depreciation and retained profits, and the proportion shows no sign of declining. And what is wrong with this? Adolf Berle, for one, approves the trend because a large corporation "has the experience, the will, the organization and the business position enabling it to take the risk and follow through to a conclusion." But such concentrations of "will" and "position" are run by human beings, and organized human beings with no incentive for doing otherwise inexorably grow sluggish and tend to use resources inefficiently. Generating capital internally can provide easy "shelter" from the discipline of both capital and consumer markets. Fortified by written-down assets, retained earnings, and the power to finance itself, a company can acquire unearned advantage over a smaller or weaker competitor with a better product. And the trend toward the internal generation of corporate equity capital has already been partly if not largely responsible for drying up the equity-capital market; stock markets, which ideally should be places where new schemes are subjected to the discipline of competition, are today mainly secondhand-security exchanges.

The present system, with its unholy trinity of the corporation income tax, the highly "progressive" personal income tax, and the maximum capital-gains tax of 25 percent, has artificially nourished the trend.[1] Since dividends are taxed in full while capital gains are not taxed until they are converted to cash, stockholders in high income brackets prefer to have their companies plow back earnings and depreciation, even if the money is used relatively ineffectively and the returns are relatively low. Later they realize the increased equity value as a capital gain. Just how much the pressure to retain its profits has driven management to invest them ineffectively is impossible to say, but the large number of companies showing inadequate earnings on their assets suggests that many firms have done so.

The stock market, which favors promising shares paying little or no dividends over unglamorous shares paying big dividends,

[1] The combination is often credited with stimulating risky investment by high-income people. When a man in the 90 percent bracket risks a dollar, the argument has it, he is really risking only 10 cents of his own, and is encouraged to stake his money in the hope of realizing a nice capital gain taxable at only 25 percent. But this argument avoids the question of how much more investment would be stimulated if there were no tax.

testifies eloquently that the pressure to plow back is there. This pressure is partly responsible for the paradoxical circumstance that many corporations today are actually plagued by an excess of investment funds. And it doubtless has been a considerable factor in the diversification movement that has featured U.S. industry since World War II. To the extent that corporate diversification has strengthened competition (and often it has not), it is eminently praise-worthy. But as an accidental benefit flowing from an unsound and unprincipled tax system, it justifies that tax no more than Al Capone's largess to poor charwomen justified his extralegal empire. When a company does not use its resources efficiently, it does not use the nation's resources efficiently. Such misuse is unavoidable and even salutary if the result of an honest mistake in a free market; when the misuse is the result of an ill-conceived tax, the joke is on the people who tolerate the tax.

The big trouble with depreciation "reform" and the investment tax credit, laudable as their intent may be, is that they intensify any misuse of resources generated by the tax. "Liberalized" depreciation of course discriminates grossly in favor of firms with a large volume of depreciable assets. Both measures give firms that cannot use capital efficiently precisely the same incentive as ones that can, and encourage all corporations to invest beyond the point at which returns justify the outlay. Among the major aims of these devices was to encourage national economic growth. But far from accelerating growth, inefficient use of capital handicaps it. The oil depletion allowance provides a tangential lesson; what is wrong with the allowance is not so much that it gives entrepreneurs "unfair" windfalls by enabling them to recover more than their costs in tax deductions, but that it wastes the nation's resources by encouraging oilmen to punch useless holes in proved oil fields.

Finally, liberalized depreciation and the tax credit, by abetting internal generation of capital, discriminate further against new, struggling long-odds enterprises with thin profit margins. "For the boys that are in, they are in more," writes an apparently tired small businessman, discussing the 7 percent credit in the *Wall Street Journal*. "But for the boys that are out, they are out further. What a discouraging prospect!" Or as Milton Friedman of the University of Chicago remarks about depreciation reform and tax credits, "It is strange to note that a tax structure, constructed in no small part with the aim of penalizing big business, in practice protects and fosters bigness and shelters established companies from competition by newcomers." What venturesome and new business needs is not subsidies and special favors, but a fair chance under the rules of the game. The only known way to avoid penalizing enterprisers with the corporate tax is to get rid of the tax. Its amendments are only making it all the more a crooked tail that wags a limping economic dog.

THE LAST-DITCH EXPEDIENT

The corporate tax has been espoused and defended as a useful way of putting a rein on wicked monopolists and oligopolists. The theory is that large corporations earn "surplus" profits, or more money than they need to attract new capital. Therefore society has a just claim to this "surplus," which should be devoted to community good; and the corporate income tax is a nice handy way of soaking up the surplus. This notion manifestly falls flat on its face if the tax is passed on because it is the strong companies with "market power" that are best able to pass it on. But even if the tax is not passed on, or to the extent it is not passed on, it remains a highly discriminatory not to say frustrating way of bagging the "surplus." Not only does the tax miss unincorporated business, but it takes the same percentage of net profit from all corporations, whether they earn "too much" or not. It is as if every driver on the road were arrested and fined to make sure of getting the traffic violators.

The only conceivable way the corporate tax could be bent to antimonopoly uses would be to change it into an excess-profits tax, adjustable for the risk taken by any given company, and this would be prohibitively complex and probably discriminatory to boot. As an antimonopoly tool, Henry Simons argued persuasively, the corporate tax is a last-ditch, ill-contrived expedient, and "any necessity to resort to it against industrial syndicalism will only reveal how small is the chance of preserving economic or political liberty."

The "tax-is-beneficial" argument may be reduced to its logical absurdity simply by imagining what would happen if it were raised to 95 percent. The federal government would in effect be a 95 percent partner of every corporation. No well-established company would have to worry about going bankrupt; nearly every company would be worth more dead than alive. Since the government would be bearing practically all the expense, there would be more arbitrary spending than at any time since Cheops built his pyramid. Unemployment would disappear as millions of bright young men entered lucrative careers as tax lawyers and accountants, and millions of people found jobs in nightclubs and *grande luxe* restaurants. But entrepreneurs would be hard put to start new companies, much less keep them going; the nation's resources would be squandered worse than they are in a totalitarian economy. In the end, living standards would probably go to pot.

HOW TO DO AWAY WITH IT

So from almost any point of view, the tax is bad. But is getting rid of it at all within the realm of possibility? The answer is that the technical (as distinguished from the political) problems are not so hard as they are sometimes made out to be. For one thing, sizable reduction or elimination would have to be gradual, say at a rate of five points a year, if only because long-standing business habits cannot be unwound in a hurry. But gradual reduction alone is not enough. To work at all, corporate-tax reform must be accompanied by an appropriate reform of the personal income and capital-gains taxes, one that could be very "unpopular." Yet such reform would almost automatically take care of the problem of where the money the corporate tax now raises will come from. And it would help allay oft-expressed fears that abolition of the tax would turn out to be a windfall for capital.

All economists agree the discrepancy between the top brackets of the personal income tax and the capital-gains tax must be eliminated before the corporate tax can be abolished or even greatly reduced. Otherwise corporations would have more reason than ever for retaining earnings and using them ineffectively, and an undistributed-earnings tax at or near the top income rate would be necessary. Henry Simons was the first to construct a system that made abolition of the corporate income tax practical, and his system is still hard to improve on. Arguing that an undistributed-earnings tax would deprive small business of its best source of capital, Simons proposed not to tax corporate earnings, distributed or undistributed. There remained, he went on, the task of weeding out biases against persons as investors and as direct participants in more risky ventures, "which task turns out to be largely one of removing present tax penalties on fluctuations of taxable annual income." So he proposed that individuals average their taxable income over the years, that capital gains be taxed as income, and that all transfers of property be taxable as "realizations" of the estimated fair market value at the time of transfer. Enterprises could keep their earnings interest-free; and individuals, at some time or other, whenever they had the cash, and inevitably at death, would have to come to a comprehensive reckoning with the government.

William Vickrey would accept this scheme, but would levy a nominal tax on retained earnings, equivalent to interest on the tax deferred. Vickrey has developed his own tax-averaging plan that renders unnecessary any tax on retained earnings. Milton Friedman would also abolish the corporate income tax, treat capital gains as income, and abolish many deductions now permitted. But to eliminate completely any tax incentive for corporations either to distribute or to retain earnings, Friedman would require shareholders to include in their income their pro rata share of the earnings of their corporation, whether distributed or not. He would also replace the present "progressive" income tax with a single flat rate of about 24 percent on all income above a certain exemption level, which he estimates would suffice to deliver all the revenues now raised by both the individual and the corporate income tax. Since retained earnings would raise the base for calculating individual capital gains, the shareholder would not be taxed twice on them. And the flat rate would largely remove any discrimination against fluctuating incomes. "More and more money would flow to the capital markets," says Friedman, "and more and more corporations would find themselves resorting to the markets. Capital would be invested where it could be used most efficiently, and business would not lack funds if its prospects were good. The number of tax experts would decline sharply, and these highly ingenious people would find far more productive use for their talents elsewhere."

WINDFALL FOR THE NATION

Such are a few of the workable schemes floating around. The point is that honest reform is possible, and that reform could abolish tax biases against equity, corporate capital, creative investment, and small and risky enterprise. It could eliminate artificial incentives either to distribute or to plow back earnings; corporate decisions on how much to distribute would depend, as they should, on efficiency and productivity.

Given such reform, the oft-expressed fear that abolishing or greatly reducing the tax would provide an unjust windfall for capital would be much less plausible than it is today. The windfall argument rests largely on the idea that corporations that have been able to pass the tax on to the consumer would be able to hang on to the proceeds of a corporate-tax cut. Even without readjustment of personal and capital-gains taxes, the facts of economic life are against such a supposition. Labor could be counted on to fight for more than its share of a tax reduction. Latest researches into corporate pricing methods and policies leave little doubt that sooner or later prices and profits would adjust to the market. No unregulated company can hang on to a monopoly position for long. Thanks to a vast corporate diversification and proliferation of capabilities, companies and industries are competing with one another as they never have before. And thoroughgoing tax reform, because it would impel companies to retain only those earnings they could use productively, would render competition all the more effective. For the same reason, it would make for larger and more productive investment, which in turn would make for higher output and lower prices.

By the same token, elimination of the corporate tax would not leave the Treasury out of pocket. Indeed, the $21-billion question of where the Treasury would get money now fetched by the tax is somewhat rhetorical. For if corporations did not pay the money directly over to the Treasury, it does not follow that the money would disappear. On the contrary, much of the money would immediately find its way into heavy industry as increased capital investment, to employees as increased wages, or to stockholders as increased dividends. A gradual corporate-tax reduction, say over ten years, could probably be more than offset by increases in these tax sources alone. What is more, price reductions would be bound to occur. And owing to the greater efficiency of tax-free corporations, real personal incomes should rise somewhat faster than the national productivity rate now enables them to. So gradual elimination of the corporate tax, far from leaving a gaping hole in the Treasury coffers, would be accompanied by a vastly enlarged tax base. The tax could be eliminated over the years without presenting any great problem to the tax collector and even without inconveniencing taxpayers.

THE UNIVERSAL JOKE

Politically, the elimination of the tax calls for a widespread realization of what a joke the tax is on everyone. The doggedly pro tax stand of labor is curious; labor leaders are *ipso facto* connoisseurs of the opportune, and should see the opportunity in going to bat for a tax reduction and at the same time plugging for a wage increase.

The tax is more of a joke on businessmen than a lot of them suspect, especially on those who may think they have pretty well passed it on even if their competitors haven't. They would be well advised to remember that what is good for, say, Consolidated Products is not necessarily good for the country. What is good for Consolidated Products is good for the economy—and over the longer run for business as a whole and Consolidated Products itself—only if Consolidated Products plays the rules of the game, and only if the government provides the legal and institutional framework under which the rules of the game can work tolerably well. The late Beardsley Ruml described many corporations as having a vested interest in the tax; more appropriate than ever, perhaps, is his observation that the biggest obstacle in the way of reforming the tax is business' own apathy.

Precisely because so many people seem to think the tax is sacred, the tax is a joke on them. It need not be. To argue that the thoroughgoing reform or abolition of the tax is very desirable but politically impossible is to argue that democracy cannot work. To make democracy work one need not believe that all people who are neither children nor insane are highly intelligent and models of responsibility; one needs to believe only that a good thing is politically feasible if enough influential opinion gets behind it. Nations do not stay great by kicking around the principles on which they are founded. The capitalist system, it should be hardly necessary to say, does not work as well as it can; if it is to earn the support of its citizens and the respect of the rest of the world, its constant improvement should be an aim of public policy. Among the many things that keep the system from working as well as it can, the corporate income tax surely ranks close to the top.

SECTION III

🎋 *Government Expenditures*

The salient characteristic of federal government expenditures is the historical upward movement in the volume of these expenditures. Any cursory evaluation of the changing size of federal outlays indicates that the central government is now responsible for the re-allocation of a larger share of personal income than at any previous time. The magnitude of these expenditures may be viewed in dollar shares of gross national product, or national income, produced by, or diverted to the public sector. However, the quantification of expenditure magnitudes is by no means a completely meaningful measure of the impact of the outlays. Government expenditures are not homogeneous, but have a variegated pattern of effects upon various sectors and economic activity. Some government expenditures are used to purchase goods and services from households and businesses, and thereby represent a claim on the volume of output. Other government expenditures simply transfer dollars from group to group and do not represent a claim on resources. The ultimate economic effects of outlays for purchases of military vehicles and aircraft may be quite different from interest paid on the national debt or monthly benefits to the aged and veterans.

Purposefully implemented, all government expenditures will bring about some type of allocation, distribution or stabilizing effects in the private sector of the economy. Dr. Samuelson's article, "Aspects of Public Expenditure Theories," points out a structure for classifying expenditures as to their general redistributive effects upon aggregative economic activity. Although Samuelson does not attempt to classify particular expenditures, he sets forth a grouping of expenditures which characterize expenditure policy in terms of outlay effects.

The three remaining readings in this section are less globally oriented than Samuelson's, but emphasize the need to introduce a qualitative orientation into expenditure analysis. Conley H. Dillon in "Government Purchases and Depressed Areas" reports on selected federal outlays which were instituted to alleviate structural employment and presents an appeal for stronger federal efforts to utilize surplus manpower.

"Federal Grants and Federal Expenditures," by Selma Mushkin, emphasizes the pattern of development and areas of concern in the selection of choice criteria for allocating federal monies to local governments. Her purpose in undertaking the research, as reported in this article, is to answer questions about the economy-wide results of the manner in which federal payments are made to other political subdivisions.

The need to continually evaluate effects of expenditures is of concern to many Americans who feel that federal outlays are too large. While the size of federal outlays is a function of basic budget policy, the objectives, given small or large outlays, may or may not be attained without careful "economizing" of expenditure dollars. The two-fold concerns of economy and performance of large budget allocations are illustrated in the last article in this section. Probably no other government agency has been as successful as the Department of Defense in achieving "efficiency" in the use of federal expenditures, and, at the same time, fulfilling the purposes of the outlay. Alain C. Enthoven's article on defense and disarmament provides a singular example of how economic analysis applied to government activities can aid in the design, control and accomplishment of the expenditure objective that requires the largest block of federal expenditures.

ASPECTS OF PUBLIC EXPENDITURE THEORIES

Paul A. Samuelson

Economic theorists have done work of high quality and great quantity in the field of taxation. Public expenditure seems to have been relatively neglected. To illustrate this, let me turn to Professor Pigou. I do so with some diffidence, remembering what Ralph Waldo Emerson said to Oliver Wendell Holmes when Holmes showed him a youthful criticism of Plato. "When you strike at a King," Emerson said, "be sure you kill him."

I have no wish to assassinate Professor Pigou. Nor even to criticize him. But immortality does have its price: if one writes an outstanding treatise such as Pigou's *A Study in Public Finance,* one must expect other men to swarm about it, picking a nugget here and probing for a weakness there.

Of a book of some 285 pages, Pigou devotes most attention to taxes. At least 200 pages to taxes; of the rest, most are concerned with fiscal policy and its impact on the business cycle.

Reprinted by permission of the publishers from *Review of Economics and Statistics,* XL, 4 (Cambridge, Mass.: Harvard University Press, November, 1958), 332-338. Copyright 1958, by the President and Fellows of Harvard College. This is a slight revision of a paper delivered at the December, 1955 meetings of the Econometric Society and the American Economic Association. Acknowledgment to the Ford Foundation for research aid is gratefully made.

What about the pure theory of public expenditure? I can find barely half a dozen pages devoted to the heart of this matter—specifically, pages 30-34. And even if we widen the category—to include Pigou's definitions of transfer and exhaustive expenditure and his discussion of pricing of state-operated public utilities—we still cannot bring the total of pages much beyond twenty.

Now it may be that this ratio of 200 on taxes to 20 on expenditure is the proper one. Perhaps there is really nothing much to say about expenditure, and so heavily overbalanced a page budget may be truly optimal. On the other hand, we must admit that fashion has a great influence in economics, which suggests that we ought periodically to survey the neglected areas of theory to make sure that they do deserve to be left in their underdeveloped and backward states.

I have previously published (*Review of Economics and Statistics,* XXXVI, November 1954, 387-89) some thoughts on public expenditure theory; and in order to widen the discussion among economic theorists, I later gave a non-mathematical exposition (*ibid.,* XXXVII, November 1955, 350-56). I do not propose here to give a detailed review of these theories. Rather, I'd like to think aloud about some of the difficulties with expenditure theory and with political decision-making. On these subjects, Richard Musgrave and Julius Margolis have done outstanding research and I must confess my obligation to them for much friendly counsel.

I

Let me first take a fresh look at the nature of government and of public finance from a purely analytical viewpoint. I must give warning: the result will be rather like a New Yorker's map of the United States, in which vast areas of the country are compressed into almost nothing and certain places—like Hollywood, Cape Cod, and Times Square—are blown up far beyond their true proportions.

Similarly, I shall commit all the sins of those bad historians and anthropologists who recreate the history of the human race according to their *a priori* conceptions of the moment. To keep from getting caught, I'll imagine a planet rather like the earth.

Once upon a time men on this planet were all alike and very scarce. Each family hunted and fished its symmetrical acres; and each ended with the same production and real income.

Then men turned to cultivating the soil and domesticating animals. This left even more of the globe vacant, but did not disturb the symmetry of family incomes.

But finally population grew so big that the best free land was all occupied. Now there was a struggle for elbow room. According to the scenario as I choose to write it, the struggle was a gentlemanly one. But men did have to face the fact that recognizing squatter's rights and respecting *laissez-faire* did result in differences of real incomes among families.

Optimal transfer expenditure. Here then for the first time, government was introduced on this planet. A comprehensive program of redistributing income so as to achieve a maximum of the community's social welfare function was introduced. The budget was balanced at a non-zero level: taxes were raised in a non-distorting lump-sum fashion, and transfer expenditure was allocated among families so as to achieve the marginal conditions necessary to maximize the defined social welfare function.

Now here on earth, things don't seem to have worked out exactly according to such a timetable. In fact, look at Adam Smith's 1776 discussion of the three duties of government—protection against external aggressors, maintenance of order at home, and erecting those public institutions and works "which though they may be in the highest degree advantageous to a great society could never repay the expense to any individual." We could interpret the last of these in so broad and tautological a way as to be compatible with anything. But if we stick to a narrower non-empty interpretation, it would appear that our planet began with redistributional governmental functions that

Smith had not even dreamed of and which would most surprise him if he were to come to life and revisit any modern nation.

Now why do I describe so bizarre a model? It is to underline this theoretical point: Given a social welfare function, and given the absence of all technological and taste externalities, and given universal constant returns to scale, there would be needed only one type of public policy—redistributive transfers. (Under some ethical assumptions, these might be from poor to rich rather than rich to poor; but only by chance alone would zero redistributions maximize a specified social welfare function that depends solely on real incomes.)

Minimal collective expenditure. But what about the neglected exhaustive elements of public expenditure that even the most thoroughgoing *laissez-faire* economy will want to make—e.g., courts of justice to enforce contracts or any of the other items under Smith's first two duties? Later I shall review a possible theory of such expenditure. But first let me mention why the problem of financing such expenditures is, so long as they remain small, secondary to that of transfers.

Even on other planets, perfectionist lump-sum taxes are rarely feasible. We tax the objects that we can feasibly tax. And this must introduce deadweight-theoretically-avoidable tax burdens in addition to the unavoidable real burden involved in having to use resources for public purposes. (This doesn't mean the public services aren't worth their costs; on well-run planets, they are.)

Years ago, when studying this problem, I encountered what was to me a surprising fact. It turns out that, so long as exhaustive expenditure is "small," the deadweight burden is "negligible" no matter what system of taxation is used. Only in the second approximation, so to speak, does it matter what tax structure we use to "cover" the needed program. At least this would be the case if incomes were already distributed optimally. *If,* as is more likely, *incomes are distributed prior to taxation in a non-optimal manner* (not as determined by me but as determined by the relevant social welfare function), *then the manner of taxing is very important even at the first level of approximation; and it is the interpersonal distributive elements that are all important in defining an optimal tax structure.*

It is because of this conclusion that my planet had to start out with transfer taxation. As I have said, this result seemed odd to me at first; but having been led there by the invisible hand of mathematical logic, I was forced to draw my map in this way.

Sizable exhaustive public expenditure. Once we admit the possibility of public collective services on our planet, we have to face the possibility that they will be large rather than small; and in any case they will be finite rather than zero or infinitesimal. So we do need an analysis of their logical nature.

We can approach this indirectly. What is our theory of *non*-public expenditure? So long as goods are producible at constant returns to scale and so long as each person's consumption of a good is measurably distinct from any other person's, the perfect-competition model of markets can be used as *an* optimal social computing device. If we deny constant returns to scale—and technology on this or any other planet may make this denial mandatory in many areas—an opening wedge for an alternative kind of social allocation arises. And if we deny that every good's consumption is purely individualistic, instead insisting on strong "external effects," we will have still another reason why the ordinary private marketing calculus must be non-optimal.[1]

To handle one difficulty at a time, let's keep to a strict assumption of constant returns to scale in all production. But let's introduce important externalities ("neighborhood" effects, etc.) into the consumption sphere. Thus, the battleship that protects your rights and investments also protects mine.

I don't suppose that anyone, upon reflection, would try to

[1] There are still other basic reasons for governmental action or interferences: e.g., "paternalistic" dissatisfaction by the electorate with the effective tastes that they will all display in their day-to-day market preference acts—leading to public policies in the field of education, capital formation, etc.; exercise of economic entrepreneurship and decision-making by public officials; and many more.

build up a theory of public expenditure without bringing in some kind of externality. Yet it is surprising that Pigou, who above all welfare economists has reminded us of external diseconomies of the smoke nuisance type, should in his brief discussion of expenditure theory have left this externality element almost completely implicit.

Now remembering that we theorists like to work with extreme polar cases, what is the natural model to formulate so as to give strongest emphasis to external effects? I have long thought that this is best brought out by the following model.

Assume that some goods, like bread, are privately consumed: this means that the total of bread can be written as the sum of the bread consumptions of each separate individual. But along with such purely private goods, assume public goods—like national defense—which *simultaneously* enter into many persons' indifference curves. Then assuming no transcendental group mind, but only a set of individual tastes and an ethical social welfare function dependent upon these tastes and ranking them in order of deservingness, we can prove that the perfect-competition market model will not work optimally. We can prove that there exists an inefficient configuration from which all men can be made better off, and a frontier of efficient points from which no universally advantageous movements are possible; of all the infinity of such efficient points, a socially best one is definable in terms of a specified normative welfare function.

It is this model that I explored in the two cited papers. And it is also this model that Sax, Wicksell, Lindahl, Musgrave, Bowen, and other economists of the last 75 years had considered under the "voluntary exchange theory of public finance" name or some other. The principal conclusions of this analysis seem to be the following:

1. Efficient, inefficient, and socially optimal configurations can be theoretically defined: a point on the efficiency frontier

requires equality between the vertically-added marginal rates of substitution of all men for the public and private goods; and the best of such points requires lump-sum redistributions of the transferable private goods until they have equal marginal social significance.

2. Although the optimum is definable, rational people will not, if left to themselves, be led by an invisible hand to the bliss point. On the contrary, it will pay for each rational man to dissemble, trying to mask his preference for the public goods and to engage in other game-strategy maneuvers which, when all do them, will necessarily involve deadweight loss to society.

Having called attention to the nature of the difficulty, I do not wish to be too pessimistic. After all, the world's work does somehow get done. And to say that market mechanisms are non-optimal, and that there are difficulties with most political decision processes, does not imply that we can never find new mechanisms of a better sort. (Example: Skillful use of the symmetry that prevails between individuals may enable us to find optimal computing algorithms. Example: Interrogate people for their tastes with respect to public goods in such large homogeneous groups as to give each respondent the feeling that his answer can be a "true" one without costing him anything extra.)

Decreasing-cost phenomena. Once people have understood the above model, they are likely to object to its unrealism. Thus, Drs. Stephen Enke and Julius Margolis have both pointed out that many, if not all, government expenditures can be qualitatively varied so as to confer more benefit on one man at the expense of another man. This raises the question whether we cannot bring back the market pricing mechanism, charging fees for public services and letting their quantity and quality be determined by money voting of the supply and demand type.

Certainly, it should be possible for the theorist to go beyond the polar cases of (1) pure private goods and (2) pure public goods to (3) some kind of a mixed model which takes account of all external, indirect, joint-consumption effects. I shall not write down such a mathematical model. But if I did do so, would we not find—as Pigou and Sidgwick so long ago warned us is true of all external economies and diseconomies—that the social optimum could not be achieved without somebody's taking into account all direct and indirect utilities and costs in all social decisions?

Now in connection with running a particular railroad, highway, or concert, we might find just the right conditions of scarcity of space and of independence of consumptions so that ordinary market pricing could lead to the optimum. In such a case, we can really reduce matters to our first category of purely private goods, and self-policing perfect competition might be an optimal social signalling and computing device.

However, generally, a mixed model that refuses to fall in my polar case of a pure public good will not thereby obligingly go into the other polar case of a pure private good. The mixed case has elements of both in it. And while we cannot by pure logic alone deduce that the intermediate case must qualitatively be a blend of the properties of the two poles, we can by logic know that ordinary pricing will be nonoptimal unless it happens to be able to pick up each indirect external marginal utility.

Here is a contemporary instance. The Federal Communications Commission is now trying to make up its mind about permitting subscription television. You might think that the case where a program comes over the air and is available for any set owner to tune in on is a perfect example of my public good. And in a way it is. But you would be wrong to think that the essence of the phenomenon is inherent in the fact that the broadcaster is not able to refuse the service to whatever individuals he pleases. For in this case, by use of unscramblers, it is technically possible to limit the consumptions of a particular broadcast to any specified group of individuals. You might, therefore, be tempted to say: A descrambler enables us to convert a public good into a private good; and by permitting its use, we can sidestep the vexing problems of collective expenditure, instead relying on the free pricing mechanism.

Such an argument would be wrong. Being able to limit a public good's consumption does not make it a true-blue private good. For what, after all, are the true marginal costs of having one extra family tune in on the program? They are literally zero. Why then prevent any family which would receive positive pleasure from tuning in on the program from doing so?

Upon reflection, you will realize that our well-known optimum principle that goods should be priced at their marginal costs would not be realized in the case of subscription broadcasting. Why not? In the deepest sense because this is, by its nature, not a case of constant returns to scale. It is a case of general decreasing costs. So long as increasing returns prevail in the actual range of consumption, we know that perfect competition will not be self-preserving and market behavior is unlikely to be optimal.

The case of decreasing costs may be empirically very important. Certainly, when you try to analyze why public utilities are public utilities and why certain activities (like railroads, water supply, electricity, and postoffices) may fall into either the category of public or private enterprise, you will usually find that some significant deviation from strict constant returns to scale is involved. I cannot then be completely satisfied with Pigou's statement:

> These are not problems of Public Finance, as I understand that term. I do not propose, therefore, to discuss at all the question over what classes of enterprise it is desirable that public operation should be extended, but to proceed on the assumption that this is already determined. (Page 24.)

> Considerations concerning waste thus enable us to say, with regard to several classes of goods and services [primarily those which do not have an inelastic demand], that, if the government decides to provide them, it should finance their provision by fees. (Pages 27-28.)

It is precisely in such cases that uniform average cost pricing will sin against the rule that prices should equal marginal costs.

As Hotelling has insisted, there is here a *prima facie* case for government subsidy. To argue, as some economists have done, that the government budget is already so loaded with necessary expenditure as to make it undesirable for it to have to take on such subsidy expenditures, is to miss the point I am trying to make. This *is* one of the needed functions of government, and in making compromises because of fiscal necessities, there is no *a priori* reason why this function should be particularly neglected.

There is a related significant point that needs stressing. It is not enough in the decreasing cost case to come closer to marginal cost pricing in the Lerner-Lange manner, making up the deficits by general taxation. As soon as decreasing cost and diversity of products appear, we have the difficult non-local "total conditions" to determine what finite mix of product is optimal. This involves a terrible social computation problem: we must scan the almost infinite number of possible products and select the best configuration; we cannot feel our way to the optimum but must make judgment at a distance to determine the *optimum optimorum.*

All this is familiar. But what I have to point out are the complications that arise when there are two or more people on the planet. I like my cider sour; you like it sweet. With constant returns we could both get what we want, or at least what we deserve. But with initial indivisibilities or other forms of increasing returns, what I get will depend on what you get. (This is true even if we pay in the form of fees the marginal costs of our separate consumption.)

Now, how can society decide on the product mix which will maximize a specified social welfare function? It must weigh in all the different individuals' utilities from each decision. And *this is a problem that is analytically almost exactly like any model of public expenditure.*

Given the individual indifference curves and the social welfare function comprising them, one could define the theoretical optimum. (In practice, finding the solution might be very tedious.) But now try to devise a system of "benefit taxation" that will in some sense make people pay for what they get—either because justice or equity requires this, or, more subtly, because the necessity of having to make such payments is thought to be a way of helping to determine the proper place for society to arrive in the end. Instantly, you will discover that the same game-theory reasons that compel rational men to hide their desires for public goods will be motivating them to hide their consumers' surpluses from different product configurations.

II

Once again, in contemplating the dilemmas that most forms of political voting involve, we are reminded of the beautiful and special simplicities of the *laissez-faire* model. But, alas, the difficulties are those of the real world. And it would be quite illogical to conclude from all this that men and technology should be different, should be such as to make the competitive game all-sufficient. That would be as silly as to say that we should all love sawdust because its production is so beautiful.

Conclusion.   Unfortunately, I have only gotten my planet started. Time hasn't permitted me to do more than describe its transfer expenditures, to relate them to the financing of small public services, and to formulate some of the analytic difficulties with a theory of public services. Though my model of pure public goods has turned out to be an unrealistic polar case, it turns out that almost all deviations from constant returns to scale and almost all externalities must inevitably involve some of the same analytic properties and dilemmas of my polar case.

We must leave to other times and other stars the exploration of those momentous coalitions of decision-making that are part of the essence of the political process. To the theorist, the theory of public finance is but part of the general theory of government. And at this frontier, the easy formulas of classical economics no longer light our way.

APPENDIX: STROTZ AND TIEBOUT DISCUSSIONS

1. *Distributional aspects of public goods.* I should like to comment briefly on two papers that have grown out of the earlier discussion. In the present issue Professor Robert H. Strotz has pointed out a formal implication of my original equations (1) and (2): they define a Pareto optimality frontier.[2]

$$u^1 = f(u^2, u^3, \ldots, u^s);$$ (A)

and each point on that frontier will generally determine a set of all public goods

$$X_{n+j} = g^j(u^2, u^3, \ldots, u^s) \ (j = 1, 2, \ldots, m).$$ (B)

Now under what conditions can the left-hand variables in (B) be regarded as independent variables? If $s - 1 = m$ and the Jacobian matrix $[g^i{}_j]$ is well-behaved, (B) can be inverted. Or if $s - 1 > m$ and the Jacobian $[g^i{}_j]$ is of rank m, m of (B)'s right-hand u's can be solved for in terms of the public goods (X_{n+1}, $\ldots$, X_{n+m}) and the remaining righthand u's. So the Strotz conclusion follows: Any public good configuration is optimal if only the "distribution of income" is such as to get us to a point on the Pareto-frontier compatible with that public good configuration.[3]

In view of the modern trend to regard mere Pareto-optimality or efficiency as incomplete necessary conditions, what follows from the above conclusion? To me, this.

It is wrong to make, as some have made, a sharp separation

---

[2] I use my original notation, which is related to Strotz's by $X_{n+j} = S_j$, $s = I$, $m = K$, $L^4 = s_4$, etc.

[3] When you reflect that the degrees of freedom to *completely specify* a single post office exceed the number of people in the United States, the case where $s - 1 < m$ may seem most realistic. In such a case, or in case people's preferences for public goods are so alike as to lead to ill-behaved Jacobians, an arbitrary choice of (X_{n+j}) will be compatible with no Pareto-optimal point.

between correct public-good decisions and correct redistribu-
tional-taxation decisions. Changing public goods *does* materially
affect the distribution of income and all decisions have to be
made *simultaneously*.

As Professor Strotz says, there is no disagreement between
our analyses.

2. *Local finance and the mathematics of marriage*. A second
paper of interest in the present connection is that of Professor
Charles M. Tiebout.[4] He argues that the public expenditure theory simplifies itself at the local level—as people spontaneously
join in forming homogeneous communities which will legislate
what each (and all) want in the way of collective goods.

This attempted solution fits in under one or another of the
"symmetry" principles that I had referred to. That it goes some
way toward solving the problem, few would doubt. As a solution, though, it raises a number of serious questions.

Thus, when you study in detail a supposedly homogeneous
suburb, you find it riddled with conflicting desires. The old, with
grown-up children, oppose the desire of the young for more
school expenditure. And so it goes. It avails little for one group to
say to another: "If you don't like it here, go back where you
came from." Ours is a fluid society, with little respect paid to
hard-to-identify charter members. People want to "improve"
their community, not abdicate from it.

Secondly, people often like heterogeneity even though it involves conflict. The old don't want to live in homogeneous ghet-
tos with their own kind, and the same goes for many other
groups. In an interdependent world, one man's privacy is another man's condemnation to loneliness.

Thirdly, there is the political and ethical question whether
groups of like-minded individuals shall be "free" to "run out"
on their social responsibilities and go off by themselves. At the
national level, society respects no such freedom: e.g., migration
control, compulsory taxation, etc.

---

[4] Charles M. Tiebout, "A Pure Theory of Local Expenditures," *Journal of Political Economy*, LXIV (October 1956), 416-24.

A simple mathematical model will illustrate a few of the intricacies of the problem. If a group of men and women have each a preference rating for members of the opposite sex, who will end up marrying whom? This assignment problem—which is stated in biological terms only for concreteness—is also faced by colleges and students choosing each other, by clubs and fraternities, etc. In real life, it is solved by dynamic reconnoiter, contact, proposal, refusal or acceptance—in short, by general trial and error, which is not guaranteed to represent any optimum.

Consider the trivial case of 2 boys A and B and two girls 1 and 2. Each boy has an ordinal preference rating of the girls, which in this simple case must be either the permutations (1, 2) or (2, 1). Each girl's rating of the boys must be (A, B) or (B, A).

Now what are the possible preference configurations? In this simple case, they are essentially only the following (where the first row lists people, with their choices shown in the columns below them:

1	2		A	B
A	B		1	2
B	A		2	1
		or		
1	2		A	B
A	A		1	2
B	B		2	1
		or		
1	2		A	B
A	B		2	1
B	A		1	2
		or		
1	2		A	B
A	A		1	1
B	B		2	2

FIGURE I

Of these four cases, the first fits Tiebout's attempt best. All the guinea pigs are in agreement: 1 and A want to marry; so do 2 and B; all get their first choices. The solution (1, A; 2, B) is Pareto-optimal; being the only Pareto-optimal solution, it is also Bergson-optimal, maximizing *any* social welfare function that respects individuals' tastes.

But now turn to the last case. A and 1 are preferred by all of the other sex. If we give persons the "property right" to form bilateral compacts, the favored ones will presumably marry each other with (1, A; 2, B) the resulting equilibrium.

However, given a social welfare function which respects tastes, this outcome is not necessarily optimal. The other possible outcome (2, A; 1, B) might be "ethically better" (e.g., where 2 has a "great" preference in favor of A but 1 is "almost" indifferent, and 2 is "ethically deserving" of great social respect). Or we can put the matter a little differently: (2, A; 1, B) is just as Pareto-optimal as is (1, A; 2, B). When you leave the former and go to the latter, you make two people happier and two people unhappier.

In the second case, there is likewise no unique Pareto-optimal point. Left to themselves with certain "freedoms" and "property rights" to make bilateral collusions, probably 1 and A will marry, ignoring 2 and B. And B will be glad. But 2 will not be glad, showing that the configuration (2, A; 1, B) is also Pareto-optimal. Of course, if you used a crude majority vote rule, (1, A; 2, B) would be the winning position. But—as Arrow, Black, and others have shown—majority-rule devices are subject to many intransitivities and drawbacks.

Finally, the third case is like the last in that both outcomes are Pareto-optimal and in going from one to the other you sadden two people and gladden two. Whether the girls or boys are to be made glad cannot be decided except in terms of a given determinate social welfare function.

I conclude from all this that there remain many important analytical problems of public-good determination that still need investigation at every level of government.

GOVERNMENT PURCHASES AND
DEPRESSED AREAS

Conley H. Dillon

The four postwar recessions have focused attention on persistent pockets of unemployment in various regions of the U.S. What programs have been attempted in recent years to alleviate this situation? To what extent have they succeeded? What can be done with existing governmental machinery to better utilize unemployed manpower?

The definition of the responsibility of the federal government for employment in our free enterprise society was legislatively established by the Employment Act of 1946. This Act commits the government to provide employment opportunities for those able, willing and seeking to work.

While indicative of national policy, this commitment was not translated into executive action until the Korean conflict. Several directives by the President and the Secretary of Defense in 1951 concerned manpower mobilization and paved the way for

Reprinted from *Challenge, The Magazine of Economic Affairs* (July, 1962), pp. 12-15, by permission of the publisher. Published by the Institute of Economic Affairs, New York University. A grant from the General Research Board of the Graduate School of the University of Maryland made the research for this article possible.

the issuance of Defense Manpower Order No. 4 (DMP 4) by the Director of Defense Mobilization. This order is still the basis for efforts to channel government contracts into surplus labor areas.

The expressed purpose of the order was to develop and maintain the necessary military and economic strength to carry out national policy and to provide for procurement by negotiated purchases from firms located in surplus labor areas. Specifically the order created the Surplus Manpower Committee, which was charged with the responsibility for making recommendations to the Office of Defense Mobilization to facilitate placing contracts in surplus labor areas—areas certified by the Secretary of Labor as having "a current or imminent surplus."

In 1953 DMP 4 underwent a major revision which altered the procedure and focus of contract placement. The authority to pay a higher price to purchasers located in depressed areas was eliminated. A new procedure was adopted whereby a part of an advertised procurement could be allocated to a firm in a labor surplus area if it met the price paid by the lowest qualified bidder. This "set aside" was awarded after negotiation with all bidders from surplus labor areas who were within 120 per cent of the price figure of the successful bidder on the unreserved portion of the contract.

In the 1954 defense appropriation legislation, Congress prohibited the purchase of *any* item with defense funds which was priced above the lowest competitive price obtainable. This legislation apparently stemmed from the fear of Congressional representatives from nondepressed areas that any shift of government purchasing toward areas with high unemployment would result in a serious loss of government contracts in their jurisdictions.

In 1960 DMP 4 was again revised. The term, "areas of current or imminent labor surplus" was changed to "areas of persistent or substantial labor surplus." In addition, this revision gave a larger role to the Department of Commerce in obtaining the cooperation of other federal agencies in channeling government contracts into surplus labor areas.

The program outlined in DMP 4 encountered serious difficulties during all stages of its development. From its inception, many officials in the Department of Defense recognized that it would be a difficult program to administer. It required revision of customary procedures, formulation of new directives and other time-consuming activities. The reluctance of policy-making and administrative personnel to push the program created slowdowns at all levels. During the Korean conflict the Labor Office of the National Production Administration acted as a "gadfly" and stimulated more activity than might have otherwise occurred.

The records of the Labor Office indicate that some officials of the Defense Department were opposed to taking the steps necessary to implement DMP 4. Since the Surplus Manpower Committee needed the agreement of representatives of participating agencies to make policy and the cooperation of responsible officials at all levels to achieve follow-through, its efforts to effectively develop a program were handicapped by this opposition.

Some officials opposed the program because they sincerely believed that the most valid overriding principle in government purchasing was to obtain the item at the lowest price. It was also generally believed that sophisticated products could be produced only by large firms, which were almost exclusively located outside the depressed areas. Consequently, the principal opportunities for firms in areas of surplus labor came through subcontracts rather than prime contracts. This placed the burden of better manpower utilization on the cooperation of prime contractors, a very slender reed.

In spite of the lack of enthusiasm for the objectives of DMP 4 in some military departments, the order was translated into the *Armed Service Procurement Regulation,* the manual prescribing the rules for contracting officers. This complicated set of operating procedures, like many statements of government policy, offered many paths to the goal of a contract award. The decision to select the "set-aside" path and divide a procurement into two parts was made by the contracting officer.

The natural tendency of this key operating official was to avoid the time-consuming, more complicated procedure of the "set aside." He was already overworked, plagued by pressure from representatives of small business and urged in the regulations to consider several other factors. Consequently, he generally failed to make surplus labor "set asides" unless there was a special program under way in his branch of the service or some superior demonstrated a strong interest in DMP 4. As these unusual circumstances rarely occurred, he was left free to make a choice—which generally resulted in contracts being placed as usual.

During the course of the last Presidential campaign, the problem of unemployment was an important issue. Sen. John F. Kennedy repeatedly asserted his strong interest in channeling more federal contracts into depressed areas. Following his election to the Presidency, he asked Sen. Paul F. Douglas (D.-Ill.) to head a task force to study the needs of these areas. This group came up with some specific recommendations for aiding surplus labor areas in their quest for more federal contracts. But when the proposed legislation came before Congress, the only provision passed was the one authorizing the compilation of data on firms in depressed areas—data to be made available to federal and private purchasing officials. This step, while important, was certainly not revolutionary.

Soon after taking office, President Kennedy issued a letter to the heads of executive offices and agencies directing them to give high priority to measures that would affect employment by spring and especially "to projects located in areas of labor surplus." The letter spelled out specific steps necessary to accomplish this purpose and directed the agencies to report their results by a dead-line date.

The President also asked the Defense and Labor Departments and the General Services Administration to recommend a feasible plan to facilitate the placement of contracts in surplus labor areas. They recommended that a certain percentage of defense contracts be set aside for firms in depressed areas. In a similar way, allotments had been made to small business, a device which had greatly increased the percentage of contracts to small businesses.

However, when it was presented to the General Accounting Office, the Comptroller General refused to approve the recommendation because of the provision in the 1954 defense appropriation legislation mentioned above. He felt that this legislation, which specifically stated that contracts were to be awarded on the basis of the "lowest price obtainable," precluded "set asides."

The next move of the President was to establish a task force in his Office under a top Presidential assistant to stimulate greater interest in carrying out the provisions of DMP 4 and to devise new techniques for this purpose. This small group is attempting to serve as a catalytic agent to inspire action on the part of policy-making and operating personnel. While this operation is still in the experimental and exploratory stage, the task force may become a permanent office whose mission would be to keep manpower utilization in the forefront of procurement administration.

In addition to these moves, White House intervention at the policy level has occasionally been evident in specific actions. For example, in the summer of 1961 it was announced that the previous policy of purchasing coal in West Germany for the needs of U.S. military forces in Europe would be discontinued and American coal substituted.

As might be expected, in view of the difficulties in administering DMP 4, it has not been too effective in stimulating employment in depressed areas. Just what do the statistics show in this regard? The Defense Department has regularly compiled data on the percentage and dollar amounts of contracts placed in surplus labor areas. While these statistics have been affected by many shifting factors (the number of surplus labor areas, changes in reporting employment figures, procurement policy, etc.), they do indicate relative trends in a general sense.

The table on page 102 shows that formal attempts (preference awards) to implement DMP 4 have not had a marked effect. These figures indicate that the message of the Administration has not reached the operating levels. Since fiscal 1957 the percentage of total procurement in depressed areas accounted for by preference awards has been approximately one per cent per year, which is a rather unimpressive trend. It is particularly unimpressive if we consider that, during these years, total procurement in depressed areas has averaged only about 20 per cent of procurement in the economy as a whole.

As I said before, any exact measurement of the impact of DMP 4 on the utilization of manpower in surplus labor areas is impossible. However, even without the support of statistics, certain significant facts are evident. The decade during which DMP 4 has been in effect has seen the number of "depressed" areas multiply. The character of the unemployment in these areas has been officially recognized in the Department of Labor's revision of the descriptive wording from "current and imminent" to "persistent and substantial." What was formerly believed to be a temporary problem of adjustment is now regarded as requiring long-range attention.

Neither statistics nor observation offer proof that the impact of the federal efforts under the DMP 4 order have been of major

Military Prime Contracts in Labor Surplus Areas, 1957-61

Fiscal Year	Contracts in Labor Surplus Areas		Preference Awards		Number of Surplus Labor Areas
	Amount	Percent of Total Procurement	Amount	Percent of Depressed Area Procurement	
1957	$ 401,413	2.2	$10,751	2.7	80
1958	3,790,658	18.0	36,592	1.0	135
1959	9,345,256	42.5	95,481	1.0	264
1960	1,958,211	9.6	22,314	1.1	153
1961	6,341,646	28.6	50,464	.8	218

SOURCE: *Department of Defense*

significance. The reluctance of Congress, the President, and the policy-making and operating agency personnel to mount a massive offensive against the chronic disease of unemployment has precluded impressive results. While the principle of federal responsibility for the achievement of full employment has been given lip service by all responsible officials, the wholehearted effort required to establish adequate machinery and to implement the policies adopted has been lacking.

The limitations of a governmental device of this character are clearly evident. At this date, after almost 10 years, the trends discernible are not encouraging. But we cannot ignore the unemployment problem, and the economy cannot afford the drain nor society the blight of "depressed" areas. What, then, must be done? Since there is evidence that the DMP 4 program could be more effective if the machinery were improved and the administrative effort strengthened, I feel it should not be abandoned.

Three approaches toward more effective utilization of idle manpower in surplus labor areas can be delineated. One is through Congressional action. Another is through executive action. The last and perhaps most important approach is to take steps to assure the full implementation of the order in all agencies.

The deletion of the provision in the defense appropriation legislation prohibiting the payment of a price differential to firms in depressed areas would remove a serious obstacle to allocating selected total procurements to surplus labor areas. This objective may be achieved during a period when major geographical regions, particularly the South and far West, are afflicted with many pockets of unemployment. Successful results in the Congress would depend on a strong, well-planned effort by executive and Congressional leaders.

It is also possible to revise DMP 4 by administrative order and to inaugurate procedures which will permit total set asides. This should be accomplished immediately in respect to nondefense contracts. Such action in regard to defense contracts would require more effort and skill as long as the limitation governing defense appropriations is in effect. A strong case for total "set asides" could be presented to the General Accounting Office. This case is based on two propositions:

1. The large number of firms currently located in surplus labor areas provides sufficient competition to satisfy the requirement of making purchases at the lowest price.

2. The special preference given these firms would amount to no more than the preference presently accorded small business firms.

"Follow-through" in executive departments could be accomplished by a combination of approaches. One is to make the temporary Presidential task force a permanent unit in the Office of the President charged with the responsibility of using its authority to obtain maximum opportunities for firms in surplus labor areas.

Within each major agency, special attention should be given this problem by assigning personnel at the planning levels the responsibility of reviewing existing procurement policies and of regularly reporting their findings to their superiors. At the purchasing level, this would require a review of all contracts by the contracting officer to determine the feasibility of "set asides." Periodic reports giving the record of surplus labor "set asides" should be required of each purchasing officer.

In addition to these actions, greater attention should be paid to developing means of helping firms in surplus labor areas to become more aggressive in seeking government contracts. For example, directories for each state with surplus labor areas should be published; more educational conferences on procurement should be held; field offices of defense and nondefense agencies should give greater technical assistance to business firms; and cooperative arrangements should be established between state and local officials to see that all interested firms are placed on appropriate bidders' lists.

Such measures, by themselves, may be insufficient to eliminate completely the pockets of unemployment which exist in the

U.S. But they could accomplish a great deal. And since the machinery for implementing them is already in place, it would seem practical to throw the switch that will set it into operation. We can no longer afford to drag our feet when it comes to making strong efforts to utilize our surplus manpower.

FEDERAL GRANTS AND FEDERAL EXPENDITURES

Selma Mushkin

In recent years there has been considerable interest in the geographic distribution of federal expenditures. In part this interest arises from current issues in federal-state fiscal relations and, more particularly, from issues surrounding federal grants-in-aid.

FEDERAL GRANTS-IN-AID AND FEDERAL TAXES

Two conflicting criticisms have run through the public debates on federal grants-in-aid.

The first is: "Grants are only a round-trip-ticket to Washington. The money comes from the taxes of the people in my state, and it is costly and unnecessary to have it travel to Washington and then back again." [1]

Reprinted from *National Tax Journal*, X, 3 (September, 1957), 193-213, by permission of the publisher. This article is an expansion of a paper delivered before the Research Section of the National Association of Tax Administrators, 25th Annual Meeting, June, 1957, Poland Springs, Maine. The basic statistical materials are those included as part of a dissertation submitted in 1956 to the Graduate Faculty of Political and Social Science of the New School for Social Research.

[1] Editorial, "$1 Aid for $2.32 Taxes," *New York Times,* July 1, 1955.

The second criticism: "My state pays more in taxes than it gets back in grants. The Federal grant-in-aid is not necessarily a bargain; . . . each dollar of Federal grants will cost my state more than a dollar in federal taxes."

The round-trip-ticket. The round-trip-ticket criticism basically assumes a distribution of federal aids on a tax-sharing basis and that states could impose the same taxes as levied by the federal government.

What types of federal revenues are shared with states or localities? They are very specialized fees and public domain land receipts which are relatively small in aggregate amount. Such sharing arrangements pertain largely to public domain lands. In the fiscal year 1953 the federal government paid to states and local governments in the form of shared revenues, mainly from the sale of federal property, products and services, the sum of $45.4 million. Of this total, three programs—the national forests funds, the mineral leasing acts, and the revested Oregon and California grant lands—accounted for $42.3 million or 93.3 per cent.[2] The federal programs that are criticized as a round-trip-ticket are not, of course, these shared revenue programs, but the welfare, health, highway, education and housing grants.

The second assumption centers on the question: Are the taxes which compose the federal tax structure available to states and localities? In the past two decades, various studies of federal-state tax coordination have explored this question and concluded largely in the negative.[3] Ease of movement across state lines and the volume of interstate transactions are barriers to effective taxation by states of sources readily available to the federal government. State tax competition and potential state tax differentials led, in fact, to federal tax-credit offsets to facilitate state use of estate and unemployment compensation levies.

[2] Commission on Intergovernmental Relations, Study Committee, *Payments in Lieu of Taxes and Shared Revenues,* Washington, D.C.: U.S. Government Printing Office, June 1955, 197 pp.

[3] Statement of Joint Conference of Representatives of the Congress of the United States and of the Governors' Conference, September 27, 1947. *State Government,* November 1947, p. 299.

The round-trip-ticket criticism ignores the specific grant objectives. Federal aids are designed to encourage or stimulate states to develop or expand public services deemed essential to the national welfare. Such aid is designed to safeguard state and local administration, while at the same time through federal support, to establish at least a minimum program standard consistent with the national interest.

Federal grants are allocated not in accord with place of tax origin, but on the basis of relative need for the public service and, in several newer grant programs, the relative capacity of states to meet this need. Need for a public service in a state is patently not related to the federal tax burdens. Various examples may be cited to show the differences between a state's tax payments on one hand, and its concentrations of public assistance recipients, classroom shortages, public health problems, hospital bed requirements, and disabled persons on the other hand. Indeed, in view of the importance of income taxes in the federal tax system, an inverse rather than a direct relationship may often be expected between program need and federal tax payments.

Because the variations in capacity among the states often led to widely divergent program performance, it became necessary to incorporate a measure of relative capacity as well as relative need in grant allocations. Accordingly, a number of post-World War II grant programs have been designed so that they are more effective than earlier grants in recognizing state capacity differences. Formulas in these newer programs have moved closer toward achievement of the twin objectives of equalization—a uniform minimum nationwide program level and uniform fiscal effort from state to state to support such a minimum program. It is intended that state and local governments will build upon these minimum standards in response to local variations in services needed and desired.

One part of the round-trip-ticket criticism, which might be mentioned in passing, is the charge of a "rake-off" for purposes of administration. Administrative costs of grant programs are difficult to define and assess in a consistent way from program to program. The variable scope of administrative costs—as Mr. Labovitz has pointed out in a recent study—requires "a detailed and specific system of cost accounting and reporting." In the absence of such a system, costs must be prorated from overhead, rentals, retirement system contributions, tax collection expenses, etc.[4]

Mr. Labovitz, in his study of nine grant programs accounting for over 80 per cent of all federal grant expenditures, employed a broad or inclusive concept of administrative expenses. For the grant programs examined, the total of directly related federal expenditures for administration and other associated activities was $36.1 million in 1956; the total was estimated to rise to $40.6 million in 1957, and to $48.8 million in 1958. These sums represent slightly more than 1 per cent of the amount of grant payments to state and local governments. If one includes, in addition, the prorated costs of federal tax collection and General Accounting Office services, the total of federal administrative expenditure is estimated at about 1.6 per cent of the grant expenditures for the selected programs. For the individual grant programs examined, the percentages of direct administrative costs to grant expenditures ranged from one-tenth of 1 per cent in the case of public assistance to between 11 and 13 per cent in the low-rent public housing program.[5]

Federal net tax "drains." The second criticism of federal grants is that these grants favor some states at the tax expense of others. The grant system is criticized for failing to be a direct tax sharing or a round-trip-ticket system. It is charged that taxes collected in New York or Connecticut, for example, are spent in Mississippi. The implication of this criticism, as Professor Newcomer has emphasized, is that a state which pays the tax has a vested right to the proceeds.[6]

[4] Labovitz, I. M., *Federal Expenditures Associated With the Administration of Programs of Grants-in-Aid to State and Local Governments,* Legislative Reference Service, Library of Congress, April 17, 1957, 34 pp.
[5] *Ibid.*
[6] Newcomer, Mabel, "Critical Appraisal of Federal and State Aid." In

To grant funds to the states in relation to where federal taxes originated as checks written, bank funds withdrawn, receipts of Internal Revenue collectors, or as tax burdens on income recipients—different places in many instances—would not be consistent with relative state needs for public services. The need for public services and the level of federal tax payments are often inversely rather than directly related, as indicated earlier.

From the earliest beginnings of non-land grants, federal allotments to states were made according to need. For example, benefits under the program of grants to the American Printing House for the Blind, initiated in 1789 to stimulate the manufacture and distribution of books and other instructional materials for the blind, were allocated to states according to the number of pupils in public institutions for the education of the blind. In general, 19th century and early 20th century grants were distributed among states either as a uniform amount per state or as a uniform amount per person in the states, and not in accord with federal tax payments.[7]

The criticism that federal grants favor some areas at the expense of others has grown with the increased use of equalization provisions in grant programs. Such provisions call for larger grant allotments or higher federal matching in states with lower incomes. While the argument that "my state is losing money" is not exclusively directed at equalization grants, equalization provisions have increased the differentials between estimated grant "take" and federal tax "drain" by widening the differences in grant allocations among states.

In recent years, the Congress increasingly has recognized that in situations where large expenditures are required to provide essential public services, federal grant funds should be distrib-

---

Federal-State-Local Tax Correlation. Symposium Conducted by the Tax Institute, December 3-4, 1953, Princeton. Tax Institute, 1954, pp. 91-100.

[7] Johnson, Byron L., *The Principle of Equalization Applied to the Allocation of Grants-in-Aid,* Bureau of Research and Statistics Memorandum No. 66, Washington, Social Security Administration, September 1947, 225 pp.

uted in larger proportion to states which have the greatest need for the services and the least financial capacity to provide them. The Commission on Intergovernmental Relations, after its study of the federal grant system, reported to the President and the Congress as follows: "During the past decade . . . the grant structure has been modified to recognize varying state fiscal capacity. In grants for hospital construction, school lunches, and public health, for example, the National Government assumes more of the financial burden in States of lesser fiscal capacity than in more prosperous ones . . . Where disparities in fiscal capacity make it unlikely that the grant's objective will be attained in low-income States without an equalizing formula, it seems only reasonable to grant more funds in relation to program need." [8] The federal-state relations task force report of the earlier Hoover Commission similarly endorsed the principle of variations in grants inversely with fiscal capacity of the states.[9]

The Congress and study commissions have favored federal equalization grants because of the unfavorable experience under earlier uniform or uniform per capita grants. They have favored these provisions because they tend to maximize the effectiveness of limited amounts of federal support in achieving nationwide program levels by putting more funds in states where the need is greatest and financial capacity least.

Recent discussions on equalization aids have sharpened two issues which are of interest since they demonstrate the need for a statistical series on federal expenditure distributions by state. These issues are equalization of state income or equalization of program financing, and efficiency in use of national resources.

Equalization through taxation. A public debate has developed among the advocates of a federal program of school construction. This debate centers on whether or not flat per capita

[8] Commission on Intergovernmental Relations, *A Report to the President for Transmittal to the Congress,* Washington, D.C.: U.S. Government Printing Office, June 1955, 311 pp.

[9] Council of State Governments, *Federal-State Relations;* a Report prepared for the Commission on Organization of the Executive Branch of the Government, 81st Cong., 1st Sess., Senate Document No. 81, 297 pp.

grants are equalization grants. The image of uniform grants as equalization grants is created by the mirror of the interstate income equalization under a uniformly applied progressive federal tax structure.

This imagery can be best explained by the long history of advocacy by educators of the application of the equalization principle, familiar in state-local relations, to federal grants to states. Much of the early research and study of equalization aid is attributable to education groups and their concern with achieving basic or foundation education programs through state and federal aids. John Norton, Paul Mort, and Leslie Chism—all pioneers in measurement of relative state capacity as a basis for federal aids—are educators. Mabel Newcomer's classic work, *An Index of the Taxpaying Ability of State and Local Governments,* was published by Teachers College of Columbia University.

Within the context of this history, it is easier to understand an educator placing the label "equalization" on proposals to distribute a major portion of federal funds on a uniform grant per school-age child basis. It is easier to understand such a statement as, "There are honest differences of opinion about what is truly 'distribution to the states according to need,' " and the statement that equalization "is inherent in the federal tax system." "Many proponents of federal funds for school construction have disregarded the effects of the federal tax system." [10]

This new meaning of equalization grants substitutes the objective of equalization of incomes among the states via federal taxes for the grant objectives of equalization of minimum public service program levels and equalization of state and local taxing burdens to finance these minimum program levels.

Federal grant-in-aid objectives are not directed to equalization of state income. As Howard Schaller, in his 1955 study of *Federal Grants-in-Aid and Differences in State Per Capita In-*

[10] Fuller, Edgar, "Paying for Schoolhouse Construction," *Nation's Schools,* January 1957, pp. 73-78.

comes, indicated after summarizing the purposes of federal grants: "Neither purpose is directed specifically toward the reduction of the per capita income differences among the 48 states." [11]

Equalization of state income and equalization of minimum program levels, paralleled by more uniform state and local taxing effort, are two different things. Moreover, they have different purposes. The design of federal grants to achieve a national minimum program level, without requiring disproportionate state and local tax burdens, needs to be considered without being confused with equalization of state income.

In fact, state income redistribution—to the extent that it occurs through the operation of the federal tax system—is a coincidental result. It is largely a by-product of the application of progressive federal income tax rate, on unequal income structures in the states. Equalization grants have been designed by the Congress to achieve the purposes of the aided program whether it be building of needed medical facilities or rehabilitation of the disabled. There is as a by-product some interstate income redistribution, but as in the case of federal taxes the redistribution is an incidental effect rather than a direct objective.

This is not to say federal taxing, on the one hand, or federal grant policy on the other, have no meaning for state income and fiscal capacity. Federal taxes, and federal grants in far lesser degree, affect states and their taxing potential. It is at this point that the interstate redistribution must be considered. Federal grants in the form of transfer payments to public assistance recipients or of salary payments to public health nurses, vocational education teachers, etc. are included in state income. Variable federal grants thus are reflected in some narrowing of interstate income differences. Interstate income redistribution resulting from federal taxes is not now fully taken into account. A

[11] Shaller, Howard G., "Federal Grants-in-Aid and Differences in State Per Capita Incomes, 1929, 1939, and 1949," *National Tax Journal,* September 1955, pp. 287-299.

correction of state income figures for federal tax payments has been suggested for some time.[12] Basically such an adjustment waits upon the development by the Department of Commerce of an income series appropriately adjusted for federal tax withdrawals. Statistical studies of this adjustment indicate, however, that the interstate redistribution resulting from federal taxes is not so large that the relative positions of the state are affected markedly.[13] The adjustment of state income for federal individual income tax withdrawals appears to have a negligible effect on the state income figures as they are used in grant-in-aid formulas.[14]

Grants and allocation of resources. Theoretical positions recently advanced by economists on the subject of equalization aids run the gamut from the contention that such grants tend to impair the efficient allocation of economic resources to the contention that these grants help to correct a distortion in such allocations. Professor A. D. Scott of the London School of Economics argues that equalization grants-in-aid impair the allocation of resources. More specifically, geographic transfer of taxes from richer states to provide "amenities to poor people in resource-poor states," he says, will deter labor mobility and "thus prevent the maximization of national production." These amenities are "largely social services and thus, through their impact upon the lower-income workers distort the supply of labor in the various areas toward relatively excessive supply just where productivity is least." [15]

[12] Wueller, Paul H., *Elements of a Variable-Grant Formula,* Bureau of Research and Statistics Memorandum No. 54, Washington, Social Security Board, November 1943, 22 pp.

[13] U. S. Department of Commerce, Office of Business Economics, *Personal Income by States Since 1929,* A Supplement to the Survey of Current Business, Washington, D.C.: U.S. Government Printing Office, 1956, pp. 29-30.

[14] Mushkin, Selma, and Crowther, Beatrice, *Federal Taxes and the Measurement of State Capacity,* Washington, Public Health Service, U. S. Department of Health, Education, and Welfare, May 1954, 91 pp.

[15] Scott, A. D., "A Note on Grants in Federal Countries," *Economica,* November 1950, pp. 416-422. *See also* "Federal Grants and Resource Allocation," *Journal of Political Economy,* December 1952, pp. 534-536.

Professor James M. Buchanan of Florida State University takes a different position. He argues that equalization grants "cannot be rejected for efficiency reasons." He says that equity, national interest, and the achievement of minimum standards of public services should be the primary trinity of motives for federal grant transfers. Professor Buchanan continues his analysis with a discussion of the tendency of state and local taxes to be higher in poorer states, and benefits from state and local services to be lower than in wealthier states. This, according to Buchanan, brings a distortion of resource allocation. Unless a remedy such as equalizing federal grants is applied to hold the resources in the poorer states, there will be movement to the high income states. Only in this way can the fiscal system be neutral "in a geographic sense." [16]

Although these points of view appear at first to differ considerably and to suggest different grant policies, essentially the major differences stem from the use of the term "poor." Professor Scott uses the word to mean an area with relatively scarce natural and other resources; Professor Buchanan means an area with relatively low current income. Experience with state-local grant policies documents the need for concern lest funds made available in a local area deter a desirable population out-migration. In the United States, however, few if any states are so small in size as to be stripped of resources in the same way that some local communities have been stripped of supporting industry because of depletion or obsolescence. Differences in the indexes of state capacity used for grant purposes are related to relative current income levels and not to underlying basic resources. Many low-income states have demonstrated they have sufficient natural resources to justify the immigration of capital and enterprise.[17] Moreover, as at least two reviews of this controversy have indicated, the amounts of income transferred through grants and the

[16] Buchanan, James M., "Federal Grants and Resource Allocation," *Journal of Political Economy*, June, 1952, pp. 208-217.

[17] These considerations, however, do not lessen the problem of maximum efficiency in use of Federal revenues.

relief of state and local fiscal pressures have not been very great.[18]

Purpose of the study. These several criticisms, in varying degrees, are based on the relationship of the geographic distribution of federal taxes and the geographic distribution of grants. Relative net grant "takes" or net tax "drains" are measured by comparing all federal grants in a state or allocations under a specific grant program with estimated federal taxes incident or paid in the state. All too frequently, total federal taxes are compared with the 4 cents or so of each federal tax dollar going out to the states in grants. But even in more careful comparisons it is assumed that each $1 of federal grants would be financed by the same complex of federal taxes as compose the total federal tax bill. Marginal tax changes to finance new aid proposals have not been considered.

Information on the state distribution of all federal expenditures should help clarify the issues underlying these several criticisms of federal grants in general and equalization aids in particular. An obvious question is: How does the state-by-state distribution of federal grants compare with the distribution of all federal expenditures for which federal taxes are imposed? Do federal tax dollars go in larger number to the poorer, or to the higher income states? Is there in the aggregate a return of federal tax dollars to their states of origin? Do federal taxing and spending processes result in a net interstate income redistribution? Is the regional income redistribution implicit in the federal tax system offset by the regional distribution of federal expenditures?

A single set of estimates cannot provide the information needed to answer these questions. Nor is a single set of estimates of federal expenditures likely to be well designed to meet the many other purposes for which state expenditure distributions have been sought.

[18] Maxwell, James A., "The Equalizing Effects of Federal Grants," *Journal of Finance,* May 1954, pp. 209-215. *See also* Schaller, Howard G., *op. cit.*

MEASURING FEDERAL EXPENDITURES IN THE STATES

There is no "correct" way of distributing or allocating federal expenditures among the states. The types of expenditures distributed, and the bases on which they are distributed essentially depend upon the purpose of the estimates. There is no simple tabulated series of federal expenditures by states similar to the tabulation of federal tax collections by Internal Revenue District. But even if there were such a series attained by counting, let us say, the amount of federal checks paid initially in each state, it would not be suitable for measuring employment impacts in a state, impacts on consumption, changes in distribution of income, or benefits received by the state residents. For example, the payment of a check in Delaware to a business office of a large corporation may represent payment for goods produced in another state. Subcontractors and factories producing the unfinished materials going into the procurement item may be located in still other states. A check paid to a land-grant college in Iowa may help finance, in part at least, education of a resident of New Jersey. Checks paid in Maryland to scientists working at the National Institutes of Health on heart or cancer diseases are not of exclusive benefit to residents of Maryland.

There is some analogy between the allocation of expenditures and the allocation of federal taxes. In the case of tax payments a distinction is usually made between collections and incidence and these two, in turn, are distinguished from the ultimate economic effects of the tax. Similarly a distinction may be made between the place where a government check is received initially and the ultimate recipient or beneficiary of the payment. Moreover, these flows may be distinguished from the intermediate and long-run economic effects of the expenditures.

Some of the methodological problems in measuring the state-by-state distribution of federal expenditures are summarized briefly below. A more detailed discussion is contained in an article in the *Review of Economics and Statistics*.[19] The supplementary documentation is presented in a paper entitled *Statistical Materials on the Distribution of Federal Expenditures among the States*, duplicated by the U. S. Public Health Service in 1956.[20]

Two concepts of geographic distribution. The location of those who benefit from federal outlays in terms of the program purposes or beneficiary groups must be distinguished from the place where federal outlays flow as dollar payments initially, or over a longer period. The first of these measures may be termed a benefit measure, the second a dollar-flow measure. In the benefit measure, emphasis is placed principally on determining who benefits from the services and where the recipients of public services are located. In contrast, a dollar-flow measure is designed to trace funds from taxpayers to federal employees, to individuals and families receiving welfare payments, to holders of the public debt, and to those who produce the goods and services which go into the commodities purchased by the federal government. In a dollar-flow measure military payrolls, for example, would be attributed to the states in which the payments are made to members of the armed forces. In a benefit measure these payrolls would be considered as a part of the national security expenditures made on behalf of citizens in all states to protect our way of life. The national security program is not designed to benefit members of the armed forces—instead it calls upon a citizen army to serve in defense of the people of all states of the union.

There have been a few studies of distribution of federal expenditures in particular states or regions. George W. McKinney undertook a study of federal taxing and spending in Virginia.[21]

[19] Mushkin, Selma, "Distribution of Federal Expenditures Among the States," *Review of Economics and Statistics.*

[20] Mushkin, Selma, *Statistical Materials on the Distribution of Federal Expenditures Among the States,* Washington, Public Health Service, U. S. Department of Health, Education, and Welfare, 1956, 79 pp.

[21] McKinney, George Wesley, Jr., *Federal Taxing and Spending in Vir-*

The Federal Reserve Bank of Boston analyzed federal cash payments and federal cash receipts, including borrowing, and currency and banking transactions for the New England Region.[22] Norman H. Jones, in a doctoral dissertation at Iowa State University, analyzed by geographic region the relationships of federal taxes and expenditures.[23] While the studies differ in scope each attempts to measure expenditures as dollar-flows rather than as benefits flowing to the people in the form of public services.

Much more extensive theoretical work has been done in connection with studies of redistributive effects of budgetary financing among income groups. Perhaps the most extensive theoretical exploration is contained in Tibor Barna's *Redistribution of Incomes Through Public Finance in 1937*—a quantitative investigation into redistribution in England before World War II.[24] Another volume of special interest is *Income Redistribution and Social Policy* edited by Alan T. Peacock.[25] This volume contains a set of studies on the nature and magnitude of the redistribution of income brought about by social policies in selected countries; it includes a study on government budgets in the United States by Alfred H. Conrad. In these studies, as well as in similar studies by John Adler[26] and Charles Stauffacher,[27] several impor-

ginia: A Quantitative Study, Advisory Council on the Virginia Economy, June 1950, 58 pp.

[22] "Federal Receipts and Expenditures in New England; Their Growth and Significance," *Monthly Review* [Federal Reserve Bank of Boston], August 1950.

[23] Jones, Norman Hugh, Jr., *The Regional Impact of Federal Fiscal Policy.* Unpublished Ph.D. dissertation, State University of Iowa, August 1954.

[24] Barna, Tibor, *Redistribution of Incomes Through Public Finance in 1937,* Oxford, Oxford University Press, 1945, 289 pp.

[25] *Income Redistribution and Social Policy,* Alan T. Peacock (ed.), London, Jonathan Cape, 1954, 296 pp.

[26] Adler, John H., "The Fiscal System, the Distribution of Income and Public Welfare," In *Fiscal Policies and the American Economy,* Kenyon E. Poole (ed.), New York, Prentice-Hall, 1951, pp. 359-409.

[27] Stauffacher, Charles, "The Effects of Governmental Expenditures and Tax Withdrawals Upon Income Distribution, 1930-39." In *Public Policy,* C. J. Friedrich and Edward S. Mason (eds.), Cambridge, Grad-

tant theoretical questions are raised: (a) the valuation of government services; (b) the content of government expenditures to be included, e.g., divisible and also indivisible benefits, total budgetary expenditures or social expenditure costs, etc.; (c) the basis of attributing government services to income groups. Except for the Stauffacher article, these studies analyze government expenditures as benefits rather than dollar-flows. John Adler, in commenting on this problem, wrote: "The money-flow concept is, by implication at least, based on the assumption that the income of government employees, for instance, would be zero if the government did not employ them. This assumption is clearly untenable if we conceive of an economy as anything even vaguely approaching a general equilibrium system in which there are forces tending toward the elimination of such maladjustments as unemployment." [28]

There are underlying conceptual differences between the problem of expenditure allocations to income classes and allocations to geographic regions. Both types of measures—benefits and dollar-flows—appear to have a meaning for geographic distributions. The translation of governmental expenditures into benefits provides a measure of the services received which are additive to other consumer goods and services consumed by the public and also quantifies the public services to the beneficiaries in accord with the purposes of the authorizing legislation. While the dollar-flow measure carries with it some implication of government use of idle manpower and resources, it is important to bear in mind that even in a period of high employment there exist resources for further growth in the states—resources which are not fully tapped. These resources include both natural resources and the potential of a better use of manpower within specific areas of the nation, as well as the shift of manpower and industrial capacity among regions.

Definition and classification of expenditures.   The choices in

---

uate School of Public Administration, Harvard University, 1941, pp. 232-261.

[28] Adler, John H., *op. cit.*

classification of expenditures for purposes of regional distribution are of at least two kinds. The overall content of the expenditure figures may be defined as total expenditures shown in the administrative budget, or as total cash expenditures. Total expenditures may be limited to only those representing current costs or may also include property purchases and property transactions. They may be gross expenditures or expenditures net of special receipts such as sales of power. Expenditures of dollar-flows may be broadly defined to include government redemptions of securities and similar transactions. Within this overall content expenditure items may be classified by agency and appropriation items, by general functional area or purpose. They may be classified as transfer payments and exhaustive expenditures with a distinction between direct payments to individuals and payments to business firms, or a special classification may be designed to reflect information available on allocators by state.

The starting point of the estimates presented here is the federal cash budget of 1952—the latest year for which expenditure data were available at the time work was begun. In 1952 the total cash budget amounted to $68.0 billion as compared with administrative budget expenditures of $66.1 billion. Cash revenues that year were about $54 million higher than the cash expenditure amounts. Two sets of estimates were developed, one a benefit measure, the other a measure approximating dollar-flows.

The use of the cash budget resulted in the inclusion of payments from trust funds to the public along with other federal outlays and avoided attributing benefits to states from interagency transfers. Cash budget-item classifications were adhered to fairly closely. This budget-item classification facilitated the use of such agency-by-agency data as existed on state distributions of federal expenditures.

Allocation indexes. The selection of allocators for distribution of expenditures among states depends upon the concept underlying the measure and the data available to match the conceptual framework.

In developing the estimates shown below, federal expenditures of each of the government agencies were allocated separately. While the detail for each of the agencies does not correspond with the detailed budget itemization, in many instances the specific appropriation served as the basic guide in arriving at the allocation detail. The detail also was determined by the nature of the expenditures and the information available on state-by-state operations of the government program.

The various indexes used in distributing federal expenditures among states may be summarized as follows:

All grants-in-aid are assigned to the states receiving the grants; all transfer payments to individuals, such as social insurance benefits, veterans' payments, and farm subsidies, are assigned to the state in which the recipient resides; all loans are assigned to the states in which the loans are made; power project costs are assigned to the users of the power; research expenditures are assigned on a uniform per capita basis throughout the nation.

International aid, military payroll and procurement costs, expenditures of the Atomic Energy Commission, and interest on the federal public debt—which taken together represent about 65 per cent of the federal cash budget—are allocated on two bases. In the benefit estimate, these expenditures—all part of a defense effort—are assumed to benefit equally people throughout the nation. In the second estimate, termed an incidence measure, the expenditures are traced through to the states in which the types of goods bought by the government are produced, both primary and secondary production effects being taken into account for the military procurement items. To illustrate, expenditures of the Atomic Energy Commission were distributed in proportion to plant and equipment costs incurred by the Commission in each of the states from the inception of the program to June 30, 1953. Military payroll expenditures were distributed to the states in which the wages, salaries and allowances were paid. Estimated disbursements for military procurement were first distributed among industries. The industrial distribution was based on the national input-output data which show for each $1 million of federal military procurement expenditures the amount going directly to farms, mines, shipyards, aircraft plants, steel rolling mills, textile mills, etc., and indirectly to these industries through the purchase of raw materials. These national totals for each industry were allocated among the states in proportion to each state's share of the wage bill in the industry. The industrial wage bill in each state was based on Employment Security data. For industries not fully covered under state employment security programs such as farming, production figures were substituted in determining the percentage distribution among the states.

Underlying this method of allocation of military purchases is the assumption that markets of all firms in an industry are influenced by federal purchases, whether or not individual producers receive a government contract. By way of illustration, let us assume that there are two states each with aircraft plants of the same size. The federal procurement contract is with plants in only one state. All civilian aircraft is produced in the second state. Federal purchases in the one state are assumed to affect the production of the plants in the other. The amount attributed to federal aircraft procurement would be allocated to both states in relation to their size, or in this example, in equal amount.

While this description is generally indicative of the approach used, it may be helpful to give some additional illustrations. For each of the federal agencies and within each agency for each program an attempt was made to determine where the people are located for whom the program is undertaken. Expenditures for programs designed to aid farmers, such as marketing and crop research, were allocated to states in relation to their relative farm or rural populations, or in some instances in proportion to the relative value of classes of aided farming operations, for example, value of wheat farms. Expenditures for veterans' programs were attributed to states in proportion to their relative numbers of aided veterans; expenditures of the Bureau of Indian Affairs in proportion to the Indian population living on Indian reservations. Expenditures of the Securities and Exchange Commission were distributed to states in proportion to income from interest and dividends. Expenses of the Tax Court were distributed in proportion to tax suits commenced in each of the states as shown in the annual report of the Director of the Administrative Office of the United States Courts.

As indicated earlier the detail of the allocation varied from agency to agency depending upon the allocation indexes available and the nature of the program. Three basic sources of information were used: *The Combined Statement of Receipts, Expenditures, and Balances of the United States Government* for the fiscal year 1952, agency annual reports, and hearings before the Appropriation Committees of the Senate and House of Representatives on the fiscal year 1954 appropriation bills. These sources were supplemented by statistical reports of the various federal departments and agencies, by estimates developed for national income purposes by the Office of Business Economics of the Department of Commerce, and by Census data on such items as population, wholesale sales, value added by manufacture, retail trade, etc.

EXPENDITURE STUDY FINDINGS

What do these findings suggest as approximate answers to the questions raised earlier?

Grants and expenditures compared. How does the state-by-state distribution of all expenditures, for example, compare with the distribution of federal grants? Do federal tax dollars go out in larger number to the low or high income states? There is more uniformity in the amounts received as federal expenditures per capita than in federal grants-in-aid per capita. Grants to states varied in 1952 from $6.83 per capita in New Jersey to $40.42 in Nevada. Per capita benefits from total expenditures varied from a high (omitting the District of Columbia) of $573 in Wyoming to a low of $403 in North Carolina.[29] For about three-fourths of the states the maximum difference is less than $60 per capita (Figure 1, on p. 135). The incidence estimates of the federal expenditure distribution, which approximate the dollar-flow, show a far wider disparity among the states. The variation of the incidence estimates, again omitting the District of Columbia, is from a high of $780 in New Mexico to a low of $240 in North Carolina.

Correlations were computed between per capita federal expenditures and per capita state income, and between per capita federal grants and per capita state income. The correlation co-efficients are summarized below:

Correlation of Per Capita Federal Expenditures in the States and Per Capita State Income, Fiscal Year 1952

All Federal Expenditures	
Benefit illustration	+ .011
Incidence illustration	+ .473
Selected Federal Expenditures	
Federal grants to states	− .082
Public assistance grants	− .257
Federal component of state income	+ .170

While the correlation between per capita incidence of federal expenditures and per capita income is + .473, there is a minor negative correlation between federal grants per capita and per capita income. This comparison, coupled with the relative size of grants and of total federal expenditures, suggests that the negligible equalizing effects achieved by federal grants are more than offset by the federal expenditure dollar-flows. The correlation between per capita federal benefits and per capita income is only + .011, a coefficient which is not significantly different from zero.

As a group, states with incomes above the United States average receive about 49 per cent of federal grants and 57 to 62 per

[29] These figures are not corrected for the budget adjustment to a daily Treasury Statement basis.

cent of all federal cash expenditures (depending upon the illustrative estimate used). States with incomes below the average receive 51 per cent of the grants but only 38 to 43 per cent of all federal cash expenditures (Table 1).

Balance of federal expenditures and revenues. Is there a return of federal revenues to states from which they come? Federal benefits and also expenditure-incidence exceed or are within 10 per cent of estimated federal revenue burdens[30] in about three-fourths of the states (Table 2).

When expenditures for national security and related major components of the federal budget are imputed as benefits to states in proportion to their populations, federal benefits are less than estimated federal revenue burdens in the major industrial states. States such as New York, California, Illinois, New Jersey, Ohio, Massachusetts, and Connecticut—with their large populations—account for almost all the estimated net revenue withdrawals in excess of the amount of imputed benefits. New York State alone is estimated to pay about 16 per cent of total federal revenues and about 40 per cent of revenue in excess of federal benefits to the states. When federal expenditures are allocated on an incidence basis, and when expenditures for national security and related programs are distributed according to place of production and employment, the relative positions of some states shift. For others there is little change. New York's and Illinois' relative balance is changed very little, although a somewhat larger percentage of the net excess revenues is estimated for these states. The difference between "take" and "drain" is widened for Pennsylvania. California's position shifts from a net tax paying state to a net receiving state. The relative estimated excess of revenue burdens in Delaware and Connecticut is reduced as compared with the benefit-burden illustration.

In both benefit and expenditure-incidence illustrations the

---

[30] The basis of estimating revenue burdens is presented in Selma Mushkin, *Statistical Materials on the Distribution of Federal Expenditures Among the States.* The incidence assumptions underlying these estimates tend to maximize the state differences in tax burdens.

states that are being aided in a comparative sense are primarily the low income states. The largest relative excess of expenditures—amounting to more than three times the revenue burdens —is indicated for Mississippi in the benefit illustration. The largest relative advantage in the burden-incidence comparison is shown for New Meixco.

As a group, states with above average incomes bear 72 per cent of all federal revenue burdens but receive about 60 cents of each $1 of federal expenditures (Table 2). The 29 states with incomes below the United States average get about 40 per cent of federal expenditures but bear 28 per cent of revenue burdens.

The geographic differences in net revenue burdens result primarily from the variation in federal taxes per capita among the

TABLE I *Federal Grants and Estimated Total Cash Federal Expenditures, by State, Fiscal Year 1952*
(Amounts in millions)

States Ranked by 1951-52 Per Capita Income[1]	Federal Grants[2]	Expenditure Illustrations	
		Benefits	Incidence
Continental United States	$2,292	$67,615	$65,712
States with incomes above U. S. average	1,116	38,751	40,412
Delaware	6	147	179
Nevada	7	97	94
District of Columbia	6	611	770
Connecticut	22	842	1,263
New York	163	6,505	6,349
California	189	5,076	6,281
Illinois	103	3,703	3,423
New Jersey	34	2,045	2,376
Ohio	98	3,391	3,620
Michigan	85	2,772	2,628
Washington	56	1,188	1,629
Massachusetts	71	2,073	1,994
Maryland	22	1,010	1,333
Montana	15	305	231
Oregon	26	818	633
Pennsylvania	110	4,562	4,124

TABLE I   (*Continued*)

States Ranked by 1951-52 Per Capita Income[1]	Federal Grants[2]	Expenditure Illustrations	
		Benefits	Incidence
Indiana	38	1,666	1,886
Wyoming	9	171	149
Rhode Island	14	353	305
Wisconsin	44	1,416	1,145
States with incomes below U. S. average	1,177	28,862	25,297
Colorado	35	665	583
Kansas	33	854	1,067
Missouri	92	1,802	1,681
Nebraska	21	579	506
Iowa	39	1,073	845
New Hampshire	8	227	144
Minnesota	46	1,295	1,396
Arizona	22	458	371
Utah	17	335	314
Texas	143	3,680	3,553
Idaho	12	311	245
South Dakota	16	335	235
Maine	15	376	326
New Mexico	21	359	558
Vermont	6	159	101
Florida	52	1,318	956
Virginia	34	1,421	1,564
North Dakota	14	315	239
Oklahoma	71	1,082	919
West Virginia	27	865	590
Louisiana	81	1,310	1,114
Georgia	66	1,502	1,137
Tennessee	49	1,493	1,552
Kentucky	47	1,292	1,114
South Carolina	33	904	909
North Carolina	52	1,657	990
Alabama	49	1,372	1,087
Arkansas	37	866	623
Mississippi	37	957	578

[1] Based on average of 1951 and 1952 per capita income from *Survey of Current Business*, August 1953.

[2] From Social Security Bulletin, June 1953.

Note: Amounts may not add to totals because of rounding.

states. For the fiscal year 1952 federal tax burdens ranged from $112 per capita in Mississippi to almost ten times that amount, or $1,015 in Delaware, reflecting the operation of federal taxing statutes on the unequal income structures in the states. While in 1952 the per capita income in the highest income state was about 2.8 times that of the lowest income state, there is far wider variation in the distribution of income and sources of income. Census data for 1949—the latest available—indicate for example, that 49 per cent of the families and unrelated individuals in Mississippi had annual incomes under $1,000 as compared with 15 per cent of the families in New Jersey and 18 per cent in New York.

Interstate income redistribution. Differences in concept between state income and the illustrative distributions of federal expenditures do not permit of direct combination of these esti-

TABLE 2   *Per Cent of Estimated Federal Cash Revenues and Expenditures in Each State, Fiscal Year 1952*

States Ranked by 1951-52 Per Capita Income[1]	Revenue Incidence	Expenditure Illustrations	
		Benefits	Incidence
Continental United States	100.00%	100.00%	100.00%
States with incomes above U.S. average	72.03	57.31	61.50
Delaware	.52	.22	.27
Nevada	.19	.14	.14
District of Columbia	1.07	.90	1.17
Connecticut	2.23	1.25	1.92
New York	15.86	9.62	9.66
California	9.00	7.51	9.56
Illinois	7.56	5.48	5.21
New Jersey	4.00	3.02	3.62
Ohio	5.81	5.02	5.51
Michigan	4.59	4.10	4.00
Washington	1.57	1.76	2.48
Massachusetts	4.10	3.07	3.03
Maryland	1.86	1.49	2.03
Montana	.34	.45	.35

TABLE 2   *(Continued)*

States Ranked by 1951-52 Per Capita Income[1]	Revenue Incidence	Expenditure Illustrations	
		Benefits	Incidence
Oregon	1.00	1.21	.96
Pennsylvania	7.29	6.75	6.28
Indiana	2.15	2.46	2.87
Wyoming	.17	.25	.23
Rhode Island	.68	.52	.46
Wisconsin	2.05	2.09	1.74
States with incomes below U.S. average	27.97	42.69	38.50
Colorado	.91	.98	.89
Kansas	.94	1.26	1.62
Missouri	2.54	2.67	2.56
Nebraska	.69	.86	.77
Iowa	1.22	1.59	1.29
New Hampshire	.34	.34	.22
Minnesota	1.69	1.92	2.12
Arizona	.41	.68	.56
Utah	.29	.50	.48
Texas	4.04	5.44	5.41
Idaho	.24	.46	.37
South Dakota	.24	.50	.36
Maine	.52	.56	.50
New Mexico	.28	.53	.85
Vermont	.21	.24	.15
Florida	1.77	1.95	1.45
Virginia	1.52	2.10	2.38
North Dakota	.23	.47	.36
Oklahoma	.89	1.60	1.40
West Virginia	.78	1.28	.90
Louisiana	1.13	1.94	1.70
Georgia	1.23	2.22	1.73
Tennessee	1.10	2.21	2.36
Kentucky	1.10	1.91	1.70
South Carolina	.60	1.34	1.38
North Carolina	1.41	2.45	1.51
Alabama	.82	2.03	1.65
Arkansas	.44	1.28	.95
Mississippi	.41	1.42	.88

[1] Based on average of 1951 and 1952 per capita income from *Survey of Current Business*, August 1953.

Note: Amounts may not add to totals because of rounding.

mates with state income. Despite the shortcomings of the estimates, an attempt was made to approximate an answer to the question raised on income redistribution, namely: Is there a net interstate income redistribution or does the income redistributive effect of federal expenditures offset the redistributive effects of federal revenues?

Private incomes after taxes and federal expenditures. An approach to the problem may be illustrated by the following simplified example. If it is assumed that there are but two states (and two people), one with a per capita income of $2,000 and another with a per capita income of $1,000, the range between them would be 2 to 1. Assuming federal taxes on a per capita income of $2,000 amount to $400 and on a per capita income of $1,000 to $100, the range of income after taxes would be reduced from 2 to 1 to 1.8 to 1. Assuming further that the total amount of tax collections—$500—is distributed uniformly between the two states as transfer payments (without any addition to total income) the per capita income of the two states after receipt of federal expenditures would be $1,850 and $1,150, respectively—a range of 1.6 to 1. Thus the redistribution of income effected by the tax differentials would be furthered by the distribution of expenditures. If the distribution of expenditures is such that $400 goes to the state with a $2,000 income before taxes and $100 to the state with $1,000 before taxes, the redistribution of income effected by the progressive tax structure would be exactly offset. If, however, the entire $500 was spent in the state with the lowest income, the maximum redistribution of income would be effected. The $2,000 income after federal operations would be reduced to $1,600 and the $1,000 income would be increased on balance to $1,400—a range of approximately 1.1 to 1.

Table 3 presents a similar type of analysis for the states based on the estimated revenue incidence and the illustrative distributions of federal expenditures. In the computation of the percentages presented in this table, Office of Business Economics estimates of income payments were adjusted for taxes not included in the estimates by adding to income payments the estimated incidence of revenue burdens assumed to be borne out of undistributed corporation earnings or to have reduced dividend in-

TABLE 3 *Per Capita Adjusted Private Income Payments, After Federal Revenue Incidence, and Per Capita Federal Expenditures as Per Cent of National Average: Illustrative Estimates*

Arrayed in Order of Per Capita Adjusted Private Income[1]	Adjusted Private Income Payments After Federal Revenues Per Capita[2]	Per Capita Federal Expenditures as Per Cent United States Average	
		I— Benefit Illustration	II— Expenditure Incidence Illustration
Continental U. S.	100	100	100
Delaware	121	100	125
Connecticut	132	93	143
New York	126	99	100
Nevada	122	126	125
Illinois	123	95	90
New Jersey	125	93	111
California	119	103	131
Ohio	119	95	104
Massachusetts	107	100	99
Michigan	116	96	93
Rhode Island	99	101	89
Pennsylvania	108	99	92
Wisconsin	110	93	77
Oregon	106	119	94
Montana	109	118	92
Washington	104	111	157
Maryland	97	93	126
Indiana	110	93	108
Missouri	99	103	99
Wyoming	100	130	116
Kansas	103	100	128
Iowa	103	94	76
Colorado	92	108	98
Nebraska	99	98	88
Minnesota	96	98	109
New Hampshire	91	97	63
Maine	84	96	86
Vermont	85	98	64

TABLE 3   (*Continued*)

Arrayed in Order of Per Capita Adjusted Private Income[1]	Adjusted Private Income Payments After Revenues Per Capita[2]	Per Capita Federal Expenditures as Per Cent United States Average	
		I— Benefit Illustration	II— Expenditure Incidence Illustration
Arizona	89	125	104
District of Columbia	39	171	221
Idaho	90	121	97
Texas	85	104	103
Florida	78	100	74
South Dakota	89	118	85
Utah	86	106	103
North Dakota	81	120	93
West Virginia	79	100	70
New Mexico	75	114	181
Oklahoma	73	110	96
Louisiana	71	109	95
Virginia	69	93	106
Georgia	68	98	77
North Carolina	69	91	56
Tennessee	68	104	111
Kentucky	66	101	90
South Carolina	64	95	99
Arkansas	60	106	78
Alabama	58	101	83
Mississippi	50	100	63

[1] The income payment series used is the average of income payments for 1951 and 1952 as reported in the *Survey of Current Business*, August 1953, with adjustments for residence. The income payments were increased by the estimated incidence of federal taxes assumed to be borne out of profits including the corporate income and profits taxes and stamp taxes (other than playing cards). From the increased total, federal income payments were subtracted to yield an adjusted non-federal income payment series.

[2] Federal receipts estimated to be borne in each state were deducted from the adjusted non-federal income payment series described in footnote 1. See table C-4 for the estimates of total incidence of federal receipts and table C-5 for receipt incidence per capita in *Statistical Materials on the Distribution of Federal Expenditures among the States.*

come. The federal income component of state income was deducted from this adjusted income base. (In this computation, unemployment benefits have been counted as a state rather than federal payment.) Having derived an adjusted income figure after deduction of federal revenues and the federal component of income payments, the net adjusted private (non-federal) income figure for each of the states was computed as a per capita amount. The range of these adjusted income figures and their relation to the United States average are compared with the relative per capita amounts of federal expenditures under the two illustrative estimates.

In the poorer states, the estimated per capita amounts derived from federal expenditures generally are a higher per cent of the United States average than are their private incomes per capita after federal taxes. This relationship suggests that federal expenditures tend to raise the incomes of the poorer states. At the same time, for many, but not all, of the wealthier states, federal benefits and expenditure incidence per capita are a lower percentage of the United States average than are their adjusted per capita private incomes after federal taxes. On balance, therefore, federal expenditures appear to result in a redistribution of income additional to that effected by federal taxes.

This method of presentation assumes away part of the income redistributive problem—the effect of federal operations on income. What would be the regional distribution of income without federal governmental activities? It is not practicable to assume the absence of federal government activities; federal activities are an integral part of the economic life of the nation and historically have altered the geographic distribution of manpower, of industry location, and economic organization from which existing income patterns developed. These activities are varied and complex and include tariff, transportation, wage, trust, patent, and other policies which are not fully reflected in budgetary spending or revenue raising.

Distribution of income, expenditures and taxes. Another method of presentation is illustrated in Figure 2. The cumulative

PER CAPITA FEDERAL EXPENDITURES
AND GRANTS, FISCAL YEAR 1952

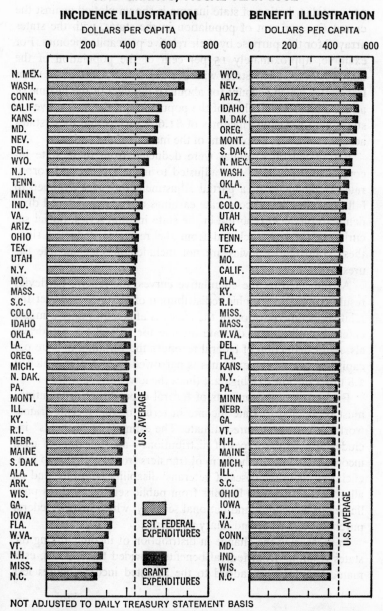

INCIDENCE ILLUSTRATION
DOLLARS PER CAPITA

BENEFIT ILLUSTRATION
DOLLARS PER CAPITA

EST. FEDERAL EXPENDITURES

GRANT EXPENDITURES

NOT ADJUSTED TO DAILY TREASURY STATEMENT BASIS

FIGURE I

per cent distribution of state income is shown plotted against the cumulative per cent of population in the states, with the states arrayed for this purpose by their relative per capita incomes. For example, approximately 15 per cent of the population of the nation is in the eight States with per capita incomes of $1,118 or less, states which account for about 10 per cent of the income of all the states. Almost half of the population of the nation lives in states with per capita incomes of $1,668 or less and these states account for about 40 per cent of the income of the nation.

Before federal revenues were deducted from these state income figures, income was adjusted to include estimated corporate tax payments as a partial adjustment for taxes assumed to fall on undistributed corporate earnings or to have reduced dividends to the level reported in the state income series. Social security taxes were excluded from the revenues deducted since these contributory levies are not included in state income figures.

As indicated by the cumulative curves, the federal tax levies result in some geographic redistribution of income. However the relative income position of the states is affected to only a minor extent by adjustment of state income for federal tax withdrawals. After deduction of federal revenues the variation in state per capita income at the extremes is narrowed from a high which is 2.8 times the low to a high 2.4 times the low.

Each of the two concepts of federal expenditure distributions must be related to state income in terms of the specific framework of the expenditure estimate. The estimate of "benefits" includes at least two types of distributions—an allocation of cash income payments in the form of transfers from taxpayers to beneficiaries, as in the cases of veterans' disability pensions, and an allocation of imputed benefits from public services such as public health, education and national security, which involve federal purchases and wage and salary payments.

In measuring the change in distribution of income among the states resulting from federal benefits provided to residents, estimated benefits were added to the adjusted income figures less federal taxes. Since transfer payments are already included in state income estimates, the federal expenditures added are exclusive of these transfers. Federal aid to the states for public

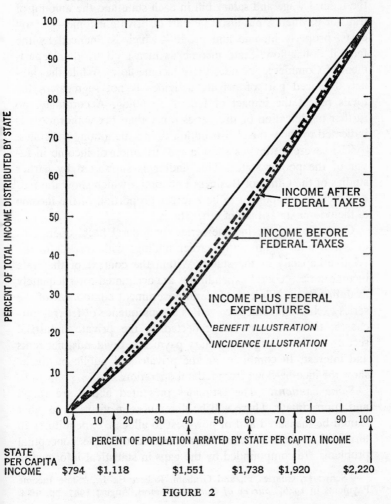

CHANGES IN DISTRIBUTION OF INCOME BY STATE

INCOME AFTER
FEDERAL TAXES

INCOME BEFORE
FEDERAL TAXES

INCOME PLUS FEDERAL
EXPENDITURES

BENEFIT ILLUSTRATION

INCIDENCE ILLUSTRATION

PERCENT OF TOTAL INCOME DISTRIBUTED BY STATE

PERCENT OF POPULATION ARRAYED BY STATE PER CAPITA INCOME

| STATE PER CAPITA INCOME | $794 | $1,118 | $1,551 | $1,738 | $1,920 | $2,220 |

FIGURE 2

assistance was classified as a transfer payment for this purpose. A successive movement of the curves to the left gives an indication of the net redistribution resulting from federal budget financing.

The second expenditure estimate is designed to show not only the federal wage and salary bill in each state and the amount of transfer payments, but also that part of private income—payroll costs, property income and profits—which is financed by the federal dollar-flow. State income as measured by the Department of Commerce includes these income-flows. While the publicly financed part of private activities is not segregated, the totals reflect the impact of federal spending. Accordingly, no further modification of this series other than tax withdrawals is indicated to show the redistribution of income among the states.

The several estimates show a redistribution of income in favor of the poorer states. This finding is supported by earlier studies of the Office of Business Economics which show the federal income component to be a larger proportion of the income of the poorer states than of other states.[31]

Correction of the income series for federal fiscal operations does not alter significantly earlier findings with respect to the relative capacity of the states. Within the context of the state income series, federal expenditures are accounted for adequately as dollar-flows. While the federal government component of the series excludes income received as a consequence of federal purchases, these amounts are reflected in the private industrial sectors—private wage and salary payments, dividends, net rents and interest. In combination, the private and public payments show the income-flows from federal operations.

Some cautions. The estimates presented above are rough and approximate. There will be differences in views as to what should be measured and of how best to allocate expenditures in terms of a given concept of measurement. These conceptual problems are compounded by the gaps in statistical information

[31] Schwartz, Charles F., and Graham, Robert E., Jr., "State Income Payments in 1946," *Survey of Current Business,* August 1947, pp. 9-24.

and the often crude indexes that are used as a substitute. Moreover, there are implicit limitations in a detailing of federal expenditures directed to the achievement of national purposes and program objectives as a series of state-by-state figures. Ease of movement of people across state lines, the dependence of industries in one state on raw materials, machinery and semi-finished goods in others, the frequency of absentee ownership of property in the state—all contribute to an emphasis on national objectives and purposes. Federal taxing and spending are governed by these national objectives and requirements. Geographic variations occurring in the taxing or spending process are a byproduct of the pursuit of these national objectives. An overlay of state boundaries on these national programs necessarily yields a distorted view of federal fiscal operations.

Furthermore, sectional interests as well as national interests are essentially parts of an overall common concern with national markets, national prosperity, and economic growth. The long-run economic interests of various sections of the nation patently coincide in the criss-crossing interstate flows of goods, funds, people and property ownership.[32]

[32] Harris, Seymour E., "Taxes and Treasury Disbursements: Regional and State Differences, 1934-1954, 1939, 1952, 1953, 1954." In *New England Textiles and the New England Economy;* Report to the Conference of New England Governors, February 1956, pp. 110-164; Press release on statement by Senator Herbert H. Lehman to the U. S. Senate, January 9, 1956; Anderson, William, and Durfee, Waite D., Jr., "The National-State Fiscal Balance." In *Intergovernmental Fiscal Relations,* Minneapolis, University of Minnesota Press, 1956, pp. 85-95.

DEFENSE AND DISARMAMENT ECONOMIC ANALYSIS IN THE DEPARTMENT OF DEFENSE

Alain C. Enthoven

INTRODUCTION

Traditionally, the economics of national defense has meant the study of economic war potential and the problems of mobilizing it to produce armaments. During the fifties, the range of national security problems treated by economists was broadened to include many topics quite unrelated to fiscal policy and monetary theory. The economics of national defense now includes studies of the organization and management of the Defense Establishment and the armaments industries, and it includes economic analysis of the requirements for weapon systems and forces; that is, the central issues of defense policy and programming. Although much of the research on these problems has been classified, enough outstanding unclassified examples have appeared to provide the economics profession in general with a good survey of the range of topics being studied.[1]

Reprinted from *American Economic Review*, LIII, 2 (May, 1963), 413-423, by permission of the author. The author acknowledges the helpful suggestions of his colleagues Wm. Niskanen, M. J. Peck, and J. A. Stockfisch.

[1] See, for example, C. J. Hitch and R. N. McKean, *The Economics of Defense in the Nuclear Age* (Cambridge, 1960). Henry S. Rowen, *Na-*

In 1961, a group of economists who had been specializing in this field joined the Department of Defense in positions which gave them the opportunity to take the initiative in applying the results of their research to the practical problems of policy planning and financial management in the Department. This paper is a progress report on some of their work.

Of course, let me emphasize, the principal military advisers to the Secretary of Defense are the Joint Chiefs of Staff. Military planning is the responsibility of the Joint Staff and the planning organizations of the military departments. However, the Secretary of Defense has the responsibility to see to it that the plans and programs of the Department of Defense are selected with proper attention to considerations of economy and efficiency, and in this he is assisted by, among others, the economists on his staff. Although this paper is about the work of economists, I do not want to suggest that we think we are doing the whole job ourselves.

I believe that it is fair to say that the economists in the Defense Department have been successful in making economic analysis an effective contributor to the efficiency of the Department's program. Such basic concepts as marginal products and marginal costs have made it possible for the economists to summarize and integrate a great deal of critical program data and other diverse kinds of information for the few key officials who must make the major decisions on resource allocation. Moreover, although we have learned much from the experience, I believe that our earlier research has stood up well under the practical tests of realism and relevance.

Economic analysis within the Department of Defense is now as diverse as economics itself. It covers many areas. We have, for example, problems of industrial organization in administer-

tional Security and the American Economy in the 1960's (G.P.O., Washington, 1960). M. J. Peck and F. M. Scherer, *The Weapons Acquisition Process: An Economic Analysis* (Boston, 1962). J. A. Stockfisch, ed., *Planning and Forecasting in the Defense Industries* (Belmont, Calif., 1962).

ing the $10 billion weapons industry which the Department of Defense has created. Determining rates of military compensation raises all the traditional problems of the labor market. The Defense Department must consider the substantial impact of its expenditures on the U.S. balance of payments. Rather than cataloguing all of the activities in which economics, or more accurately economists, have proved useful, I have chosen to focus in this paper upon the problems of determining requirements for weapon systems and forces; that is, the allocation of the defense budget. While this application of economics is relatively novel, I hope to make clear that economic analysis here is simply traditional marginal analysis, compounded, however, by real life uncertainties, data problems, problems of complex interactions between many diverse elements, and the continuing dialogue with the politically and legally responsible decision-makers.

THE PROGRAMMING SYSTEM

Before economic analysis could be applied systematically to the problem of allocating the defense budget, it was necessary to install a financial management system that provided the right kind of information for top-level decision making. The system we found did not do this. It had several important defects, perhaps the most important of which was the almost complete separation between planning and decision making on weapon systems and forces, on the one hand, and budgeting on the other. What Arthur Smithies found in 1954 was still true six years later. To use his words: "Planning and programming precede budgeting, and programs provide the basis on which budgets are prepared. Programs, however, are prepared in terms of military concepts and not in terms of dollars. When a program is completed, the cost in dollars is not known." [2] In other words, the long-range plans for weapon systems, forces, and all of their supporting elements were made by the services on the basis of

[2] *The Budgetary Process in the United States* (New York, 1955), p. 241.

their estimates of the forces required to assure our national security. Generally speaking, costs were not introduced systematically, either to test the feasibility of the whole program or for purposes of evaluating the efficiency of allocation.

Budgeting, on the other hand, had as its point of departure the guideline dollar totals laid down by the Administration and based on estimates of the burden the economy could or should bear. The result was a gap. The "required forces" always cost much more than the Administration and the Congress were willing to pay. The process by which the conflicting interests were resolved was unsystematic and wasteful because it led to unbalanced programs.

Furthermore, the Secretary of Defense did not receive adequate cost data. The budgetary system identified costs by object classes—Procurement, Military Personnel, Installations, etc.—the inputs to the Defense Department, rather than by weapon systems and forces, such as B-52 wings and Army divisions which are the tangible outputs of the Department. The identification by object classes is suitable for purposes of appropriations and for management of a program already decided upon, and we have retained it for those purposes, but it is not suitable for top-level decision making on such questions as the proper mix between B-52 wings and Army divisions. Moreover, cost data were presented and financial management was conducted at the Defense Department level on a year-at-a-time basis. The full time-phased costs of the proposed forces were not presented to the Secretary of Defense. Because the costs of most programs are small in their first years, this led to the starting of many programs that could not be completed at anything like existing budget levels. Although a certain amount of this is a desirable hedge against uncertainty, it is clear that there were a great many wasteful stretch-outs and cancellations of programs that would not have been started if the costs of all of the approved programs had been anticipated.

Another problem was that the cost data that were presented when a program was being "sold" to the Secretary of Defense were not related in any systematic way to the costs used for budgeting. This meant that the services had a very powerful incentive to understate the costs, without the offsetting incentive of knowing that they would be held accountable for the same estimates when it came to budget preparation. Still another problem with the cost data was that the estimates that were made of the marginal costs of the various programs were incomplete and generally very low. For example, in 1961 the Congress appropriated a half billion dollars to buy another wing of B-52's, apparently in the belief that that appropriation would "pay for" the wing. As the Secretary of Defense pointed out in his announcement of his decision not to procure the extra bombers, the half billion represented only procurement costs. The total cost to buy and operate the bombers and their associated equipment for a period of five years would be three times that much. The understatement of marginal costs has a sort of "Duesenberry effect"; it makes increases appear to be relatively attractive and it makes program reductions appear to be unrewarding in terms of savings.

There were other problems also. Program decisions were made largely unilaterally on a single-service basis. For example, the Navy and the Air Force decided on their long-range ballistic missile programs largely independently of each other. To the extent that there was interaction, it was more competitive than cooperative.

Finally, the system did not provide data on marginal utilities or marginal products. The traditional military requirements study was typically a calculation of the forces required to achieve a single hypothesized objective. To give an oversimplified example, suppose that the objective were to achieve an expectation of destroying 97 per cent of 100 targets, using missiles having a 50 per cent single-shot kill probability. The requirements study would conclude that 500 missiles were required, without pointing out that the last 100 missiles only added an expectation of killing about 3 extra targets. We are now finding that it is just the latter kind of information that is required to close the gap I referred to earlier.

To correct these deficiencies, we established the Programming System. Reduced to simplest terms, the Programming System consists of a five-year projection of all forces, weapon systems, and other activities described in physical (or nonfinancial) terms, together with their costs, all as approved by the Secretary of Defense, plus a set of regular procedures for modifying the plan.

The key to the Programming System is decision making by program elements and major programs; that is, by the outputs of the Department rather than by the inputs. A program element is an integrated activity combining men, equipment, and installations whose effectiveness can be related to our national security policy objectives. The list includes B-52 wings, infantry battalions, and combatant ships, taken together with all the equipment, men, installations, and supplies required to make them effective military forces. The program elements are assembled into major programs which contain interrelated elements which closely complement each other or are close substitutes for each other and which must therefore be considered together in arriving at top-level decisions. The entire defense program is now divided into major programs, as follows: (1) Strategic Retaliatory Forces, (2) Continental Air and Missile Defense Forces, (3) General Purpose Forces (primarily intended for the nonnuclear defense of overseas theaters), (4) Airlift and Sealift Forces, (5) Reserve and Guard Forces, (6) Research and Development, (7) General Support, (8) Civil Defense, and (9) Military Assistance.

The key point about a program element is that it has both costs and benefits associated with it. The benefits are the ways in which it helps us to achieve broad national security objectives. The costs are primarily the appropriations in all categories that will be required for its execution, not only in the current year, but throughout the lifetime of the program.

The Programming System has made it possible to unify program decisions and budget decisions. Budgets are still prepared annually in much the same way as before. However, the Five-Year Force Structure and Financial Plan is used as guidance to the military departments for the preparation of their budgets. During the annual budget review, the approved five-year plan is translated into requests for appropriations, by object classes, and there is a detailed review of the cost estimates and the manner in which the approved program is being carried out.

The programming approach is based on an over-all Department of Defense look at national security requirements, not a single service approach. Decisions about Polaris and Minuteman, Army divisions and tactical fighters, and other closely related programs supported by different services are made by the Secretary of Defense. This has made possible better balanced forces for the Department as a whole.

The Programming System frees the Department from year-at-a-time decision making, and forces us to look systematically at our plans and programs over a longer period of time. For defense planning, a year is arbitrary and short. The leadtime for most weapon systems is at least several years. The decisions that were made in 1961 about the fiscal 1963 budget will not have their full impact on our military posture until the period 1965 to 1967. We need an economically realistic plan for the future, so that long-lead decisions on program components will have a reasonable chance of turning out to be right.

Finally, and perhaps most important, the Programming System has formed the foundation for a systematic approach to the problem of reconciling "military requirements" and "reasonable budget levels." In the Programming System, costs and benefits are looked at together at the same time and by the same people rather than at different times and by different people. What is required militarily is looked at in the light of its costs, and estimates of what the country can or should afford to pay are considered in the light of the requirements of national security. Estimates of marginal costs and marginal products are provided for the Secretary of Defense, so that he and his principal advisers can concentrate their attention not so much on such questions as whether we need a capability to destroy 97 per cent of the 100 targets, with the alternatives unspecified, as on such questions as whether the capability to raise expected target destruction from 94 to 97 per cent is worth the cost of 100 extra missiles. Of course, data on marginal costs and marginal products do not imply mathematically what the number should be. We have no equivalent to the point at which marginal cost equals marginal revenue. A complex judgment still has to be made. But data of this kind contribute a great deal to making that judgment an informed one.

THE ECONOMICS OF OUR POSTURE FOR THERMONUCLEAR WAR

The U.S. military posture for thermonuclear war includes our Strategic Retaliatory Forces, Continental Air and Missile Defense Forces, our Civil Defense Program, parts of our theater-based forces, plus research and development and weapon production programs to support them. An economic theory is required to allocate resources among these components.

By 1961, a great deal of progress had been made in the development of an economic theory for our posture for thermonuclear war. Many possible objectives had been explored, the important criteria had been clarified, and a reasonably good understanding had been developed of how the various elements of the program are related to the objectives.[3] It should be emphasized, however, that although the analytical methods were developed to a point of high sophistication, the theory rests on very little empirical data, and hopefully will remain so. There is no lack of awareness of this point among top-level policy-makers in our government.

[3] See, for example, A. J. Wohlstetter, "The Delicate Balance of Terror," *Foreign Affairs* (Jan., 1959); H. S. Rowen, *op. cit.;* and Herman Kahn, *On Thermonuclear War* (Princeton, 1960).

Briefly stated, the objectives sought for our posture for thermonuclear war are twofold: First, we seek to make war unlikely; and, second, if despite our best efforts a war should occur, we seek to limit the damage caused to U.S. and Allied population and industry and to put ourselves in a position to achieve a speedy and favorable termination of the war. For the most part, these objectives can be translated into the quantitative criteria of damage to U.S., Allied, and Sino-Soviet population and industry and the balance of surviving military forces occurring under various different circumstances of outbreak and conduct of the war.

Although there is obviously much more to the problem of thermonuclear war than economic analysis of efficient and inefficient postures, I will comment here only on two lines of advance that we have made in the past two years in the economics of the problem. First, we have made a great deal of progress in the translation of our broad objectives into specific quantitative criteria that can be applied in a systematic and practical way to the evaluation of alternative proposed forces and postures. This has been a matter of translating research results into practical operating procedures.

Second, prior to 1961, very little was done on the questions of budget level and total requirements. Economic research was limited almost entirely to questions of allocation within existing budgets and force levels. Although the problem of determining the budget level cannot be separated altogether from the efficiency of allocation, it was easier for economists to assume a given budget level and address exclusively the question of efficiency of allocation. However, when the Secretary of Defense made it clear that he was not going to begin with a predetermined budget level, but rather was going to address the problem of requirements directly, it became necessary to change somewhat the focus of the analysis. Instead of working in terms of marginal rates of transformation and substitution, in effect we switched to marginal products and marginal costs. This allowed the Secretary to make his own judgments as to the point at which the various marginal products were no longer large enough to justify the incurring of extra costs.

CONVENTIONAL FORCE REQUIREMENTS

Although the determination of conventional (i.e., nonnuclear) force requirements, in the sense of forces required to do a particular well-defined task, has traditionally received thorough study by the military profession, the broader problems of relating alternative conventional force levels to national security objectives and of determining the over-all U.S. conventional force levels had not received much systematic treatment. Of course, as in the case of our nuclear forces, nonmilitary considerations such as those of foreign policy and domestic economic policy and political factors must enter into the decision.

There are several factors that make the economic analysis of conventional force requirements a very different kind of problem from the economics of our posture for thermonuclear war. First, the uncertainties appear to be much greater and intangibles play a larger part in the case of conventional forces. I say "appear" to be "much greater" because it is altogether possible that our ability to put quantitative limits on the effects of nuclear weapons is based on ignorance of some crucial aspects of the problem. On the other hand, the United States has fought many nonnuclear wars. From the study of these and many other wars, the military profession has developed empirical generalization about the effects of various force ratios, weapons, terrain, and other factors. But, as they are quick to point out, the averages are surrounded by very wide variances. The uncertainties are large because of the critical importance of such factors as morale, leadership, surprise, etc., and the fact that the outcomes of conventional land-air battles are the product of very large numbers of complex interacting elements.

Another important difference is that the specific objectives sought by conventional forces lend themselves much less easily to quantitative treatment than do the objectives of our posture for nuclear war. The economic theory of our posture for nuclear war can be described in terms very similar to the economic theory of a multiproduct firm. There are smooth continuous rates of transformation and substitution and almost ubiquitous diminishing marginal returns. The objectives for conventional forces must generally be defined in terms of seizing or holding specific pieces of terrain in or for specified periods of time against specified enemy forces.

The approach we have adopted has been to formulate, in collaboration with the military planners, a range of carefully defined limited war problems in each of the various theaters in which our security requires a capability for major military operations. The questions are of the form, "What is the minimum amount of forces that would be required to hold, with high probability, for X weeks (perhaps indefinitely) at the Y line against an attack by Z forces?" After examining various limited wars in each theater, mixes of wars in two or more theaters are examined. Then alternative forces, together with their required logistic support, are assembled to deal with the various assumed limited wars, their costs estimated, and the results presented to the Secretary of Defense. Although much remains to be done, these military-economic studies have given the civilian leadership a much clearer picture than they had before of over-all force requirements to implement the desired strategic objectives.

PRACTICAL WAYS OF DEALING WITH UNCERTAINTY

I have referred several times to the numerous and major uncertainties present in this kind of work. There are good ways and bad ways of dealing with the problems of decision making under uncertainty. Economists have the advantage of familiarity with an extensive and sophisticated literature on the subject. I would like to outline here some of the practical quantitative methods we have adopted to deal with uncertainties in our work.

One encounters many different kinds of uncertainties in empirical studies of weapon systems and defense policy. Most of them fall into the following categories. There are uncertainties about operational factors such as the accuracy and reliability of missile systems, the hardness of targets, or the range of future aircraft. These are closely related to uncertainties about the time and cost to develop weapon systems. There are uncertainties about enemy behavior, his weapon systems and forces, and the behavior of other countries. How many ICBM's will the Soviet Union have in 1968? Will country X continue to grant us base rights in 1967? There are also conceptual uncertainties. How will the weapon systems we are buying now for the late sixties be related to our national security objectives then? If past experience is a reliable guide, it is almost certain that our strategy will change between now and then. If we fail to anticipate the change and allow for it now, our weapon systems may be quite inappropriately designed for the strategy of 1968, and the deficiency may have to be remedied at great cost later on.

Without attempting to give a complete catalogue of the tricks of this trade, let me indicate some of the methods and rules we follow.

First, there seems to be a widespread belief that the safe thing to do, in cases of doubt, is to overestimate one's opponent and underestimate one's own capabilities. If uncertain about the reliability of the enemy's missiles and ours, so this belief would have it, one should pick from the high end of the range of uncertainty for the opponent's and from the low end for our missiles. In fact, we have learned that it is just as dangerous to overestimate the enemy's capabilities relative to our own as it is to underestimate them. Overestimates do not necessarily lead to insurance and safety. They are just as likely to lead to despair, to pricing of important policy objectives out of the market, and to strategies of desperation.

Next, we have found that in cases of uncertainty, it is often useful to carry three sets of factors through the calculations: an "Optimistic" and a "Pessimistic" estimate that bracket the range of uncertainty and a "Best Estimate" that has the highest likelihood. These terms are not very rigorous. A subjective judgment is required. But it is surprising how often reasonable men study-ing the same evidence can agree on three numbers where they cannot agree on one. In fact, one of the great benefits of this approach has been to eliminate much senseless quibbling over minor variations in numerical estimates of very uncertain magni-tudes.

I pointed out earlier that the relationship of marginal prod-ucts to marginal costs is usually of central importance in deter-mining force levels. Interestingly enough, we have found that it is frequently the case that although there are major uncertainties about total products and costs, the marginal products and costs will be much less sensitive to variations in the factors.

In the case of uncertainties about enemy behavior, we have often found it useful to play a simple two-person game in which the enemy is permitted to adjust to variations in our posture, in order to evaluate our own alternatives. Of course, thinking through the enemy's countermove is a time-honored part of mili-tary procedure. The trick, in the long-range planning business, is to apply realistic technical, budgetary, lead-time, bureaucratic, and other constraints to the enemy's hypothesized freedom to react. A frequent error here is to allow him too much freedom to adjust; the consequences are those of overestimating the oppo-nent, described earlier.

With respect to conceptual uncertainties and uncertainties about strategic context, another error to be avoided is becoming locked in tightly by current strategic concepts and assumptions. We therefore make a conscious effort to evaluate alternative postures under a wide range of different hypothetical future cir-cumstances and policies. Although this procedure doubtless is not nearly as good as actually knowing the future, it does help our decision-makers to build into our posture a certain amount of flexibility that might not otherwise be included.

CONCLUSIONS

I would like to conclude with three general observations.

First, the tools of analysis that we use are the simplest, most fundamental concepts of economic theory, combined with the simplest quantitative methods. The requirements for success in this line of work are a thorough understanding of and, if you like, belief in the relevance of such concepts as marginal products and marginal costs, and an ability to discover the marginal products and costs in complex situations, combined with a good quantitative sense. The advanced mathematical techniques of econometrics and operations research have not proved to be particularly useful in dealing with the problems I have described. Although a good grasp of this kind of mathematics is very valuable as intellectual formation, we are not applying linear programming, formal game theory, queuing theory, multiple regression theory, nonlinear programming under uncertainty, or anything like it. The economic theory we are using is the theory most of us learned as sophomores. The reason Ph.D.'s are required is that many economists do not believe what they have learned until they have gone through graduate school and acquired a vested interest in marginal analysis.

Second, I observed earlier that economic analysis cannot determine the optimum allocation or size of the defense budget. It stops with informing the legally constituted officials who have to make the critical judgments. Because the range of possible alternatives is so great, economic analysis in the Office of the Secretary of Defense has become a continuing dialogue between policy-makers and economists, in which the policy-makers ask for alternative solutions to their problems, make decisions to exclude some in order to focus attention on the most interesting candidates, and make value judgments and policy decisions, while the economist attempts to clarify the conceptual framework in which decisions must be made, to define alternative possible objectives and criteria, and to explore in as clear terms as possible (and quantitatively) the cost and effectiveness of alternative courses of action.

Finally, the range of interesting and important problems urgently requiring the attention of economists is very great. As well as the many unsolved problems remaining in the area of weapon systems and force requirements, we have problems of personnel compensation, requirements and utilization, problems of internal organization and pricing, inventory management, contracting for research and development and procurement, and many others. For economists interested in the field of national security, the Defense Department offers excellent and exciting opportunities for public service.

SECTION IV

✖ Criteria for Evaluating Government Financing

The goods and services made available to the citizens of the United States are produced or provided by either the private sector or the public sector. These goods may be classified on the basis of whether they are private, collective, quasi-collective, social, or private goods publicly provided. The benefits or utility from private goods are divisible among the users. The assignment of benefit or worth to individuals from collective, quasi-collective and social goods and services is extremely difficult. The action of the price mechanism allocates the resources to users or purchasers of private goods through the traditional goods-price-offer, market forces. But since price assignment cannot be readily made for goods and services that are not divisible among users, some central decision-making agency must make resource allocation decisions outside of the traditional market environment.

Thus the level of resources to be used by government for defense, foreign aid, national parks, law and order, business regulation, education, school lunch programs, and social insurance must be determined by social choices implemented through our democratic political system. However, the extent to which resources *should* be devoted to providing non-private goods is singularly important when total outlays by governments approximate one-third of national income. Given the magnitude of today's governmental activities, we must seek guidelines for evaluating the quality of performance of federal processes and the "proper" limitation on the extent of government resource use. The criteria for evaluating government finance are the topics discussed in the following section.

Issues central to the political and market determination of resource use for collective goods are discussed by James Buchanan in the first reading, "Social Choice, Democracy and Free Markets." Buchanan's article emphasizes the nature of the problem of translating political decisions into specific identification with free market functions. In the second reading, "Welfare Aspects of Benefit-Cost Analysis," a more specific and pragmatic method of channeling resources to the public sector is presented by Professor Krutilla. The article provides a summary and review of contributions by various authors on the extent to which "welfare" can be changed if public expenditures are predicated upon benefit-cost analysis. Underlying such an approach to government expenditure decisions is the value judgment that government activity should improve the allocation of resources.

The concern with efficient government use of resources is pursued by Julius Margolis in the reading entitled, "Secondary Benefits, External Economies and the Justification of Public Investment." Professor Margolis discusses the analytical tools employed by the government's Bureau of Reclamation in allocating public funds among its projects. The emphasis is on analysis of the indirect benefits that accrue to large sectors of the economy because of federal projects that were planned to benefit regional economies.

John Kendrick's article provides additional insight into the standards by which government performance should be evaluated. Kendrick asserts that it is the function of public administrators to achieve and increase the productivity of public agencies. Problems pertaining to measures, concepts and the meaning of productivity must be solved before any efficiency standard can be applied to "public management."

Standards for evaluating the features and structure of income taxation are the contribution of the noted fiscal theorist, Henry Simons. The excerpt from his well-known book, *Personal Income Taxation,* outlines the elements without which income taxation will not have attained a "millennium."

Budget surpluses and budget deficits have been frequently used as a measure of the overall performance of federal fiscal activity. But the presence of a budget surplus or deficit is an extremely superficial standard for assessing any government activity. Of more importance to the fiscal theorists are the guidelines that provide for minimizing adverse effects of persistent deficits. Earl R. Rolph in his article on "Principles of Debt Management" provides such a guideline—his principle of efficiency. The principle, developed by Rolph, is simply that the composition and size of national debt is optimal when the marginal utility of each type of debt instrument is made proportional to its marginal cost.

The final reading in this section adds institutional and historical perspective to the pattern of choice in federal government economic policy, beginning with the Employment Act of 1946. Professor Colm's summary of the type and extent of economic problems, which required government fiscal and other policy actions, provides a suitable framework to structure the pragmatic success criteria provided in the wording of the 1946 Act. The article presents illustrative cases of the great venture to prove that "free" economic institutions can adapt sufficiently well to meet the exigencies of modern problems. Colm's conclusion is noteworthy: new policy formulation and machinery are required since the standard of performance as tested by experience shows the need for bolder government policy.

SOCIAL CHOICE, DEMOCRACY, AND FREE MARKETS

James M. Buchanan

Professor Kenneth Arrow's provocative essay, *Social Choice and Individual Values*,[1] has stimulated a great deal of comment and discussion during the two years since its publication. Reviewers and discussants have been primarily concerned with those formal aspects of Arrow's analysis which relate to modern welfare economics. This concentration, which is explained by both the stated purpose of the work and the tools with which it is developed, has resulted in the neglect of the broader philosophical implications of the essay.[2] In this paper I propose to examine the arguments of Arrow and his critics within a more

Reprinted from *Journal of Political Economy*, XLIII (Chicago: University of Chicago Press, April, 1954), 114-123, by permission of the publisher. Copyright 1954 by the University of Chicago. The author acknowledges the helpful suggestions of Marshall Colberg and Jerome Milliman, of Florida State University, and Proctor Thomson of the University of Chicago.

[1] New York: John Wiley & Sons, 1951.

[2] Little's stimulating review article and, to a somewhat lesser extent, Rothenberg's subsequent critique provide partial exceptions to this general statement (see I. M. D. Little, "Social Choice and Individual Values," *Journal of Political Economy*, LX [1952], 422-32; and Jerome Rothenberg, "Conditions for a Social Welfare Function," *Journal of Political Economy*, LXI [1953], 389-405).

inclusive frame of reference. This approach reveals a weakness in the formal analysis itself and demonstrates that some of the more significant implications drawn from the analysis are inappropriate.

I shall first review briefly Arrow's argument, in order to isolate the source of much of the confusion which has been generated by it. Following this, I shall raise some questions concerning the philosophical basis of the concept of social rationality. In the next section I shall attempt to show that the negative results of Arrow's analysis as applied to voting represent established and desirable features of the decision-making process embodied in constitutional democracy. From this it follows that if the conditions required by Arrow were satisfied, certain modifications in the underlying institutional structure would become imperative. Finally, I shall develop the argument that the voting process is fundamentally different from the market when the two are considered as decision-making processes rather than as bases for deriving social welfare functions. Here it will be demonstrated that the market does produce consistent choices and that the market does not belong in the category of collective choice at all.

I. ARROW'S CONDITIONS FOR THE SOCIAL WELFARE FUNCTION

Arrow first defines his problem as that of constructing an ordering relation for society as a whole which will also reflect rational choice-making. This construction requires the establishment of a weak ordering relation among alternative social states. He then defines the social welfare function as a *"process* or rule which, for each set of individual orderings . . . *states* a corresponding social ordering" (italics mine).[3] The language is extremely important here, and the use of the word "process" seems singularly unfortunate. This usage has apparently been the source of the confusion, which is present in both the original

[3] Arrow, *op. cit.*, p. 23.

essay and most of the criticism, between the definition of the social welfare function and the actual *processes* of choice: voting and the market. As will be shown in this paper, the decision-making *process* may produce consistent choice, even though the *rule* which *states* the social ordering from the individual values may not exist.

Having defined the social welfare function, Arrow proceeds to set up the conditions which are necessary to insure that it will be based on individual values. These conditions have received the bulk of attention in the discussion of Arrow's work and are so generally familiar that they may be merely listed here. They include the requirements that (1) the function shall not be imposed; (2) it shall not be dictated by any one individual; (3) if one individual prefers one social alternative to another and everyone else is indifferent between the two, the preferred alternative shall not stand lower in the social ordering; and (4) irrelevant social alternatives shall not affect the ranking of relevant alternatives.[4]

Having set up these necessary conditions, Arrow develops his General Possibility Theorem (p. 59) which states that, if there are at least three alternatives, every social welfare function satisfying the rationality conditions along with requirements 3 and 4 above must violate the condition either of nonimposition or of nondictatorship. The theorem is proved to be applicable to the method of majority decision *as a welfare function* and to the market *as a welfare function*. It is inapplicable only when there exists unanimous agreement among all individuals concerning alternative social states, when the required majority of individuals possess identical orderings of social alternatives, or when individual orderings are characterized as "single-peaked." Since each of these possibilities appears somewhat remote, the weight of Arrow's argument is to the effect that the individual values which are implicit in the normal decision-making mechanisms of

---

[4] For the most concise listing of these conditions see William Baumol's review in *Econometrica*, XX (1952), 110.

society do not provide methods of deriving social welfare functions that are neither imposed nor dictatorial. So far, so good.
But Arrow extends the argument to say that these ordinary decision-making mechanisms do not allow rational social choice.[5]
Now this is a horse of quite a different color, with which the
Arrow argument should not legitimately concern itself at all. Arrow is not at all clear as to which of these two animals he is
chasing. The title of his essay implies that he is concerned with
decision-making processes, and he begins his work by reference
to the democratic means of decision-making—voting and the
market. He states his General Possibility Theorem in terms of
"moving from individual tastes to social *preferences*" (italics
mine).[6] Yet he slips almost imperceptibly into the terminology
of social-ordering relations or social welfare functions when he
sets up his required conditions. He fails to see that his *conditions, properly interpreted, apply only to the derivation of the
function and do not apply directly to the choice processes.*[7]
As will be shown in Section III, this distinction is not important
in application to voting, and this appears to be the root of some of
the difficulty. As will be shown in Section IV, when the market
is considered, this distinction is fundamental. It will be proved
that the existence of an Arrow social welfare function is not a
necessary condition for consistent decision-making.

Unfortunately, but understandably, the Arrow argument has

[5] *Op. cit.,* p. 59.

[6] *Ibid.*

[7] Little objects to Arrow's failure to draw a distinction between the social welfare function and the decision-making process on quite different
grounds from those advanced here. His objections are primarily centered
on Arrow's labeling the ordering as a "social welfare function" rather
than merely as the resultant of the decision-making process (Little, *op.
cit.,* pp. 427-30). He thus fails, along with Arrow, to make the necessary
distinction between an ordering of social states possessing certain properties and a decision-making process which is consistent, that is, rational.

Rothenberg, on the other hand, explicitly defines the results of the
choice process as the social welfare function (*op. cit.,* p. 400). He fails,
however, to trace through the effects of this definition on the Arrow analysis.

been widely interpreted in the erroneous sense of proving that the decision-making processes are irrational or inconsistent.[8] To the critics and reviewers of his analysis, almost without exception, Arrow appears to have subjected voting and the market to the test for rationality and to have found both these processes wanting.

II. THE CONCEPT OF SOCIAL RATIONALITY

It is difficult to know exactly what is meant by "rational social choice" in the Arrow analysis. Social rationality appears to imply that the choice-making processes produce results which are indicated to be "rational" by the ordering relation, that is, the social welfare function. But why should this sort of social rationality be expected? Certainly not because it is required for the derivation of the function in the first place. The mere introduction of the idea of social rationality suggests the fundamental philosophical issues involved. Rationality or irrationality as an attribute of the social group implies the imputation to that group of an organic existence apart from that of its individual components. If the social group is so considered, questions may be raised relative to the wisdom or unwisdom of this organic being. But does not the very attempt to examine such rationality in terms of individual values introduce logical inconsistency at the outset? Can the rationality of the social organism be evaluated in accordance with any value ordering other than its own?

The whole problem seems best considered as one of the "either-or" variety. We may adopt the philosophical bases of individualism in which the individual is the only entity possessing ends or values. In this case no question of social or collective rationality may be raised. A social value scale as such simply does not exist. Alternatively, we may adopt some variant of the organic philosophical assumptions in which the collectivity is an

[8] See, e.g., J. C. Weldon, "On the Problem of Social Welfare Functions," *Canadian Journal of Economics and Political Science,* XVIII (1952), 452-64.

BUCHANAN/*Social Choice, Democracy, Free Markets* (*163*

independent entity possessing its own value ordering. It is legitimate to test the rationality or irrationality of this entity only against this value ordering.[9]

The usefulness of either of these opposing philosophical foundations may depend upon the type of problems to be faced.[10] But the two should always be sharply distinguished, and it should be made clear that any social value scale may be discussed only within an organic framework. Once this approach is taken, the question as to whether or not the social value scale may be based on individual values may properly be raised,[11] and the individual orderings of all possible social states may be the appropriate starting point in the construction of a social ordering that is to be based on individual values. But the appropriateness of such individual orderings for this purpose does not depend on the fact that these are sufficient to allow the ordinary decision-making processes to function.

Voting and the market, as decision-making mechanisms, have evolved from, and are based upon an acceptance of, the philosophy of individualism which presumes no social entity. These processes are related only indirectly to the individual values entering into any welfare function. This was true even in the pre-Robbins state of welfare economics. The measurability and comparability of utility did provide a means by which individual

[9] By this statement that "every value judgment must be someone's judgment of values" (*op. cit.*, p. 427), Little appears fully to accept what I have called the "individualistic assumptions" and, in doing so, to deny the possible existence of an organic social unit. In his critique Rothenberg seems to adhere to the organic conception, when he states that "social valuation as opposed to solely individual valuation is an existential reality" (*op. cit.*, p. 397).

[10] The point involved here is closely related to a central problem in the pure theory of government finance. The whole body of doctrine in this field has suffered from the failure of theorists to separate the two approaches (see my "The Pure Theory of Government Finance: A Suggested Approach," *Journal of Political Economy*, LVII [1949], 496-505).

[11] Whether or not the degree of dependence on individual values is or is not a good criterion of appropriateness for a social ordering depends, in turn, on one's own value scale. We may or may not agree with Rothenberg when he says that consensus is required for a good social welfare function (*op. cit.*, p. 398).

psychological attributes could be amalgamated into a conceptual social magnitude. The social welfare function of the utilitarians was based, in this way, on components imputable to individuals. But the welfare edifice so constructed was not necessarily coincident with that resulting from the ordinary choice-making processes. It was made to appear so because the utilitarians were also individualists[12] and, in one sense, philosophically inconsistent.

Arrow's work, correctly interpreted, consists in rigorously proving that the individual orderings of alternatives which are sufficient to allow the decision-making processes to function produce no such measuring stick as was provided by the measurability of utility. The overthrow of such measurability destroyed the conceptual social welfare function; there are no longer any units of account.[13] Arrow's analysis appears to consist, however, in proving that the decision-making processes themselves define no social welfare function, that is, do not produce rational social choice. And here the implication is strong that this is true only when an ordinal concept of utility is substituted for a cardinal concept. Actually, the decision-making processes do not produce rational social choice, even in the utilitarian framework, until and unless certain restrictive assumptions are made.

If social rationality is defined as producing results indicated as rational by the welfare function, that is, maximizing total utility in the utilitarian framework, a market decision is socially

[12] Cf. Lionel Robbins, *The Theory of Economic Policy in English Classical Political Economy* (London: Macmillan & Co., Ltd., 1952), p. 182.

[13] Several of the attempts to modify Arrow's conditions in such a way as to define an acceptable social welfare function involve, in one form or another, a revival of the interpersonal comparability of utility (see Murray Kemp and A. Asimakopulos, "A Note on Social Welfare Functions and Cardinal Utility," *Canadian Journal of Economics and Political Science,* XVIII [1952], 195-200; Leo Goodman and Harry Markowitz, "Social Welfare Functions Based on Individual Rankings," *American Journal of Sociology,* LVIII [1952], 257-62; Clifford Hildreth, "Alternative Conditions for Social Orderings," *Econometrica,* XXI [1953], 81-95).

rational only if individuals are rational and individual utilities are independent. A voting decision is socially rational only if individual voting power is somehow made proportional to individual utility. Cardinal utility allowed the economist to construct a social welfare function from the individual utilities; it did nothing to insure that market or voting choices were socially rational. Here the distinction between a rational choice process and an acceptable social welfare function becomes evident.

The proper approach to social welfare functions appears to begin with the frank admission that such functions are social, not individual, and therefore are of a fundamentally different philosophical dimension from individual values or from individualistically oriented decision-making processes. It seems meaningless to attempt to test such choice processes for social rationality. But if the idea of acceptable social welfare functions and of social or collective rationality is completely divorced from the decision-making processes of the group, what is there left of the Arrow analysis? It is still possible to test these processes for consistency;[14] but consistency or rationality in this sense must not be defined in terms of results obtainable from a social ordering. Consistency must be defined in terms of satisfying "the condition of rationality, as we ordinarily understand it." [15] This implies only that choices can be made (are connected) and that the choices are transitive. The implications of the Arrow argument appear to be that such consistency of choice, could it be achieved, would be a highly desirable feature of decision-making. I shall attempt in the following section to show that possible inconsistency of collective choice as applied to voting is a necessary and highly useful characteristic of political democracy.

[14] Cf. Little, *op. cit.*, p. 432.
[15] Arrow, *op. cit.*, p. 3.

III. MAJORITY DECISION AND COLLECTIVE CHOICE

The reaching of decisions by majority vote provides the simplest example of voting. In the historical and philosophical context, majority decision evolved as a means through which a social group makes collective choices among alternatives when consensus among the individuals comprising the group cannot be attained. Correctly speaking, majority decision must be viewed primarily as a device for breaking a stalemate and for allowing some collective action to be taken. A decision reached through the approval of a majority with minority dissent has never been, and should never be, correctly interpreted as anything other than a provisional or experimental choice of the whole social group. As a tentative choice, the majority-determined policy is held to be preferred to inaction,[16] but it is not to be considered as irrevocable. The fact that such decisions may be formally inconsistent provides one of the most important safeguards against abuse through this form of the voting process.[17] If consistency were a required property of decision, majority rule would not prove acceptable, even as a means of reaching provisional choices at the margins of the social decision surface.

One of the most important limitations placed upon the exer-

[16] For a discussion of the basis for majority decision see Robert A. Dahl and Charles E. Lindblom, *Politics, Economics, and Welfare* (New York: Harper & Bros., 1953), pp. 43 f.

[17] Throughout this section the term "inconsistency" will be used in the formal sense without specific reference to the question of time dimension. This is admissible if it is assumed that all individuals have sufficient knowledge of alternatives to enable each to rank all alternatives and if it is assumed further that neither these individual orderings nor the available alternatives change over time. These assumptions, which are central to the Arrow analysis, allow the time dimension of the voting paradox to be neglected. When knowledge of alternatives is not perfect, however, and when the individual orderings do change over time (cf. below) or the alternatives presented vary, the concept of inconsistency itself becomes extremely vague. The argument of this section is applicable, however, whether or not the conditions required for the formal analysis are satisfied.

cise of majority rule lies in the temporary or accidental nature of the majorities. One social alternative may be chosen during a legislative session, but a new and temporary majority may reverse the decision during the same or the next session. A majority may reject C in favor of B, and then select A over B, but still select C over A when put to yet another test. The obvious result of this so-called "paradox" of voting is that the social group cannot make a firm and definite choice among the alternatives offered.[18] Thus the voting process does not necessarily produce consistency of choice, and, within the Arrow framework, the individual rankings required for voting cannot be translated by the economist into a satisfactory social welfare function. The implication is that both these results are undesirable; the transitivity property is not present.

But, certainly, majority rule is acceptable in a free society precisely because it allows a sort of jockeying back and forth among alternatives, upon none of which relative unanimity can be obtained. Majority rule encourages such shifting, and it provides the opportunity for any social decision to be altered or reversed at any time by a new and temporary majority grouping. In this way, majority decision-making itself becomes a means through which the whole group ultimately attains consensus, that is, makes a genuine social choice. It serves to insure that competing alternatives may be experimentally and provisionally adopted, tested, and replaced by new compromise alternatives approved by a majority group of ever changing composition. This is democratic choice process, whatever may be the consequences for welfare economics and social welfare functions.

The paradox is removed, and majority rule produces consistent choices, in the formal sense, if the individual components of

[18] Dahl and Lindblom accept fully this interpretation of the paradox when discussing it in specific reference to Arrow's work. They also dismiss the logical difficulty involved in the paradox as "minor" and "not an empirical observation of a common difficulty." In this latter respect, they apparently fail to see that the potential intransitivity property of ordinary majority voting provides a means of removing one of the greatest of all difficulties in the structure of majority rule (*op. cit.*, pp. 422 f.).

a majority possess identical orderings of all social alternatives. If, for example, Joe and Jack both prefer A to B to C, and Tom prefers C to B to A, Joe and Jack can always outvote Tom and adopt A. The selection of A would represent definite and irreversible choice as long as the individual orderings remain unchanged. This is one of the situations in which Arrow's General Possibility Theorem would not hold; a social welfare function may be derived, and the implication appears to be that such a situation would prove a more desirable one than that in which inconsistency is present. In one of the most revealing statements in his essay Arrow says: "Suppose it is assumed in advance that a majority of individuals will have the same ordering of social alternatives. . . . Then the method of majority decision will pick out the agreed-on ordering and make it the social ordering. Again all the . . . conditions will be satisfied. These results reinforce the suggestion . . . that like attitudes toward social alternatives are needed for the formation of social judgments." [19] The above statement also shows that Arrow is primarily interested in individual values as the units of account to be used in deriving social welfare functions. It is the collective rationality with which he is concerned; his approach includes no consideration of individual values as ends as well as means.

If one examines the choices made in this case of identical majority orderings, it becomes evident that collective rationality or consistency is secured here only at a cost of imposing a literal "tyranny of the majority." Minorities under such conditions could no longer accept majority decisions without revolt. If there should exist policy areas in which specific majority groupings possess identical orderings of social alternatives, it would become necessary to impose additional restraints upon the exercise of majority decision. This was one of the considerations which led Wicksell to advocate the adoption of the principle of unanimity in the approval of tax bills. He reasoned that in the imposition of taxes the given majority in power would tend to be

[19] *Op. cit.,* p. 74.

too cohesive and would, therefore, be able permanently to impose its will on the minority.[20]

The form in which Arrow states his condition of nondictatorship is closely related to the point discussed above. This condition, as applied to group decision, states that no one individual must dictate the choice without regard to the values of other individuals.[21] From the individual minority member's point of view, however, the acceptance of irrevocable majority decision is not different from the acceptance of irrevocable authoritarian decision. In either case the choice is dictated to the individual in question, since his values are overruled in the decision-making. If one thinks in terms of individual values as ends, "dictated to" seems a more meaningful concept than "dictated by."

The reason that majority rule proves tolerably acceptable and individual authoritarian dictatorship does not lies not in the many versus the one. It is because ordinary majority decision is subject to reversal and change, while individual decision cannot readily be made so. With identical majority orderings, the majority would, of course, always choose the same leaders, and this advantage of majority rule would be lost. It is not evident that we should summarily reject the rule of one individual if we could be assured that every so often a new dictator would be chosen by lot and that everyone's name would be in the lottery.

The attempt to examine the consistency of majority voting requires the assumption that individual values do not themselves change during the decision-making process. The vulnerability of this assumption in the general case has been shown by Schoeffler.[22] Individual values are, of course, constantly changing; so a postdecision ordering may be different from a predecision ordering. The assumption of constancy may, however, be useful in certain instances. For example, the assumption of given

[20] Knut Wicksell, *Finanztheoretische Untersuchungen* (Jena: Gustav Fischer, 1896), p. 122.

[21] Arrow, *op. cit.*, p. 30.

[22] Sidney Schoeffler, "Note on Modern Welfare Economics," *American Economics Review*, XLII (1952), 880-87.

tastes in the decision-making represented by the market is essential for the development of a body of economic theory. But the extension of this assumption to apply to individual values in the voting process disregards one of the most important functions of voting itself.[23] The definition of democracy as "government by discussion" implies that individual values can and do change in the process of decision-making. Men must be free to choose, and they must maintain an open mind if the democratic mechanism is to work at all. If individual values in the Arrow sense of orderings of all social alternatives are unchanging, discussion becomes meaningless. And the discussion must be considered as encompassing more than the activity prior to the initial vote. The whole period of activity during which temporary majority decisions are reached and reversed, new compromises appear and are approved or overthrown, must be considered as one of genuine discussion.

In a very real sense collective choice cannot be considered as being reached by voting until relatively unanimous agreement is achieved. In so far as the attainment of such consensus is impossible, it is preferable that the actual choice processes display possible inconsistency to guaranteed consistency. The molding and solidifying of individual values into fixed ordering relations sufficient to make ordinary majority voting fit the Arrow conditions for consistency would mean the replacement of accepted democratic process by something clearly less desirable. The danger that such solidification will take place becomes more imminent as functional economic groups, subjecting members to considerable internal discipline, seek to institutionalize individual values.

The unanimity requirement need not imply that consistent choice can never be reached by voting. Relatively complete consensus is present in the social group on many major issues, and

[23] The difference in the validity of the constancy assumption in these two situations is stressed by L. J. Richenburg in his review of Duncan Black and R. A. Nevins, *Committee Decisions with Complementary Valuation*, in *Economic Journal*, LXIII (1952), 131.

the securing of such consensus need not involve the concept of a Rousseau-like general will. As Arrow points out,[24] the unanimity required may be reached at several levels. There may exist relatively general support of the framework within which change shall be allowed to take place, that is, the constitution. This in itself insures that a genuine attempt will be made to attain consensus on controversial issues and, more importantly, to insure that the changes which are made are introduced in an orderly and nonrevolutionary manner. This relative consensus on procedure, however, will exist only so long as majorities on particular issues do not solidify; in other words, as long as ordinary decision-making may be formally inconsistent.

IV. COLLECTIVE CHOICE AND FREE MARKETS

In his discussion Arrow fails to make any distinction between voting and the market mechanism as decision-making processes, and he specifically defines both as "special cases of the more general category of collective social choice." [25] He is led to this conclusion because he is unable to define a satisfactory social welfare function from the individual orderings required for either process. In the consideration of voting, it is a relatively simple step to discard the social rationality or social welfare function implications and to utilize the Arrow conditions in testing the consistency of the choice process. When this is done, it is found that ordinary majority rule does not necessarily produce consistent choices. Thus the voting process serves neither as a basis for deriving a social welfare function in the Arrow sense nor as a means of producing consistent choices if tested by the Arrow conditions. When the market is considered, however, a different result arises when the process is tested for consistency of choice from that which is forthcoming when one seeks to derive a social welfare function. A necessary condition for deriving a social welfare function is that all possible social states be or-

[24] *Op. cit.*, pp. 90 f.
[25] *Op. cit.*, p. 5.

dered *outside* or *external to* the decision-making process itself. What is necessary, in effect, is that the one erecting such a function be able to translate the individual values (which are presumably revealed to him) into social building blocks. If these values consist only of individual orderings of social states (which is all that is required for either political voting or market choice), this step cannot be taken. This step in the construction of a social welfare function is the focal point in the Arrow analysis. This is clearly revealed in the statement: "The relation of known preference or indifference is clearly transitive, but it is not connected since, for example, *it does not tell us* how the individual compares two social alternatives, one of which yields him more of one commodity than the second, while the second yields him more of a second commodity than the first" (italics mine).[26]

By the very nature of free markets, however, the only entity required to compare two social alternatives when a choice is actually made is the individual. And, since individual orderings are assumed to be connected and transitive,[27] the market mechanism does provide a means of *making consistent choices* as long as individual values remain unchanged. If, given this constancy in individual tastes (values), the economic environment is allowed to change, consistency requires only that the same social state result always from similar environmental changes. Of course, there is no way of telling what a market-determined result will be (even if we know the individual orderings) except to wait and see what the market produces. The market exists as a means by which the social group is able to move from one social state to another as a result of a change in environment without the necessity of making a collective choice. The consistency of the market arises from what Professor Polanyi has called the system of "spontaneous order" embodied in the free enterprise economy. The order "originates in the independent actions of

[26] Arrow, *op. cit.*, p. 61.
[27] *Ibid.*, p. 34.

individuals." [28] And, since the order or consistency does originate in the choice process itself, it is meaningless to attempt to construct the ordering. We should not expect to be told in advance what the market will choose. It will choose what it will choose.

The market does not estabish the optimum social state in the sense that individuals, if called upon to vote politically (act collectively) for or against the market-determined state in opposition to a series of alternatives, would consistently choose it. This may or may not be an important conclusion, depending on the value-judgment made concerning the appropriateness of majority approval as the criterion of optimum collective choice. But the essential point here is that the market does not call upon individuals to make a decision collectively at all. This being the case, market choice is just as consistent as, and no more consistent than, the individual choice of which it is composed.

V. SUMMARY

It is necessary to distinguish between the problem of deriving a social welfare function from the individual orderings required for the operation of the decision-making processes of our society and the problem of testing these processes themselves for consistency. I have shown that the failure to make this distinction clear is the source of much of the confusion surrounding the Arrow analysis. A second distinction must be made between social or collective rationality in terms of producing results indicated by a social ordering and the consistency of choice produced by the mechanisms of decision-making. If rationality is taken to mean only that the choice-making is consistent, the Arrow analysis shows that voting may be inconsistent. But I have argued that possible inconsistency is a necessary characteristic of orderly majority rule. The market, on the other hand, has been shown to produce consistent choice, in spite of the fact that

[28] Michael Polanyi, *The Logic of Liberty* (Chicago: University of Chicago Press, 1951), p. 160.

a "satisfactory social welfare function" cannot be derived from the individual rankings implicit in the market mechanism.

The consistency of market choice is achieved without the overruling of minority values, as would be the case if ordinary political voting were made consistent. Therefore, in a very real sense, market decisions are comparable to political decisions only when unanimity is present. The question as to what extent this lends support to the utilization of the market as the decision-making process when it is a genuine alternative to voting opens up still broader areas of inquiry which cannot be developed here.[29]

[29] So far as I know, the differences between the market and political voting as choice processes have never been clearly and precisely analyzed. I hope to explore some of these differences in a forthcoming paper.

WELFARE ASPECTS OF BENEFIT-COST ANALYSIS

John V. Krutilla

I. INTRODUCTION

In recent years there has been substantial interest in developing decision rules for public expenditures under a variety of conditions. To a large extent in the literature dealing with governmental expenditures in the United States the interest has been confined to the field of resource development and the activity known in general as benefit-cost analysis. Benefit-cost analysis can be characterized as the collection and organization of data relevant by some conceptually meaningful criteria to determining the relative preferredness of alternatives (24 Parts II, III).[1] As is typical of much of economic analysis, the objective is to attempt by analysis to indicate how a particular desideratum can be maximized—accomplished by comparing the differences in the relevant costs and benefits associated with alternatives

Reprinted from *Journal of Political Economy*, LXII (Chicago: University of Chicago Press, June, 1961), 226-235, by permission of the publisher. Copyright 1961 by the University of Chicago. Acknowledgments are made to Robert Dorfman, Otto Eckstein, Francesco Forte, George Hall, Orris Herfindahl, and Vernon Ruttan. The substance of this paper was presented as one in a series of lectures given in the training program sponsored by the United Nations Economic Commission for Latin America at the University of Mexico, summer, 1960.

[1] Parenthetical data refer to bibliographical listing on pp. 190-192.

among which choices are to be made. This activity, of course, does not differ in kind from the economic analysis employed in reaching decisions with respect to production or other policies of the firm. Nevertheless, while the analytic activity does not differ in *nature*, the desideratum and the choice variables on which it depends will differ. Essentially, a private cost-gains calculus is employed in deciding private firms' policies; externalities and other divergences between private and social product are neglected. Benefit-cost analysis, on the other hand, seeks to take account of such divergences as a basis for guiding public action either when market prices do not accurately reflect social value or when, by virtue of the indivisible nature of collective goods, no market exists from which to observe directly objective evidence of the community's valuation of the social marginal product. Speaking loosely, while the decision rules of the theory of the firm aim at profit maximization, the decision rules of benefit-cost analysis seek to maximize "public benefits" or "general welfare" within the area of responsibility (29, p. 3).

In this connection the normative nature of the analysis needs to be emphasized. Unlike the assumption of profit maximization, which is a descriptive hypothesis having explanatory value (but cf. 28, 38), benefit-cost analysis is intended to be prescriptive. Underlying the analysis is the value judgment that, if governmental intervention is justified in part [2] by virtue of the market's failure to achieve an efficient allocation of resources (1, 3, 16, 22, 23, 26, 34), public officials ought to apply decision rules which tend to improve the allocation, that is, to improve the *general* welfare rather than their personal or specially interested clientele's welfare.[3]

[2] That part of governmental intervention characterized by Musgrave's "allocation branch" (26).

[3] For a positive theory of political behavior, which may more accurately mirror actual rather than "desirable" behavior of public officials, see Downs (4).

II. INITIAL CONDITIONS AND SIDE EFFECTS

While intervention is required to correct divergences between private and social product and cost, both the initial conditions and the associated side effects of intervention are of relevance in assessing the welfare implications of supramarket allocations of resources. Public intervention to redirect the use of resources involves costs. Assuming that the gross benefit achieved exceeds associated opportunity costs, if, in addition: (*a*) opportunity costs are borne by beneficiaries in such wise as to retain the initial income distribution, (*b*) the initial income distribution is in some sense "best," and (*c*) the marginal social rates of transformation between any two commodities are everywhere equal to their corresponding rates of substitution except for the area(s) justifying the intervention in question, then welfare can be improved by such intervention. And, to the extent that the objective is pursued to the point where the social marginal rates of transformation between commodities in this area and other sectors are likewise equal to the rates of substitution for correspondingly paired commodities, welfare is maximized.

However, since condition (*a*) is only partially feasible in the majority of cases dealt with by benefit-cost analysis, the likelihood of condition (*b*) has been subject to considerable question, and in the world of reality condition (*c*) is improbable, consideration of these stringent conditions is necessary to assess in pragmatic terms the welfare implications of supramarket allocation of resources suggested by benefit-cost comparisons.

III. IMPLICATION OF REDISTRIBUTIVE EFFECTS FOR THE MEASUREMENT OF WELFARE

Considering condition (*a*), we may recognize that the practical possibility of multipart pricing or corresponding special assessments is limited; and thus we must retreat to weaker positions. This retreat will require, at best, that the analyst rely on interpersonal comparisons of utility before he can hazard any judgment with respect to welfare, *plus* a degree of faith that the redistributional consequences for the measurement of welfare are of the second order of significance, or (at worst) that the analyst abstain from saying anything about the magnitude or even the direction of the change in either wealth or welfare, that is, about the change in the size of the national real income or its welfare implications.

To claim that welfare has increased, when the *ex ante* distribution is not automatically preserved by the mechanism of intervention, requires that those who gain are able to *and do* compensate those who lose, and still have something remaining. However, if we are uncertain about the "goodness" of the original distribution of income (condition *b*), we cannot contend that failure to compensate would not result in a greater gain in welfare. Such failure means only that the issue cannot be resolved without making interpersonal comparisons (31).

If we are content to attach no greater normative significance to the result of "maximizing" decision rules, however, than to aver that the national income has been increased, taking the distribution as given, we can envisage a broader application of benefit-cost decision rules. We are then content to accept the "production-distribution" or the "efficiency-ethics" dichotomy of the Kaldor-Hicks-Scitovsky line of development (9, 10, 15, 36, 37). We say that, if those who benefit by virtue of the increase in production can overcompensate those who suffer losses (but do not actually make the compensating payments), the "aggregate real income" has been increased irrespective of its distribution and, accordingly, of its welfare implications.[4]

Kaldor's production-distribution dichotomy and the resulting test of an increase in real income appear supportable for the more or less marginal adjustments for which benefit-cost criteria

---

[4] Of course, it is not to be inferred that Hicks ignores the welfare issue, since he attempted a defense of such an interpretation of the rise in social income. Among others, Hotelling (14) preceded and Wantrup (2) followed Hicks in providing a defense of such welfare implications.

were originally developed and typically applied in the United States. This remains true, I believe, despite Samuelson's and De Graaff's criticism of the proposition in general (33, pp. 10-11; 8, p. 90 ff.). At the most fundamental level is De Graaff's criticism, namely, if we wish to base our economics on an individualistic rather than an organic conception of the community and its welfare, and if there is more than one commodity, then the "aggregate real income" cannot be evaluated without weighting components, which in turn is not independent of the income distribution. We may resort to the "size-distribution" dichotomy, but it has no operational significance, for "we do not know the size unless we know the distribution" (8, p. 92).

De Graaff's concern with the distributional implications for aggregate real income corresponds to Scitovsky's concern with the *re*distributional consequences for measuring the *change* in real income. Consideration of only the latter and lesser question will suffice for our immediate purpose. Scitovsky's critical point can be summarized somewhat as follows: an indicated net increase in real income when valued in terms of prevailing prices may not prove so when valued in terms of prices reflecting the attendant income redistribution. Admittedly, for a structural reorganization of the magnitude implicit in the repeal of the corn laws, the effect of the income redistribution on the constellation of relative prices cannot be ignored. On the other hand, the relative magnitude of the redistribution associated with investment decisions for which benefit-cost expenditure criteria have been traditionally employed will be of the second order of smalls in terms of its implication for measuring the change and, for practical purposes, can be ignored (16, p. 50).[5]

[5] This is not necessarily meant to imply that the redistributive implications for welfare (discussed in the following section) can be similarly ignored. Such welfare effects might be important, especially if redistributive effects from expenditures for development of resources were cumulative. But cumulation hardly seems likely in the area of such expenditures. Additional annual expeditures of the Bureau of Reclamation, for example, do not benefit individuals previously favored because such additional expenditures represent predominantly extension of the program to new areas and, accordingly, to different individuals.

Thus, while the absolute size of the national income may not be independent of its distribution, a relatively small change in its size, for practical purposes, can be considered independently of its *re*distributional consequences in determining the magnitude and direction of the change. The distinction for benefit-cost analysis, of course, is significant, as it provides the theoretical basis for benefit-cost practices. For, if the more simple criteria of Kaldor and Hicks had to be supplemented even by Scitovsky's extension alone—not to mention Samuelson's all-possible-distributions test (33)—no *ex ante* judgment with respect to the anticipated change in economic efficiency resulting from a contemplated supramarket allocation could be supported by benefit-cost analysis. This follows because the analyst does not have the power to manipulate the distribution of income experimentally before rendering a judgment; nor does there exist sufficient information regarding individual preference maps to stimulate results from hypothetical distributions.

Samuelson's requirement that an improvement in efficiency must be tested not only against the *ex ante* and *ex post* income distributions but against all possible hypothetical distributions stems from two partially distinct considerations. The first involves the degree to which an implicit value judgment has been made in either Kaldor's and Hicks's criterion or Scitovsky's double criterion in spite of the intended preoccupation solely with production or efficiency. That is, to take the *ex ante* distribution (or in the case of Scitovsky the *ex post* as well as the *ex ante*) as a datum confers too significant a normative status on these particular distributions. For, as Fisher has observed:

> The refusal to make a value judgment . . . is in itself a value judgment, not only in the sense that one is saying that one ought to abstain from making value judgments, but also in the sense that the results obtained are those that would result from glorifying the present distribution [7, p. 394].

The second consideration underlying Samuelson's position seems to be concerned with the distinction between the "utility possibility frontier" and the "utility feasibility frontier," that is, between potential and feasible welfare. Here, while the utility-possibility function may be shifted outward uniformly or welfare potentially increased by a policy prescription, the implementation of the policy may cause such distortion of marginal conditions and "undesirable" income redistribution that the utility-feasibility frontier twists inward (33, pp. 18-21).

The first of these observations is related directly to condition (*b*), whereas the second bears obliquely on condition (*c*).

IV. THE WELFARE STATUS OF THE STATUS QUO

Considering condition (*b*), I believe it fair to say that the redistributive consequences of small changes of the sort encountered in benefit-cost analysis in the United States are negligible. But, as Fisher points out, this does not mean that benefit-cost analysis is free of distributional value judgments. For equating incremental benefits and costs in the designing of projects and "scoping" of programs relies on price data, which in turn are dependent on the prevailing distribution. Accordingly, if for no other reason than this, a judgment is implied regarding the normative status of the existing distribution.

A proper question to raise at this junction, however, is: "Can the prevailing distribution indicate, as a pragmatic approximation, the socially sanctioned one in a democratically organized society?" There are at least three ways in which to answer this question. One can reply with a qualified "yes," following a line of reasoning to be sketched below. One can maintain that it is really not possible to know, but that the answer may not be too important, given the level and distribution of income approached in the United States. Finally one might argue, as does Little, that the prevailing distribution of income does not enjoy a social sanction, so that any judgment with respect to efficiency must be in the nature of a second-best solution contingent also on a value judgment that the resulting income distribution is "good."

It can be argued that the prevailing distribution of income is approved by the community, since in a democracy the community has the means of changing it. Little discounts this rationale, apparently on the basis of the observed historical tendency toward persistent reduction of inequalities in income in modern industrial nations (19, p. 114). Yet the degree of income equality sought by a community may not be unrelated to the level of per capita income, and the reduction of inequality over time may be only a function of technological advances and the increase in efficiency of economic organization.

Differential rewards of income appear to be compatible with a Jeffersonian conception of democracy which accommodates an aristocracy of ability. Indirect evidence that the community sanctions some inequality of income has been reflected perceptively in the writings of Perlman (27, pp. 164 ff.). Anthony Downs, in a wholly different fashion, provides an interesting rationale for the existence of income inequality in a political democracy (4, pp. 199-200, but also cf. p. 94).[6] If I interpret Downs correctly, it seems probable that the income distribution resulting from the explicit redistributive activities of the government is, assuming that the incidental redistributive consequences of other governmental activities are non-cumulative, a reasonable approximation to the socially sanctioned distribution.[7]

A second possible argument, related to the first, is that, although there may be reasons for rejecting the prevailing distribution as in some sense "best" reflecting a social welfare function, at the present level of income distributional (and redistribu-

---

[6] For a comprehensive survey of recent thoughts on egalitarianism which, though exhaustive, is not conclusive, see Lampman (17).

[7] Musgrave, in his discussion of voting methods (26, chap. vi), observes the numerous difficulties of implementing an unadulterated social ethic and concludes that perhaps majority voting in a democracy comes as close to achieving the desired end as the mechanics of social organization will permit.

tional) questions are not dominant considerations.[8] This does not imply that all members of society have their non-frivolous needs met equally amply, but only that the associated dead-weight losses of moving toward greater equality would be judged to exceed the compensating distributional gains.

A third possible argument is that advanced by Little. Little abandons interest in a welfare maximum, regarding such an aspiration as utopian. Considering the existing distribution as non-optimal,[9] he focuses on conditions *sufficient for an improvement* in welfare rather than on conditions *necessary for a welfare maximum* (19, pp. 115-16). To render an improvement in efficiency desirable, that is, for it to improve welfare, the attendant redistribution of income must be acceptable. To pursue the matter to its ultimate conclusion, one could accept the frankly ascientific approach suggested by Meade (25, chaps. v, vii) and assign distributional weights based on interpersonal comparisons of welfare in order to incorporate redistributional aspects into a multidimensional objective function. In a similar, if more restricted, sense there is the possibility, consistent with Little's position, of maximizing a one-dimensional benefit function subject to an income-redistribution constraint.[10]

[8] Of course, while such an argument can be advanced following, or perhaps interpreting liberally, Fisher's argument (7, pp. 407-8), at such levels of income considerations of efficiency may also be of the second order of significance; that is, freedom from extension of governmental intervention may be purchased at the expense of some relative reduction in potential national income. On the other hand, maximum efficiency may be viewed as a possible good in its own right irrespective of the level of opulence if the welfare function depends on the relative rate of growth vis-à-vis some ideologically competitive society.

[9] Although Little rejects the notion that the prevailing distribution of income is sanctioned, his willingness to rely on prices as indicators of value suggests that its departure from optimality is not sufficient to affect relative prices—or else that individuals' preferences are sufficiently similar that redistributions will not affect the constellation of relative prices appreciably.

[10] To implement these suggestions, however, the benefit-cost practitioner would require supplemental legislation suspending the congressional directive in the Flood Control Act of 1936 to the effect that dollar democracy is to prevail.

V. WELFARE IMPLICATIONS OF NON-OPTIMAL INITIAL CONDITIONS OF PRODUCTION AND EXCHANGE

The third possibility noted immediately above touches on maximization problems best treated in connection with an evaluation of general condition (c), problems associated with the non-existence of the necessary conditions for a Pareto optimum. Here it must be acknowledged that, by reason of market imperfections and distortion of marginal conditions owing to government activities (both explicit redistribution and the financing of supramarket allocations), the Pareto-optimum conditions (c) are at best only approximated in practice and at worst are universally breached, so that the slopes of Samuelson's feasibility frontiers have little relation to prices and marginal costs (33, p. 18). The significant problem then remains of evaluating the welfare implications of benefit-maximizing criteria under real world conditions.

Of the major participants in the post-war discussion of welfare economics, only Little (later joined by Meade) attempts to come to grips with problems of this nature. These problems appear to be at least as great in practical importance as is the issue of interpersonal comparisons and income distribution; and they are, if anything, less susceptible of an intellectually satisfying solution. This is brought home decisively by the pessimistic conclusions of the statement by Lipsey and Lancaster of the general theory of the second best (21). They have demonstrated that, if any one of the conditions for a Pareto optimum is not attainable, it is in general not desirable to achieve any of the remainder (18, pp. 11, 26-27). The following quotation reflects the flavor of their nihilistic conclusions:

> The problem of sufficient conditions for an increase in welfare, as compared to necessary conditions for a welfare maximum, is obviously important if policy recommendations are to be made in the real world. Piecemeal welfare

economics is often based on the belief that a study of the *necessary* conditions for a Paretian welfare optimum may lead to the discovery of *sufficient* conditions for an increase in welfare. In his *Critique of Welfare Economics,* I. M. D. Little . . . says, ". . . necessary conditions are not very interesting. It is *sufficient* conditions for improvement that we really want." But the theory of second best leads to the conclusion that there are in general no such sufficient conditions for an increase in welfare. There are necessary conditions for a Paretian optimum. In a simple situation there may exist a condition that is necessary and sufficient. But in a general equilibrium situation, there will be no conditions which in general are sufficient for an increase in welfare without also being necessary for a welfare maximum [18, p. 17].

And, to erode further the faith of the innocent, they conclude that, in general, there is no proof of the existence of a second-best solution (18, pp. 27-28).[11]

Non-existence of a second-best solution in a technical sense, however, does not mean that, if an additional constraint is imposed on the welfare function, there is no actual relative maximum. Intuitively, we perceive that some adjustments in response to the given constraints will be better than others and that there must be an actual peak whether or not we can stipulate what conditions must obtain at the margin for all permutations. But the question remains whether or not supramarket allocations, guided by marginal equalities rather than the unknown appro-

[11] Professor Dorfman, in private correspondence, has taken exception to this conclusion. In his opinion, a second-best optimum exists under the same conditions that a Pareto optimum does, but in general the familiar Pareto-marginal equalities will not hold at a second-best optimum. Therefore, under the second-best conditions, an allocation of resources that satisfies some of the Pareto-marginal equalities is not necessarily preferable to an allocation that satisfies none of them. Nevertheless, there does exist a second-best optimum, that is, an allocation of resources that satisfies the distorting constraints that make "second-besting" necessary and that is socially preferable to any other allocation that satisfies those constraints.

priate inequalities, will tend to move the economy further away from such an actual relative maximum when similar marginal equalities are absent elsewhere in the economy. While it follows that, in general, supramarket allocations guided by marginal equalities will prevent the economy from achieving the constrained maximum, it does not follow that abstention from intervention would permit the economy to remain closer to the constrained maximum.

The possibility always exists that an observed inefficient situation is dominated by an attainable more efficient situation (12, p. 98; 13, p. 208). An example drawn from the field of resources may illustrate this point. Three alternative plans of development were proposed for the Hell's Canyon reach of the Snake River, the third of which was a privately advanced plan of development. For the three plans of development the following conditions hold:

$$O_1 > O_2 > O_3$$

and

$$I_1 > I_3 > I_2,$$

where O and I refer respectively to physical output and inputs, and the subscripts to the respective plans of development (16, chap. v). As between the second and third alternatives, it is obvious that the efficiency of the former dominates the latter. Hence, we can argue by dominance that, subject to an economic demand for the output, appropriate public intervention is a sufficient condition for an improvement without regard to necessary conditions for a welfare maximum. On the other hand, since the first alternative requires more inputs to achieve the greater output than does either the second or the third, and the value of the difference in output is greater than, equal to, or less than the opportunity costs of the inputs depending on a critical factor price, we cannot make a decision without recourse to prices. Now, if prices are not exact measures of opportunity costs—a condition implicit in the negative theorem of the general theory of the second best—they do not provide an unambiguous criterion.

Three partially distinct positions can be discerned in the approaches adopted by benefit-cost analysts in such cases. McKean takes the following position:

Those conditions [Pareto optimum] are not completely realized and moving toward the achievement of *one* alone is not necessarily a step in the right direction. However, if a frequency distribution of the possibilities is imagined, it seems likely that increased production where price exceeds cost would usually be a step toward efficiency, even though the other conditions are only partially fulfilled. The conclusion here is that prices and costs show how to "maximize production" [24, pp. 130-31].

Eckstein (5, p. 29), following Little (20, pp. vii-xiv), approaches the problem in the following manner:

[Insofar as there are monopoly elements, prices will exceed marginal costs, but from a quantitative point of view, these deviations are both widely—also perhaps evenly—diffused and relatively small, particularly in the range of markets most relevant to water resource development. Projects in these fields produce outputs which in largest part are producer goods, such as raw materials, electric energy and transportation services. In these areas, advertising, consumer loyalty and asymmetric market power concentrated on the side of the seller are less prevalent than in markets for consumer goods. Thus while prices do not serve their function perfectly, we hold that they are generally adequate for the range of policy decisions with which we are concerned. At the same time, in any application of the methods of this study, we must keep in mind the assumptions which validate the use of prices, and we must not hesitate, in certain situations, to reject them in favor of other measures of social benefit and cost.[12]

[12] Consistently with the latter part of the statement, Eckstein has done much original work in developing benefit maximizing criteria subject to a

A third position supporting the use of prices (adjusted for obvious divergences) as measures of opportunity costs, and of criteria based mainly on the presumption of the existence of marginal equalities is the following (16, p. 73, n. 32). While the benefit-cost analyst must recognize that he does not institute utopian reforms simply by an act of analysis, he must also recognize that his criteria, in the dynamic context of the real world, should be consistent with the higher-level aims which dominate the work of those public servants responsible for policing monopoly, improving market performance, and otherwise monitoring the economy with the objective of increasing the efficiency of its operation. And, while he must recognize the prevalence of departures from ideal conditions, he should not feed such departures systematically back into the optimizing calculations. For, in contrast to the static situation to which the negative theorem of Lipsey and Lancaster applies, such feedbacks can have a cumulative effect, resulting in progressive divergences from conditions of optimum production and exchange.

The choices in which one alternative clearly dominates another (or all others), while they may be numerous absolutely, must still represent a small proportion of the total of choices which face the economic decision-makers. And the positions advanced above to deal with the more representative situation can neither rest on formal proofs nor claim much by way of an intellectually satisfying status. Also, while the analyst must be sensitive to "higher-level aims," he must by virtue of the nature of his problems and analysis work largely in a suboptimizing or partial-equilibrium context (24, pp. 30 ff.). Conclusions reached by analysis at this level of generality need not hold in more general cases, and may require substantial reconsideration (see, for example, 21, 30, 32). The application of criteria for improving welfare therefore cannot be a mechanical or a compellingly logical activity. Rather, it requires perhaps more intimate knowl-

---

variety of constraints in addition to the resource-technology constraint (5, 6). This effort has been extended and generalized by Steiner (39), Marglin, and other members of the Harvard Water Resources Seminar.

edge of the economy, experience, and highly developed intuitive sense than analysts commonly possess—which suggests the quality of results and degree of precision to be anticipated.

VI. CONCLUSIONS FOR PRACTICAL CHOICES "IN THE PUBLIC INTEREST"

Does the array of positions advanced previously provide an adequate rationale for attempts to evaluate the benefits and costs of resource-development alternatives? Or are the comments herein transparent rationalizations which leave little conviction that analysis of benefits and cost and of their distribution can help significantly to improve welfare through public intervention? One's view, of course, will differ depending on the nature of one's experience, one's temperament, and perhaps also one's personal situation. The academic theorist without responsibility for policy can afford to (and probably should) be puritanical without regard to whether or not this is immediately constructive. On the other hand, the practicing economist in government, charged with responsibility to act under constraints of time and information, will often be grateful for perhaps even a perforated rationale to justify recommendations "in the public interest." Since the alternative is not to retire to inactivity but, rather, to reach decisions in the absence of analysis, we may take some comfort from the belief that thinking systematically about problems and basing decisions on such analysis are likely to produce consequences superior to those that would result from purely random behavior. Nonetheless, the utility and welfare effects of benefit-cost analysis are likely to be viewed differently, depending on the end of the telescope through which the affected party is privileged to look.

REFERENCES

1. BAUMOL, WILLIAM J. *Welfare Economics and the Theory of the State*. Cambridge, Mass.: Harvard University Press, 1952.

2. CIRIACY-WANTRUP, S. V. "Concepts Used as Economic Criteria for a System of Water Rights," *Journal of Land Economics,* XXXII (November, 1956), 295-312.

3. COLM, GERHARD. "Comments on Samuelson's Theory of Public Finance," *Review of Economics and Statistics,* XXXVIII (November, 1956), 408-12.

4. DOWNS, ANTHONY. *An Economic Theory of Democracy.* New York: Harper & Bros., 1957.

5. ECKSTEIN, OTTO. *Water Resource Development: The Economics of Project Evaluation.* Cambridge, Mass.: Harvard University Press, 1958.

6. ————. "A Survey of the Theory of Public Expenditure Criteria," paper read at Universities-National Bureau Conference on Public Finance, April, 1959, University of Virginia, Charlottesville.

7. FISHER, FRANKLIN M. "Income Distribution, Value Judgments and Welfare," *Quarterly Journal of Economics,* LXX (August, 1956), 380-424.

8. GRAAFF, J. DE V. *Theoretical Welfare Economics.* Cambridge: Cambridge University Press, 1957.

9. HICKS, J. R. "Foundations of Welfare Economics," *Economic Journal,* XLIX (December, 1939), 696-712.

10. ————. "The Valuation of Social Income," *Economica,* N.S., VII (May, 1940), 105-24.

11. ————. "The Rehabilitation of Consumer's Surplus," *Review of Economic Studies,* VIII (February, 1941), 108-16.

12. HITCH, CHARLES. "Suboptimization in Operations Problems," *Journal of the Operations Research Society of America,* I (May, 1953), 87-99.

13. ————. "Economics and Military Operations Research," pp. 199-209 in "Economics and Operations Research: A Symposium," *Review of Economics and Statistics,* XL (August, 1958).

14. HOTELLING, HAROLD. "The General Welfare in Relation to Problems of Taxation and of Railway Utility Rates," *Econometrica,* VI (July, 1938), 242-69.

15. KALDOR, NICHOLAS. "Welfare Propositions of Economics and Interpersonal Comparisons of Utility," *Economic Journal,* XLIX (September, 1939), 549-52.

16. KRUTILLA, JOHN V., and ECKSTEIN, OTTO. *Multiple Purpose*

River Development: Studies in Applied Economic Analysis. Baltimore: John Hopkins Press, 1958.

17. LAMPMAN, ROBERT J. "Recent Thoughts on Egalitarianism," *Quarterly Journal of Economics,* LXXI, No. 2 (May, 1957), 234-66.

18. LIPSEY, R. G., and LANCASTER, KELVIN. "The General Theory of the Second Best," *Review of Economic Studies,* XXIV (1956-57), 11-32.

19. LITTLE, I. M. D. *A Critique of Welfare Economics.* Oxford: Clarendon Press, 1950.

20. ————. *The Price of Fuel.* Oxford: Clarendon Press, 1953.

21. ————. "Direct vs. Indirect Taxes," *Economic Journal,* LXI, No. 243 (September, 1951), 577-84.

22. MARGOLIS, JULIUS. "A Comment on the Pure Theory of Expenditures," *Review of Economics and Statistics,* XXXVII (November, 1955), 347-49.

23. ————. "Secondary Benefits, External Economies and the Justification of Public Investment," *ibid.,* XXXIX (August, 1957), 284-91.

24. MCKEAN, ROLAND. *Efficiency in Government through Systems Analysis, with Emphasis on Water Resource Development.* New York: John Wiley & Sons, 1958.

25. MEADE, J. E. *The Theory of International Economic Policy,* Vol. II: *Trade and Welfare.* New York: Oxford University Press, 1954.

26. MUSGRAVE, RICHARD A. *The Theory of Public Finance.* New York: McGraw-Hill Book Co., 1959.

27. PERLMAN, SELIG. *A Theory of the Labor Movement.* New York: Macmillan Co., 1928.

28. REDER, M. W. "A Reconsideration of the Marginal Productivity Theory," *Journal of Political Economy,* LV (October, 1947), 450-58.

29. REGAN, MARK, and TIMMONS, JOHN F. "Benefit-Cost Analysis," paper presented before a joint session of the Economics and Engineering Section of the American Association for the Advancement of Science, Berkeley, California, December 27, 1954. Reproduced by the Committee on the Economics of Water Resources Development of the Western Agricultural Economics Research Council.

30. ROLPH, EARL, and BREAK, GEORGE. "The Welfare Aspects of Excise Taxes," *Journal of Political Economy,* LVII (February, 1949), 46-54.

31. RUGGLES, NANCY. "The Welfare Basis of the Marginal Cost Pricing Principle," *Review of Economic Studies,* XVII, No. 2 (1949-50), 29-46.

32. ————. "Recent Developments in the Theory of Marginal Cost Pricing," *Review of Economic Studies,* XVII, No. 3 (1949-50), 107-26.

33. SAMUELSON, P. A. "Evaluation of Real National Income," *Oxford Economic Papers,* N.S., II (January, 1950), 1-29.

34. ————. "The Pure Theory of Public Expenditures," *Review of Economics and Statistics,* XXXVI (November, 1954), 387-89.

35. ————. "Aspects of Public Expenditure Theories," *ibid.,* XL (November, 1958), 332-38.

36. SCITOVSKY, TIBOR. "A Note on Welfare Propositions in Economics," *Review of Economic Studies,* IX (1941), 77-88.

37. ————. "A Reconsideration of the Theory of Tariffs," *ibid.,* IX (1942), 89-110. Reprinted in pp. 358-89 of *Readings in the Theory of International Trade,* ed. Howard S. Ellis and Lloyd A. Metzler. Philadelphia: Blakiston Co., 1949.

38. SIMON, HERBERT. "A Behavioral Model of Rational Choice," *Quarterly Journal of Economics,* LXIX (February, 1955), 99-118.

39. STEINER, PETER O. "Choosing among Alternative Public Investments," *American Economic Review,* XLIX (December, 1959), 893-916.

SECONDARY BENEFITS, EXTERNAL
ECONOMIES, AND THE JUSTIFICATION
OF PUBLIC INVESTMENT

Julius Margolis

One argument often used to justify public services is that the benefits of the activity cannot be limited to the direct recipients of the services—those who would purchase the product if it were privately produced. These benefits, which are presumed to accrue to a large sector of the nation, are referred to as secondary or indirect benefits. There are many formulations of these secondary benefits. This paper will focus on the use of this concept and its measurement by the Bureau of Reclamation. In the case of the Bureau of Reclamation the development of this concept and its measurement is more than an argument for an extension of the public sector. The measurement is claimed to be part of the planning process, since it is supposed to enter into the determination of the scale of investment in water projects and the allocation of public funds among projects.

There are several other formulations of the appropriate concept of secondary benefits in use in federal agencies, but these

Reprinted by permission of the publishers from *Review of Economics and Statistics,* XXXIX (Cambridge, Mass.: Harvard University Press, August, 1957), 284-291. Copyright 1957, by the President and Fellows of Harvard College. This work was supported by the Office of Naval Research under contract N6 onr-25133.

will receive only passing attention.[1] As background it should be mentioned that those who advocate the use of the secondary benefits concept in project justification are today on the defensive. The current position of several staff coordinating agencies in Washington is to minimize the importance of secondary benefits. In this paper we shall restrict our attention to one type of public investment—dams and distribution systems for irrigation projects. The conclusions of this paper are that the procedures followed by the government agencies are confusing and incorrect, but that secondary benefits can be significant. The proper framework within which to discuss the secondary benefits is the theory of external economies.

I

Projects in the area of water resources development are expected to justify themselves by the computation of a benefits/ costs ratio. In general the benefits assigned to a project are the difference in the national income with and without the project. The increase in the national income is then broken into two groups, primary and secondary benefits. The primary benefits are the increases in the net incomes of the project farmers, after a full allowance has been taken for their costs including an imputed return on their own capital, land, and labor. No one challenges this increase in productivity as a benefit though there persist unresolved problems of how to measure the income, how to

---

[1] For a sample of different viewpoints see: Bureau of Reclamation, *Draft of Revision of Reclamation Manual, Vol. XIII, Benefits and Costs,* June 27, 1951; Federal Inter-Agency River Basin Committee, Subcommittee on Benefits and Costs, *Revised Statement on Secondary Benefits,* January 1952; J. M. Clark, M. M. Kelso, and E. Grant, *Secondary or Indirect Benefits of Water-Use Projects,* Report of Panel of Consultants to the Bureau of Reclamation; S. V. Ciriacy-Wantrup, "Benefit-Cost Analysis and Public Resource Development," *Journal of Farm Economics,* XXXVII (November 1955); House Committee on Public Works, Subcommittee to Study Civil Works, *Economic Evaluation of Federal Water Resources Development Projects,* 82nd Cong., 2nd Sess., House Committee Print No. 24, 1952.

forecast the increase, and how to compare the income of different time periods. The secondary benefits are quite different.[2]

At a general level there is little disagreement about the meaning to be attached to the concept of secondary benefits. This is surprising since there does not exist a clear theoretical or statistically operational definition. "Secondary benefits . . . are the values added by incurring secondary costs in activities stemming from or induced by the project." [3] Almost all parties to the discussion of the role of secondary benefits accept this two-way classification of "stemming from and induced by," though there is no defense of the meaningfulness of the classification. Essentially the "stemming from" benefits are the net incomes in the secondary activities which transport, process or sell the products of the project area. Benefits "induced by" the project are less clearly stated. Their major characteristic is that they are the net incomes in activities which sell to the project area, though in some formulations they include the incomes of the activities whose products or services are utilized by those who derive income from the activities involved in producing, transporting, processing, or selling the products of the project.[4]

The Manual of the Bureau of Reclamation presents the secondary benefits in the following detail:

5. Indirect irrigation benefits comprise the increase in:
   A. Profits of local wholesalers and retailers from handling increased sales of farm products consumed locally off the project without processing.

[2] The secondary benefits discussed in this paper refer to national benefits. There is another formulation of secondary benefits which refer to local benefits, the growth in economic activities in the area of the project. For an example of the analysis of local secondary benefits see: H. C. Holje, R. E. Huffman, and C. F. Kraenzel, *Indirect Benefits of Irrigation Development, Methodology and Measurement* (Montana State College, Agricultural Experiment Station, Technical Bulletin No. 517, March 1956).

[3] Federal Inter-Agency River Basin Committee, *Proposed Practices for Economic Analysis of River Basin Projects* (Washington, D.C., May 1950), 10.

[4] F.I.A.R.B.C., *Revised Statement on Secondary Benefits*, 2-3.

    B. Profits of all other enterprises between the farm and the final consumer, from handling, processing, and marketing increased sales of farm products locally and elsewhere.

    C. Profits of all enterprises from supplying goods and services for increased farm purchases for family living and production expenses.

    D. Land value of local residential property.

6. Like direct farm benefits, indirect irrigation benefits will be calculated from summaries of farm budget data representing future conditions with and without the project. Indirect benefit factors will be applied to increases or decreases in the value of individual commodities listed in the budget summaries. The indirect benefit from increased land value of local residential property will be calculated separately.

7. The following factors will be used to derive indirect irrigation benefits from summaries of farm budget data:

Indirect Benefit A	5 percent
Indirect Benefit B	
Cotton	83 "
Wool	78 "
Grain (wheat, oats, corn, barley)	48 "
Oil crops (flax, cottonseed, soybeans)	30 "
Sugar beets	26 "
Fruits and vegetables	24 "
Dry beans	23 "
Rice	13 "
Livestock (meat)	11 "
Seed crops	10 "
Dairy products	7 "
Poultry products	6 "
Indirect Benefits C	18 "

A factor of 4 percent will be applied to the increase in

land value of local residential property to derive an annual value for Indirect Benefit D.

8. Improvement in non-commercial land value of property in towns on or near irrigated areas will create an indirect benefit to persons other than project farmers. For example, twenty acres of unimproved land worth $100 an acre might be subdivided for residential purposes and sell for $800 an acre. Higher-grade use of the land would then have increased its value from $2,000 to $16,000. The indirect benefit would be 4 percent of the $14,000 increase, or $560 per year.[5]

It is difficult to characterize in analytical terms the above listed benefits. The first confusion surrounds the word "profits" which is used in the Manual. Other statements indicate that the incremental incomes are not restricted to profits but include "wages, and salaries, rents, interest and profits before income taxes." [6] Explanations of an earlier version of the Manual clearly state that the increments to be included in indirect benefits are to include all factor incomes.[7] But the secondary benefit factors to be applied to gross value of farm products used in the earlier Bureau reports are uniformly greater than the factors in the Manual. This would indicate that only profits are used in the Manual.[8] But in some cases the differences are too small to sup-

[5] U.S. Bureau of Reclamation, *Draft of Revision of Reclamation Manual Vol. XIII, Benefits and Cost,* June 27, 1951, ch. 2.2. In addition to these indirect benefits they also claim intangible public benefits as: increased farming opportunities—$1,000 for each new family farm; employment of seasonal or otherwise unemployed labor; the increase in property tax payments as a community service benefit, . . .

[6] House Committee on Public Works, op. cit., 15. The description of the Bureau of Reclamation's methods in this report was published a year and a half after the Manual was published.

[7] F.I.A.R.B.C., *Measurement Aspects of Benefit-Cost Practices* (Washington, D.C., November 1948).

[8] Mr. Alfred R. Golzé, Chief of the Division of Program Coordination and Finance of the Bureau of Reclamation says that, *"In general,* the Bureau has not used wages and interest in computing indirect benefits." Private letter of June 25, 1956. Italics added.

port the belief that there has been a change in definition. The cotton and wool factors fell from 124 and 91 to 83 and 78 per cent respectively. Clearly this is not a change from all income payments to profits. But compare the changes in livestock and dairy products, which fell from 55 and 71 to 11 and 6 per cent respectively. Whichever definition is used in practice, the restriction of the benefits to the profits of the supplying and processing industries is more consistent with the rationale of the concept than the use of all factor incomes.

If all factor incomes were included in benefits, and this was certainly done prior to 1951, the secondary benefits could be best characterized as the value of the incremental product on the project farms, valued as a final product in the national income sense, less the increased income on the farm attributable to the incremental project waters. With the inclusion of the primary direct benefits, the total benefits would be the increases in project farms' product valued as a final product. The Bureau procedure would value the final product at factor costs rather than at market prices. To see the applicability of this characterization consider the product produced on the farm and valued at the price it brings when it enters into the final product as inventory accumulation, exports, or in the pantries or closets of households. This price is equal to the sum of all incomes paid out to the productive factors plus the indirect taxes paid. If we summed all the incomes associated with bringing a physical product to the point where it reaches final consumption, it would be equivalent to valuing it at factor costs. This involved method is used by the Bureau if "profits" refer to factor incomes.

If "profits" refer to the net income of the firms processing the farm output or supplying the farm input, then implicitly the Bureau has valued (primary plus secondary benefits) the incremental product as final product at business (including farm) net income costs. This may seem a stranger measure than factor costs, but it is more defensible, though it is rejected in this article. It is more defensible since it assumes that there is an opportunity cost to most of the complementary resources in either further processing the farm product or preparing the farm inputs. These factors are paid according to their productivity in producing the agricultural final product, and their productivity in these activities approximates their productivity elsewhere. Therefore the payments these factors receive cannot be claimed as incomes created because of the incremental project output. The logic of this argument should extend to the factor payment, profits, since there is no reason to assume that there will be anything other than normal profits in the complementary industries.

The substitution of profits for factor incomes goes a long way toward surrendering the secondary benefits as a major contribution of the project. The Federal Inter-Agency River Basin Committee has gone even further in reducing secondary benefits. They retain the same structure of "stemming from" and "induced by" benefits. They expand the concept of induced benefits to include quasi-Keynesian effects.

Induced benefits in the case of the Bureau are the profits of the suppliers of the project area, while the induced benefits of the F.I.A.R.B.C. include the incomes to the suppliers of the materials and services used in producing, processing, transporting, and marketing the materials grown on the farms. Though the F.I.A.R.B.C.'s stream of benefits exceeds the Bureau's they quickly reduce them by saying that the alternative investment undertaken by the government other than the irrigation project in question would have given rise to a similar stream of benefits. The secondary benefits without the project are subtracted from those with the project to derive the net secondary benefits attributable to the project. The net secondary benefits are linked to the project's primary benefits. The proportion of the secondary benefits which they credit to a project is determined by the ratio of net primary project benefits (farm net income) to the government's project costs. Why this ratio has any meaning in terms of secondary benefits is not given. It would seem irrelevant since the secondary benefits are presumed to be a function of gross farm production rather than the rate of return on public investment in the project. Therefore the secondary benefits with the project as against the secondary benefits without the project have no relationships to the amount of primary benefits or the ratio of primary benefits to project costs.

Though the F.I.A.R.B.C. reduces the amount of secondary benefits by this peculiar linkage to the rate of return on the project, they are in agreement with the Bureau of Reclamation in claiming that secondary benefits develop because of expansion in complementary industries. How legitimate is this claim? Three types of arguments can be used in defense. First is the crude argument, implicit in the measurement procedures adopted, which state that supply creates its own demand. A second level of argument is that there exists a large volume of unemployed resources for which the opportunity costs are zero. A final level of argument, which is implicitly used though more frequently implicitly rejected, is the existence of external economies. The latter argument, we would hold, is the only valid defense of the inclusion of secondary benefits, but unfortunately economic analysis is still too primitive to allow for an accounting of these external economies.

II

The first argument, supply creating its own demand, is on the surface absurd. The Bureau of Reclamation assumes that there will be an increase in production on the farms in the project area and that this increment will be a net increase of production of all similar goods. Further they assume that the increment of goods will be processed and will require for processing complementary inputs used under conditions of constant costs so that the same incomes per unit of commodity will be generated. These assumptions violate the basic axioms of economic behavior. If we ignore the reality of agricultural price supports and surpluses which make a mockery of using current market prices as a basis to evaluate agricultural products, any expansion of production must lead to the competitive reduction of agricultural incomes and production elsewhere. Therefore no more goods would be processed and no further complementary inputs would be required. In the short run, if we accept the common assumptions of inelasticity in the demand for most agricultural goods and the immobility of farmers, we can expect a reduction of both farm and market prices with reductions in incomes for both farms and processing industries.

Price and income reduction may not be necessary consequences if the economy is expanding and demand curves are generally shifting upward so that the additional project products would not force a reduction in prices. But what would happen if the project had not been initiated? Agricultural prices would have risen and there would have been an expansion of agricultural production thus giving rise to all of the indirect benefits credited to the irrigation project.

There is one possible defense of the above argument. It could be claimed that the irrigation project is more efficient and that for the same investment more production is forthcoming, thus restraining the rise in price, allowing more sales, and thereby more employment in the secondary industries. In this case secondary benefits are dependent upon the existence of an economically justified primary investment in the project works and upon a further assumption that the additional employment of resources to be used had no alternatives. Both are probably unwarranted. The large public investment in irrigation systems in the West if valued solely in terms of the returns to the project farmers is probably inefficient.[9] The assumption of no alternatives to the resources used in secondary activities would similarly be improper, given the argument of the government that the projects are based upon assumptions of general expansion and growth in the economy.

The second defense of indirect benefits is closely related to the above. It is argued that there exists a large body of unem-

[9] We cannot hope to document this point in this brief article. One striking evidence of the inefficient investment is the poor repayment histories of the projects. See Bureau of Reclamation, *Repayment Histories and Payout Schedules*, 2nd ed. (Washington, D.C., 1953).

ployed resources. Therefore there exist no opportunity costs for the use of these resources. Therefore the costs assigned to factor inputs in industries servicing the project area, as well as the "stemming from" activities, should not be so considered but are instead benefits. In national income terms, the project product is being valued at market prices, and since the inputs complementary to the project product have no alternatives the full market value could be assigned to the project product. This argument violates in general the assumption underlying the irrigation program—that there is a general growth of the economy requiring further agricultural goods.

Further one might question the basic assumption underlying this argument—that employment effects should be considered in choosing irrigation projects. Irrigation projects are very inefficient counter-cyclical measures. They take a long period in planning and in construction so that they have none of the flexibility necessary for counter-cyclical programming. Further, it is certainly not obvious that one should encourage certain projects just because they give employment to otherwise unemployed resources. It might be more in line with social policy that the resources be made more mobile and move to more efficient locations or occupations. Further, even if the irrigation projects could be used in an effective counter-cyclical program there is no reason to assume that the unemployed resources which would be employed would be any greater than in many other forms of public or private investment.

III

The final argument, the stress on possible external economies, is defensible but it cannot be used to defend the measurements used by the Bureau of Reclamation or the F.I.A.R.B.C. The conventional formulation of Marshallian external economies and diseconomies is to restrict them to the changes in the supply price of factor inputs to a firm as the industry expands. It is common to extend the frame of reference beyond firm-industry relationships and discuss firm-local-area or industry-national economy relationships. In these cases the expansion of an industry may not lead to a reduction in factor costs to that industry, but external economies are said to exist if there are reductions in factor costs to other industries. Beyond this simple statement of external economies and diseconomies the discussion becomes very confused.[10]

It is usual to distinguish between technological and pecuniary external economies. When the discussion centers around the problems of the divergence between social and private costs and benefits the writers point out that they are

> interested in what have been referred to as technological economies or diseconomies of scale, i.e. economies or diseconomies in the use of resources by other firms (usually taken to be in the same industry) resulting from an increase in the output of one particular firm. There are also what have been called pecuniary diseconomies of scale (which caused the main difficulties in the early discussion of Marshall and Pigou), and which refer to increases in money costs of production resulting from increases in the remuneration of those factors already employed as their scarcity value increases with increasing output of the firm in which they are employed. These costs are not directly relevant to the question of the technical efficiency with which the goods are produced and hence they do not enter into the discussion of social cost.[11]

The pecuniary external economies are not social benefits since they are transfers of rent among specialized factors. The gains to

---

[10] There are repeated references to external economies in economic writing but Ellis and Fellner were being over-cautious when they "confessed that the theoretical treatment of this subject still leaves much to be desired." H. Ellis and W. Fellner, "External Economies and Diseconomies," *American Economic Review*, XXXIII (1943), reprinted in G. Stigler and K. Boulding, *Readings in Price Theory* (New York, 1952), 255.

[11] W. J. Baumol, *Welfare Economics and the Theory of the State* (Cambridge, 1952), 32.

one group are offset by the losses of another group—there is no net increase in the efficiency of the economy. In the case of technological external economies we do have a set of benefits to the nation which extend beyond the product of the firm or the industry.

The sources of external economies as stressed in the literature are manifold. The "balanced growth" literature relies on an assumption of a growth of productivity as the size of the market increases. Allyn Young elaborated on a theme of Adam Smith—the division of labor. The division of labor is necessary for increasing returns. The degree of specialization is a function of the extent of the market. Young was explaining some of the causes of historical growth and thereby correctly assumed that the economy was never at an equilibrium. This theme has been continued by the more recent writers, though they have added the moral for planners that induced growth along many lines would be self-justifying. Rosenstein-Rodan in addition to the Marshallian external economies adds the reduction in risk attendant on the planned creation of a complementary industrial system.[11a] This argument has provided much of the basis for the espousal of balanced growth which sometimes is urged independently of considerations of economies of scale.

The usual assumption made in the balanced growth and development literature is that there exists a large volume of underemployed resources, both human and natural. At the same time there exists a storehouse of technology which is not being applied. The problem, as seen in this literature, is one of social engineering to program the installation of the technology in order to convert the underutilized resources to optimal employment. The possibilities of external economies in this case are tremendous. Rather than marginal effects, any new investment bringing new industrial techniques is a school of industrial, financial, and marketing techniques for labor, managers, and entrepreneurs. The costs of the plant are markets for unutilized

[11a] P. N. Rosenstein-Rodan, "Problems of Industrialization of Eastern and South-Eastern Europe," *Economic Journal,* LIII (1943), 206.

factors. These "external economies" are also present in the alternative model offered to underdeveloped areas—the development of services to facilitate the basic export industries. Government will often undertake this form of "social overhead" capital on the assumption that this will improve the competitive position of their export-oriented industries and the presence of a large volume of underutilized resources will enable the expanded export base to generate investment in many allied fields. Care must be taken that the claimed external economies do not degenerate into an equivalence with some sort of "snowballing" effect. If the "snowball" effects do involve opportunity costs, if they use factors which have alternative uses, the benefits of the external economies are likely to be overstated.

Though one might establish grounds for the presumption of external economies in the case of underdeveloped areas, is it reasonable to assume that the same type of reasoning would be applicable in the United States? First let us recall that there are no special "economic laws" dealing with external economies for underdeveloped areas. In every case it must be established that we are not dealing with transfers but with a reorganization of the economy which makes better use of resources. Therefore, the question cannot be answered by a statement that the United States is developed and therefore the analysis is not applicable, but we must look at the specific circumstances and see whether the investment creates external economies.

The secondary benefits listed by the Bureau of Reclamation are instances of complementarities, but complementarities can result in both simple transfers as well as more efficient organizations. We must assume that the alternative to irrigated agriculture would be an expansion of production of similar agricultural products in other regions of the country. The case for secondary benefits would then depend upon the presumption of special conditions in the West giving rise to external economies, or the existence of a supply of underutilized resources in the West. The "stemming from" benefits extending to processing and marketing at distant points would be indefensible since the alternative production would bring the same volume of materials to the market.

The question therefore is reduced to one spreading fertilizer in the Mid-West or water in the arid West. On a primary benefits basis the choice probably would be for the Mid-West. The return to the Mid-Western farm would be greater than the return to a Western irrigated farm. A study which compared returns in Mecklenburg County, Virginia with those on the Columbia Basin Project of central Washington estimated that 7.5 acres of land could be cleared and developed in Mecklenburg County for the cost of each acre brought into production on the Columbia Basin Project.[12] The defense of the irrigation project in terms of the goal of economic efficiency would have to rely on secondary benefits arising from the use of unused resources, or external economies enabling a more efficient organization of the resources.

In general it would seem plausible to argue that regional redistributions of income through direct transfers or government expenditures would have positive efficiency effects. The highly unequal per capita incomes among the states imply that a reshuffling of resources would bring the economy closer to a Paretian optimum. The inequality indicates a distance from equilibrium which is a necessary condition for the developmental types of external economies. The underdeveloped regions usually have a much lower capital to labor or capital to land ratio. The usual proposal is that the mobile factors shift. Irrigation by the federal government is essentially a capital subsidy to an underdeveloped region and therefore a shift of capital. Commonly these regions lack capital, entrepreneurial talents, highly skilled workers, and similar necessary ingredients for an expanding economy.[13] The

[12] R. Ulrich, "Relative Costs and Benefits of Land Reclamation in the Humid Southeast and the Semiarid West," *Journal of Farm Economics,* xxxv (February 1953) 72.

[13] In a study of comparative returns to farming in Montana, Iowa, and Alabama it was concluded: "Our estimates are for farmers in Alabama with capital in a form representing 'poor techniques.' The same amount

irrigation expenditures have induced effects not only by the employment of labor on construction and operations but also in bringing capital funds in the area. The farmers selected for the project are expected to be capable of managing the difficult tasks of the more intensive irrigated farming. Labor skill will be improved and capital will become more accessible in an area which lacked them. The more dense settlements characteristic of irrigated farming will permit improvements in transportation, reductions in public costs, and population growth extending the market. All of these are conditions of economies of scale.

An additional consideration might be the pattern of growth of the Western states where the projects are located. Their population has grown rapidly relative to the United States, but their manufacturing industries have lagged. They export lumber and agricultural products and import manufactured goods. They are sparsely settled so that the distances between urban places are large. How do irrigation projects fit into this picture? The increased crops provide an expansion of the export base of the area, but this one may claim is only a regional benefit—a transfer—and can only be used to justify national investment if it leads to such external economies as increased capital funds, transport economies, enhanced labor and entrepreneurial skills, and so on. The projects result in a shift to an intensive agriculture with more dense settlement patterns. New urban places develop and older urban places grow. This development has two consequences. The urbanization is an extension of the market which permits economies of scale for the development of manu-

of capital in 'improved techniques' might give much higher returns. While Alabama is near the 'tail end' in capital productivity, returns on this resource could actually be very great if more capital were also invested in educational resources for farmers; more capital also would allow livestock production on a commercial basis rather than as a semi-household enterprise. A reorganization of agriculture to give larger farms would also bring about higher productivity in capital." E. O. Heady and R. Shaw, "Resource Returns and Productivity Coefficient in Selected Farming Areas," *Journal of Farm Economics*, XXXVI (May 1954), 253.

facturing in the West, and it also enables efficiencies in transportation to be realized. These are less likely to occur in the settled areas of the East.

The existence of these economies is dependent on an assumed shift of population to the West—an areal preference function which is not that of the government but implied in the large migration of recent decades. The population will be under-equipped with capital, public facilities, supplying industries, or jobs. Irrigated agriculture will provide some external economies under these conditions, especially when one considers that the alternative would be importing food, thereby creating a very heavy leakage to any investment undertaken in the area. But the extent of the economies that could be justified under this sort of argument is small compared to the actual practices of the Bureau. Labor resources are not free in spite of their possible willingness to take a smaller wage in order to live in the West. The labor moving to the West is mobile and could return. The full opportunity costs should be assessed against labor as well as the interest on the entrepreneurial capital. In this case the only "induced by" or "stemming from" effects which can be considered legitimate are those which create external economies—the major part of the indirect benefits being transfers. Unfortunately no one has devised a general method by which these economies could be measured.

Though theory has not progressed to the point where the statistical counterparts of theoretical concepts can be constructed, the discussions of external economies can provide some insights into what the analyst should investigate when looking for economically justifiable secondary benefits. One major source of external economies is the growth of the market. The local market will grow both because of the project farmers and the service industries associated with them. The question for the analyst is: Has the market grown to the point where it is sufficiently large to support an optimum-sized plant, instead of requiring local imports and high transport costs from the production centers of the dense Eastern market areas? [14] The argument that the new firm is an "economy" for the nation is dependent upon the assumption of a continued existence of population in the underpopulated West.

A second source of external economies is use or expansion of social overhead capital. In some cases, roads, schools, urban centers, and so on may have excess capacity. They are in the nature of a decreasing-cost industry. An expansion may be provided without an increase in these social costs.[15] This is probably not an important case since the irrigation investment and associated expansion is usually large relative to the local economy, so that an expansion of overhead capital is usually required. This growth of overhead capital and its implications for the establishment of efficient plants instead of importing should be investigated.

These studies of external economies involve an analysis of the local area, but the results will bear little relationship to the local secondary benefits estimated by the Bureau of Reclamation.[16] The major technique of the Bureau is to compare the trends of many economic indexes in counties with irrigation as against nearby comparable counties without the projects. It is possible

[14] See Joe S. Bain, *Barriers to New Competition* (Cambridge, 1956), for a discussion of minimum-sized efficient plants in twenty industries. An extension of the number of industries and an estimate of the regional markets for the industries would enable the analyst to judge the possibilities of introducing efficient firms in the area rather than importing.

[15] See W. C. Wheaton and M. J. Schussheim, *The Costs of Municipal Services in Residential Areas,* Housing and Home Finance Agency (Washington, 1955), for the differences in public marginal costs to service population growth in established cities as against unpopulated peripheral suburbs.

[16] Holje, Huffman, and Kraenzel, op. cit., M. E. Marts, *An Experiment in the Measurement of the Indirect Benefits of Irrigation, Payette, Idaho,* Bureau of Reclamation (Boise, Idaho, June 1950); M. K. Strantz, *Reclamation Accomplishments, 1905-53, Klamath Project, California,* Bureau of Reclamation, 1953; and M. S. Bentson and R. E. Struthers, *Accomplishments of Irrigation, Weld County, Colorado,* Bureau of Reclamation (Denver, February 1952).

that the difference in the levels may be attributed to the project, but this difference is not a national benefit since a large part of this enhanced income would have arisen wherever the project had been located.

To gain insight into the incidence of external economies, rather than comparing nearby counties with and without irrigation, the Bureau should compare the economic growth of Western areas with irrigation against Eastern areas with soil-treatment programs. It is the speculation of this paper that the Western investment will show larger external economies than the Eastern.

EXPLORING PRODUCTIVITY MEASUREMENT IN GOVERNMENT

John W. Kendrick

The most distinctive function of management, whether in private industry or government, is innovation. In today's world, in which nothing is certain but change, management must continually be adapting to change, or, since the best defense is a good offense, producing changes favorable to the organization. This involves research, invention, and development of new or improved products or cost-reducing innovations in the instruments and organization of production.

In private industry, it is obvious that firms must innovate or perish, subject as they are to the discipline of competitive markets and the cost-price relation. In a broad sense, governmental units are also competing for scarce resources—with private industry and with each other—when public taxation and expenditure decisions are made by legislators and, ultimately, by the sovereign consumer-citizen in a democracy.

It is the peculiar function of public administrators to secure and increase the productivity and service standards of public

Reprinted from *Public Administration Review*, XXIII, 2 (June, 1963), 59-66, by permission of the American Society for Public Administration. It is taken from a talk to the ASPA National Capital Area Chapter, March 20, 1963.

agencies and enterprises. In this way, functions can be performed with decreasing inputs of men and other resources, or, to state it differently, given human and material resources can be made to yield increasing outputs of public services.

As a result of measured productivity increases in the private economy, since World War II advances in productive efficiency have accounted for approximately two-thirds of the 3.3 per cent a year average increase in the real gross national product (G.N.P.). We do not now know how rapidly government productivity has been rising—official real G.N.P. estimates include government at its real cost without allowance for productivity change. But it is clear that our total economic growth will be greater, and our resources made to go further, the greater is the rate of increase in the productivity of government. And it is unnecessary for me to embroider the theme that our national security and welfare depend in large measure on our rate of economic growth.

Or, to look at it purely from the viewpoint of the government administrator, as real unit costs of government services are decreased by innovations, and the quality of the services improved, agencies are in a stronger position to compete with other sectors of the economy for scarce resources. This must be so to the extent that the public, directly and through its elected representatives, rationally weighs the relative costs (per unit) of both privately and publicly produced goods and services against the relative satisfactions, or benefits, they receive from each.

THE DEVELOPMENT OF PRODUCTIVITY MEASURES

Administrators of both public and private enterprises have a variety of techniques for enhancing efficiency, but business management is more fortunate (unfortunate from the standpoint of peace of mind) in having the continuing discipline of the profit and loss statement both as a record of performance and spur to achievement. Administrators have been ingenious in devising other means of measuring performance as background for improvements, the most recent of which is the organizational productivity index. Productivity indexes—which relate output to input in real, physical volume terms—are of particular significance in government agencies, but private firms have also been experimenting with this type of measure as an adjunct to the usual financial operating statements.

Actually, productivity measures were first developed intensively for private industry groups, and the private economy as a whole—notably by the National Bureau of Economic Research and the Bureau of Labor Statistics Division of Productivity and Technological Developments—beginning in the 1930's. Company measurement programs began to spread in the 1950's. In government, a few attempts had been made to calculate agency labor productivity ratios prior to 1962, notably by the Bureau of Old Age and Survivors' Insurance and the Railroad Retirement Board.

A major impetus to agency productivity studies came in January 1962, when a Management Analysis Conference held at Cacapon Springs was devoted to the theme "Managing Government Productivity." At this conference it was pointed out that, as a result of advances in performance budgeting, work measurement, and cost accounting, sufficient internal data were available to permit construction of productivity measures in many agencies at a small cost. Basically, what was required was a recasting of data largely available into the conceptual framework of productivity accounting.

In the spring and summer following, the Management Research and Improvement Branch of the Office of Management and Organization in the U. S. Bureau of the Budget (BOB) made plans for and obtained the cooperation of five Federal agencies to set up pilot studies of productivity to determine the feasibility and usefulness of such measures. Mr. William Rapp of the BOB and the author worked closely on this preparatory phase of the project. A small staff of productivity specialists was then set up under the direction of Dr. Nestor Terleckyj to work with agency technicians to develop estimates for recent years.

In October of last year, a two-week orientation course was held for the agency representatives. After this, they went to work on their own, with guidance from the BOB staff in regular weekly conferences. During February preliminary results were obtained and written up for review by an Advisory Committee to the BOB on the project. In general the Committee and the Bureau staff have been encouraged by the preliminary results of the pilot studies. These studies will be used to illustrate the general discussion of agency productivity measurement today. A full evaluation of the pilot studies will have to await completion of the project in June. Assuming favorable assessment, it is planned to issue the case studies and a general handbook to guide other agencies.

THE CONCEPT AND MEANING OF PRODUCTIVITY

Broadly defined, productivity estimates compare the output of an organization with one or more of the associated inputs, in real physical volume terms, through time (or with similar organizations). When output is related to total input, the productivity ratio shows changes in the efficiency with which resources are converted into final products. The productivity ratios are usually expressed in index numbers, relative to a given base year as 100.

Changes in the productivity ratio primarily reflect innovations in the instruments and organization of production, and in the short run, changes in the degree to which resources are utilized. Changes in the ratio of output to any one class of inputs, such as labor alone, not only reflect changes in productive efficiency, but also the substitution of the unmeasured nonlabor inputs for labor. The ratio of output to all associated inputs has been dubbed "total productivity," while the ratios of output to labor, capital, or materials inputs singly are "partial productivity" ratios. Obviously output per manhour, or any other partial productivity ratio, does not measure the efficiency of labor, or any other single factor, but rather the efficiency with which the factor is used in production. In showing the savings achieved over time per unit of output in the consumption of basic resources, the productivity ratio is perhaps the best overall measure of the innovational performance of management. It does *not* replace, but supplements the other management performance measures, by giving a summary picture of productivity changes within an agency as a whole, and/or its organizational divisions.

To bring the nature of productivity measures down to earth the measurement of output and input will be discussed with concrete examples from the agency studies. Then it will be practical to consider the potential uses of the indexes.

MEASURING OUTPUT

Output measurement involves: 1) identifying all the various classes and specific types of final output—those services, or goods, which implement the basic mission of the agency; 2) defining the various outputs in terms of measurable, standard units; 3) assembling data on the numbers of these standard units of output of each type of service produced currently and over the years covered by the historical study; 4) adjusting the units, where necessary, for changes in characteristics in order to achieve consistency over time, and 5) estimating base-period unit costs for purposes of combining, or "weighting" the various output units into an aggregate—the choice of weights depending on the cost items, or inputs, to which the output indexes are to be related.

With regard to identification of the final outputs of an agency, a useful by-product of our study has been that it forced the agency representatives to re-think the basic mission and end-products of their agencies—to identify those outputs that correspond to the sales categories of a private enterprise. Now, to give a quick run-down on the outputs selected by the five agencies, in order of ascending complexity:

In the *Division of Disbursement* of the Treasury Department, the output measure is quite simple—the volume of checks, and of savings bonds, issued. Checks are by far the more important output.

In the *Insurance Service,* Department of Veterans Benefits, in the Veterans Administration, five final output classes were identified. The most important, and basic, service is provision of insurance protection, as reflected in the average number of policies in force during the period. Other services are: waiver of premium payments in cases of total disablement, as measured by numbers of initial claims and review decisions; the numbers of terminations, involving final settlements, by four types; the number of loan applications processed; and the number of new policies issued—although the last-named service has been very small since 1958.

In the *Post Office,* by far our largest cooperating agency, or, perhaps, "public enterprise," output is measured in terms of 14 types of mail handled—first class, second class, parcels, etc., generally expressed in terms of the number of pieces of each—and seven types of special services, such as money orders and postal savings, measured in terms of numbers of transactions.

In the *Systems Maintenance Service* (S.M.S.) of the Federal Aviation Agency, output consists primarily of maintaining in operation the various types of devices used to maintain the airways navigation system and to regulate and control air traffic, plus some non-aeronautical facilities that service the personnel. The output is measured in terms of facility-years, broken down into 82 major groups and over 250 classes of facilities by model, size, and geographical function (each of which is associated with different unit labor requirements).

Finally, in the *Bureau of Land Management* (B.L.M.) of the Interior Department, current outputs were measured in preliminary form for five major programs. In land and minerals there are six types of land activities measured in terms of acres placed into use or numbers of transactions and five types of mineral activities, chiefly numbers of leases, licenses, permits, and sales. The range program output is "animal unit months" of grazing. Forestry output is quantified in terms of the board feet of timber offered for sale. Cadastral surveys involve miles of line and number of monuments set and the relatively minor recreational function can be gauged by the average daily number of visitors.

B.L.M. is at the top of the list in terms of complexity, since a problem is posed by the fact that a major portion of the outputs is of an investment character, such as construction, or additions to forests and other natural resource reserves. Either ways must be found of measuring these outputs, or else the inputs associated with the investment outputs should be excluded, and the current outputs related to current inputs. Work is proceeding along these latter lines.

SPECIAL PROBLEM AREAS

Identification of final outputs does not mean listing all the types of activity in which the personnel are engaged. Some of these may be intermediate, representing staff functions, or stages in the process of turning out the final services. For example, in the V.A. Insurance Service, there are about 150 types of workload used in the work measurement system, while only 8 activities were classed as final outputs.

Of course, some of the outputs which are final to a division of an agency, such as maintenance of air traffic control facilities by the S.M.S., are intermediate to the agency as a whole. When these outputs, or the associated inputs, are related to final agency output (in this case, primarily a measure of the volume of air traffic) the apparent productivity increase may be quite different from the division measure. If there were a consolidated

Federal government measure, then much or all of the outputs of many entire agencies, such as the Civil Service Commission or the Executive Office of the President, would work out as intermediate, and only the services rendered to other sectors of the economy remain as final.

In measuring units of different types of work over time, it is important to use the right unit—the one that most nearly describes the final service rendered or function performed. Thus, in the Post Office, for most categories of mail and special services, the number of pieces carried or processed is sufficient. In the case of parcels and freight, however, the cubic volume and weight were dimensions that had to be added to the number count. In some of the initial B.L.M. measures, *approvals* of applications and other cases was taken as a unit, but on review it was felt that the numbers of cases processed (whether approved or disposed of otherwise) was the basic service since the Bureau was required by law to consider all applications, etc., but obviously the percentage approved is a matter of discretion.

Production may be for stock—i.e., to add to inventories or fixed capital—as well as for current consumption, and the investment outputs should be included if possible. Some agencies perform construction with their own force. A major problem in the Bureau of Land Management is that the Bureau not only supervises the use of public lands but also is concerned with building up and improving the public's natural resources. To some extent, current use and adding to resource stocks are inversely related.

In the range and forest management programs, for example, in recent years grazing and cutting of timber have been restricted in order to build up the resource base. Unless the Bureau is able to include in the output measure the changes in resource inventories represented by vegetative cover and forest stands, their output and productivity estimates would tend to be understated.

Another kind of investment is represented by changes in work-in-progress. When, for example, applications are being considered, there is a time lapse between initiation of work and final action or disposition. If the work-in-process increases during a period, the additional resources embodied in this inventory should be counted as output. Otherwise, the time lag between output and input can cause erratic fluctuations in the productivity ratio.

One of the most difficult aspects of measuring output is to take account of changes in the *quality* of services. One way is by adjusting output units for the difference in work content when the nature of the service changes. Thus, if an Act of Congress increases the amount of information required on a given form necessitating 10 per cent more processing time after shake-down of the operation, the new work units would be adjusted to represent 110 per cent of the output of the old units.

Some changes in quality aspects of services are not associated with unit cost increases. For example, use of electronic equipment in processing checks (and documents) reduces errors and increases speed of processing, while at the same time cutting unit cost. In the cases where it is not feasible to quantify the contribution of quality improvements, it is desirable where possible to present subsidiary indexes of qualitative aspects of performance along with the basic productivity measures to assist in their interpretation.

WEIGHTING

Finally, measures of the relative importance of the various outputs of an agency for a base-period must be obtained in order to combine the units into an aggregate output measure. For several technical reasons I will not go into now, it is desirable to have a recent base—fiscal year 1962 is used in this study. It is desirable that the unit weights correspond to the inputs with which the output is to be compared. Thus, for an output per manhour index, the unit manhour requirements for each type of output should be obtained, and for a total productivity index, unit dollar-cost measures are appropriate. These weights are usually available from the work measurement or cost accounting records.

Consistency between output weights and inputs ensures that shifts from lower cost to higher cost outputs will result in corresponding increases in the total output and input measures, and that productivity will show an increase only if efficiency in turning out component outputs rises—not as a direct result of shifts in the product-mix.

It would be possible to weight outputs in terms of their requirements for each of the several inputs which are separately measured. Mr. Schachter, now with the Post Office, has done an interesting job preparing 12 different aggregate output measures corresponding to each of the 12 types of manpower for which manhour estimates were made.

INPUT MEASUREMENT

Inputs of the basic factors of production, labor, and capital are generally measured in terms of the hours the factors are available for service, weighted by the average hourly compensation (or cost) in the base period. Inputs of intermediate goods or contract services are measured (like outputs) in terms of the quantities of each type consumed weighted by the base-period price or unit costs.

The estimator must be sure that his inputs match the outputs. For example, hours spent on research and development or other investment activities that do not affect current output should be excluded (unless the investment outputs are measured and included with current output—which does not seem practical in the case of R. & D.).

Unlike outputs, in measuring specific inputs we do *not* want to take account of quality changes, but rather to measure the inputs in units of standard efficiency over time—like manhours of a given grade weighted by base-period average hourly earnings. We wish the changing productive efficiency of the inputs to show up as changes in the output-input ratio.

The chief input in the economy generally, and particularly in Government, is labor. If average hours data are not available, full-time equivalent manyears may be used to approximate labor input, although manhours worked are generally considered a more precise unit. The Division of Disbursement and B.L.M. used manyear equivalents, while the other three agencies were able to calculate manhours. A further refinement is to break manhours down into occupational categories and grades, and to weight each by base-period average earnings. When this is done, a relative shift of employment towards higher-pay categories shows up as an increase in labor input, as in the Division of Disbursement case. In the Systems Maintenance Service of F.A.A., to the contrary, there was a relative shift to lower grades, which showed up as a smaller increase in weighted than in unweighted manhours.

The Division of Disbursement, the Post Office, and the V.A. Insurance Service have attempted to measure non-labor as well as labor costs. This is not the place to go into detailed techniques. But generally the purchased goods or services—such as transportation in the case of the Post Office, or machine rentals in the case of Treasury—were deflated by appropriate price indexes. Equipment purchases were converted to constant (1962) dollars, and amortized over their estimated lives. The real annual depreciation, or "capital consumption," was counted as the input.

In addition to capital consumption, a real interest charge for the use of capital should also be computed. This can be estimated as the real net stock of capital goods at the disposal of the agency weighted by an imputed base-period interest charge. But it may not be feasible on this round for the agencies to include this aspect of capital input.

All of the inputs can be combined in terms of constant (1962) dollars. Output then can be related to total input, as well as to each class of inputs separately, to show the economies achieved through time in real costs per unit of output.

USES OF THE PRODUCTIVITY RATIOS

Once productivity estimates for an agency have been made, what can they be used for? I should like to discuss two major sets of uses of productivity measures. The first is for cost analysis, budgeting, and projection.

Cost Analysis, Budgeting, and Projection. The availability of aggregate output estimates makes possible the estimation of past changes in unit costs—which, as suggested earlier, promote more rational program decisions. The associated input and productivity estimates make possible the breakdown of unit costs $\left(\dfrac{\text{Cost}}{\text{Output}}\right)$ or $\left(\dfrac{C}{O}\right)$ into the productivity $\left(\dfrac{\text{Output}}{\text{Input}}\right)$ or $\left(\dfrac{O}{I}\right)$ and the price of input elements $\left(\dfrac{\text{Cost}}{\text{Input}}\right)$ or $\left(\dfrac{C}{I}\right)$; or, $\left(\dfrac{C}{O}=\dfrac{C}{I}\times\dfrac{I}{O}\right)$. That is, costs per unit of output rise in proportion to the prices of the inputs (primarily the wage rate) *reduced* by the degree of productivity advance. This analysis can be applied to as many different categories of cost as there are real input estimates.

Take as an example the labor cost per check and bond issued by the Division of Disbursement—over the 5-year period between 1957 and 1962, unit labor cost fell 17 percent. This was the net result of a 31 percent increase in average employee compensation (including benefits) more than offset by a 58 percent increase in output per manhour.

This sort of analysis is of particular relevance as a background for budgeting and longer-term projections.

In projecting costs, one starts with the projected final workloads (or outputs) of the agency. Then, based on past trends, modified by the expected effect of planned technological change, productivity can be projected. The projected index of output divided by the projected index of productivity gives the input requirements for the period ahead. If no changes of input prices (particularly wage or salary rates) are expected, the input requirements can be multiplied by their most recent prices to get at the cost budget or projection. Or, if input price changes are probable, these can easily be fitted into the calculation.

The productivity estimates, by making it possible to break the cost changes into their basic components, make possible a more logical budget or long-term projection than is possible without specific output and input estimates. And it is of assistance not only in budget making, but also in budget review, where summary-type statistics are particularly helpful.

Management Control. Productivity measures *cannot* be used to set standards for one agency, let alone the entire Federal establishment, and Budget Bureau officials have no such scheme in mind. Irresponsible talk of requiring all agencies to achieve the 3 percent a year average annual productivity advance that typifies private industry reveals considerable ignorance as to how productivity advances take place.

In the private sector itself, as documented in the author's National Bureau study, there is a wide range of trend rates of productivity advance—ranging from less than 1 percent a year to well over 5 percent.[1] Over short periods of time, variations in annual changes are considerably greater. In fact, while over long periods no industry has shown declines, between two years productivity drops are not uncommon, particularly if output itself declines. Preliminary results show the same picture among governmental agencies.

Thus a standard productivity requirement would bear unevenly and inequitably among agencies. Even in one agency, a given productivity gain cannot be set as a standard in any rigid way, although it could be set loosely as a *goal* with due consideration for the technological and human possibilities in the given agency. In some agencies, projection, or goal setting, can be more accurate than in others. In the Division of Disbursement, for example, output per manhour has been calculated for each

[1] John W. Kendrick, assisted by M. R. Pech, *Productivity Trends in the United States* (Princeton University Press, 1961).

of the nine technological processes used in check issue. Most of the historical productivity advances have been achieved by shifts from lower-to-higher-productivity technologies—very little by increasing productivity *within* a given technology. So when equipment acquisition plans and associated personnel allocations are made for a coming period in terms of the alternative technologies, the associated productivity change is simple to compute. In agencies with more complex outputs, and less detailed productivity estimates (by technology), the projection would not be so simple and greater reliance would have to be placed on past trends as modified broadly by general factors such as anticipated changes in workloads and rates of utilization of capacity, anticipated changes in equipment, etc.

Of greater value to management than setting targets, in my opinion, is the fact that recent changes in the productivity indexes, when unfavorable, will lead management to ask questions about the operation. In some cases, an unfavorable productivity change can be explained satisfactorily; in others, it may uncover developments that require further study and corrective action. Favorable productivity movements will often stem from innovations that should be given publicity.

The more comprehensive and detailed the productivity measures, the more useful they are in this regard. Thus, when output is related to labor and other inputs, broken down by categories, it can be seen at a glance what specific inputs have been rising relative to output, or decreasing less than average. Frequently, the change in the input mix may represent *planned* substitutions of one input for another in order to achieve least-cost combinations. In other instances, however, the suspiciously behaving partial productivity ratios may, upon investigation, reveal that certain cost items have not been brought into line with new technology or organization, or that they have gotten out of line and need to be cut back.

For example, one year the productivity measure of one of the agencies showed a significant drop. Investigation revealed that, during this period of substantial expansion, hiring of new personnel had proceeded more rapidly than the installation of the facilities with which these new personnel were to work. Also, it had become necessary to hire somewhat less experienced employees. But it was a reasonable expectation and target to expect significant productivity advances in subsequent periods as the facilities caught up with personnel, and the average training and experience of the work force increased.

If cost accounts make possible a compilation of productivity ratios by product, this adds a further analytical dimension. In an agency with field offices, or a regional organization, it is useful to estimate productivity changes in each. This is being done by the Systems Maintenance Service, and the Post Office may do likewise at a later date. Inter-office, inter-plant, or inter-regional comparisons are tricky, and due allowance must be made for differences in scale, and in the composition of workloads, or other relevant factors. But here, too, the persistence of relatively unfavorable productivity experience in certain offices certainly calls for further scrutiny.

In concluding this point, let me emphasize that the productivity indexes themselves do not indicate whether or in what respect management action is called for. They merely provide signals that further questioning and investigation are called for, which may uncover situations requiring further study and positive actions.

A final aspect of the productivity measures as a management tool, which should be mentioned briefly, is their psychological impact. Measurement of productivity and dissemination of the results in an agency helps to promote "productivity-mindedness," and the search for new and more efficient ways and means of doing things becomes more of an ingrained attitude. This effect is enhanced when intra-agency comparisons are made, and a competitive element is introduced.

If, and when, the Bureau of the Budget sponsors additional rounds of agency productivity studies, it might be useful, if results for the several agencies are compiled and circulated within the government. This is said in full awareness that inter-agency comparisons have no normative implication. The measures should be accompanied by historical data, supplementary measures of qualitative factors, and descriptions of the technological and organizational changes that have accompanied the measured changes. So presented, such compilations, possibly on an annual basis, would help further promote "productivity-mindedness" and would help disseminate information on specific management advances that could prove helpful to other agency administrators in the unending search for new and better ways of accomplishing more for the taxpayer's money.

SUGGESTIONS FOR FUTURE WORK

Based on the preliminary estimates and reports of the several agencies cooperating with the Bureau of the Budget in its pilot study, it is clear that productivity measurement is both feasible and useful in those Federal agencies whose work is of a generally recurring nature. Of course, a definitive evaluation will have to await preparation of the final report, scheduled for June.

But, if the final general appraisal coincides with this current view, hopefully productivity measurement systems will spread widely throughout government. Based on a quick survey, it appears that civilian agencies employing more than two-thirds of all government workers are susceptible to productivity measurement. In making the decision in this area, administrators should bear in mind that, given the existing data reporting systems, the cost of measuring productivity is not high, since it chiefly involves processing, rearranging, and weighing existing data within the conceptual framework of the productivity relation. On an average, even to set up new systems, less than two full-time equivalent manyears have been required in the pilot agencies, and about the same expenditure in the Bureau of the Budget. Maintenance of the estimates on a current basis will require less time.

Hopefully in June, following completion of the present pilot studies, the BOB will start a new round. Or, with the help of the handbook that emerges from the present studies, a number of agencies should be in a position to proceed on their own, with technical advice from the BOB staff. The BOB staff plays an important role in promoting general consistency of method, and bringing to bear technical competence, plus the experience gained from the pilot studies, on the problems of an agency newly starting in this field.

In conclusion, the distinctive, creative function of management is innovation, and innovation manifests itself in productivity advance. Only by developing measures of organizational productivity can we know how we are doing in managing real costs in relation to output! The measures are of value regardless of their outcome—whether they afford ground for self-congratulation or for self-examination. In either case, they provide a needed background for planning future progress.

PERSONAL INCOME TAXATION

Henry Simons

There is an important (though subordinate) place for strictly impersonal, *ad rem* levies in a good tax system. On the basis of the presumption against governmental subsidies to particular groups, one may argue decisively for the indefinite continuance of real-property taxes without change in the established effective rates; for continued imposition of ordinary special assessments (what are sometimes called "cost assessments"); for the heavy taxation of gasoline and other fuels used in highway transport; and for other benefit levies where reliable minimum estimates of benefits are possible and where convenient forms of levy are available. All taxes which fail of justification on these grounds may properly be judged mainly in terms (*a*) of their effects upon the degree of economic inequality and (*b*) of their fairness between and among persons of similar economic circumstances.

Such considerations point to the income tax as the proper source of those necessary revenues which cannot be provided by the few good impersonal taxes. The personal income tax should

Reprinted from *Personal Income Taxation* (Chicago: University of Chicago Press, 1938), pp. 205-220, by permission of the University of Chicago Press. Copyright 1938 by the University of Chicago.

be progressive; it should be levied according to simple general rules or principles (complexity in detailed applications is, of course, unavoidable); and, subject to this latter requirement, it should be as equitable as possible among individuals. Thus, it must proceed from a clear and workable conception of personal income; and it must be constructed in such manner as to minimize the possibilities, both of lawful avoidance (defined in terms of the basic conception of income) and of successful evasion through false declarations.

The appropriate general conception of income, for purposes of personal taxation, may be defined as the algebraic sum of the individual's consumption expense and accumulation during the accounting period. Taxable income, properly, is a kind of measure of the individual's prosperity—or, in the language of Professor Haig, a measure of "the net accretion of one's economic power between two points in time" (if one includes power exercised for consumption purposes). Money affords, of course, a very imperfect unit for purposes of such measurement; but any attempt to allow systematically for monetary instability in the measurement of taxable income seems altogether inexpedient; and the establishment of a monetary system which was reasonably satisfactory in other respects would largely dispose of this special problem in personal taxation. The measurement of consumption also presents grave difficulties of principle, especially in the case of receipts in kind. These difficulties largely disappear in practice, however, when "earned income in kind" is exempted or disregarded; and the omission of such receipts is defensible not only as a concession to administrative necessity but also as a desirable offset to the disregard of leisure as a form of consumption. The measurement and inclusion of income in kind from consumer capital used by the owner presents only minor practical difficulties which can be dealt with adequately.

In principle, all receipts from gifts, inheritances, and bequests should be included in determining the basis of individual contributions under income taxes. This procedure is desirable (*a*) to avoid arbitrary and casuistic distinctions in the underlying definition of income, (*b*) to make the system more nearly fool-proof by introducing a larger measure of automatic cancellation with respect to the inevitable errors in property appraisal, and (*c*) as part of a scheme for rescuing the whole enterprise of inheritance taxation from confusion, unfairness, and futility. Complete inclusion of all gifts, however, is unthinkable, especially in the case of small gifts in kind; tax legislation must stop short of folly, by deliberately disregarding minor gifts in most instances. Just how far and in what cases such items may wisely be disregarded is a difficult practical question; but reasonably satisfactory solutions can surely be worked out through careful experiment and experience.

The proper underlying conception of income cannot be directly and fully applied in the determination of year-to-year assessments. Outright abandonment of the realization criterion would be utter folly; no workable scheme can require that taxpayers reappraise and report all their assets annually; and, while this procedure is implied by the underlying definition of income, it is quite unnecessary to effective application of that definition. Our income taxes, as a matter of declaration, of administration, and of adjudication, rest upon great masses of business records and accounts; and they simply must follow, in the main, the established procedures of accounting practice. Thus, they must follow the realization criterion, but not so blindly and reverently as in the past. The recognition of capital gains and losses may wisely be postponed while the property remains in an owner's possession; but postponement should not be allowed to eventuate in evasion. Thus all accrued gains must be taxed as income to the individual owner whenever the property passes out of his hands, whether by sale or by gift, and as income to his estate when the property is transferred to his heirs or legatees. By such arrangements, the same total of taxable income may be reached for every taxpayer during his lifetime as would have been reached by direct application each year of the procedure implicit in our fundamental definition. The distribution of his taxable income between particular years would be different, to be sure, under the two procedures; but the taxpayer would be free so to manage his affairs that the distribution would not work greatly to his (or his heirs') disadvantage; and, apart from successful gambling on rate changes, he could not manipulate the distribution unfairly to his own advantage.

A strong if not decisive case can be made for not introducing the corresponding (consistent?) provisions as to "unrealized capital losses." If deductible losses could be established by gift, there would be a strong temptation for false reporting, especially in the case of transfers to persons of smaller means or to exempt institutions; and adequate policing of the law at this point would be difficult and expensive. Moreoever, the denial of deductions in such cases would only compel the taxpayer to establish his loss through bona fide sale. If this consideration is less decisive in the case of estates, the fact remains that individuals could easily protect their heirs by systematically avoiding large accumulations of potential loss deductions, i.e., by rather nominal shifting of their investments or merely by parting occasionally with particular securities for short periods (over thirty days— see sec. 118). A strictly limited deduction for unrealized losses, however, might reasonably be allowed in the case of estates— but not in the case of gifts.

Such cases apart, there should be no limitations whatever upon the deduction of bona fide losses, and no limitations or concessions with respect to the inclusion of capital gains. Any special treatment of particular gains and losses by kind is utterly incompatible with the proper purposes and functions of the income tax—just as incompatible in principle as, and more so in practice than, the exemption of interest on state and local debts. And any one-sided restrictions as to losses are too ridiculous and inequitable for serious consideration. That such restrictions are somewhat defensible in our present income tax only testifies to the existence of flagrant shortcomings at other points; they can find no justification as part of a good law.

Other features of the general scheme of levy need be mentioned only in summary statements of specific proposals:

1. All exemptions of receipts by kind (save those of "earned income in kind" and minor gifts) should be eliminated entirely—notably, the exemption of interest on governmental obligations.

2. Income in kind from the more durable forms of consumer capital used by the owner should be included in determining his taxable income, at least in the case of real property used for consumption purposes.

3. All gifts, inheritances, and bequests should be treated as part of the recipient's taxable income for the year in which they are received (with such limited and carefully devised exemptions for minor gifts as are required by administrative necessity).

4. A supplementary personal tax, in the cumulative form of our present tax on donors, should be levied upon the recipients of gifts, inheritances, and bequests, to eliminate any advantage which might otherwise be obtained, under a progressive annual tax, by gradual distribution of property. (Amounts actually paid as additional income tax by virtue of such receipts should be deductible from the taxes as imposed by this supplementary levy.)

5. The law should provide for full inclusion of all gains on assets which have appreciated in the owner's possession, the gains being taxable at time of bona fide sale or, at an amount determined by fair appraisal, on the occasion of any other disposition of the property. In the case of property passing through probate, any appreciation should be taxed as income to the estate in the same manner as it would have been taxed to the decedent if, living, he had given the property to the beneficiary on the date when it actually passes to the beneficiary from the estate. Full deduction should be allowed for all *realized* capital losses; but no deduction should be allowed to donors with respect to estimated losses on property transferred by gift; and only limited deductions, if any at all,

should be permitted to estates with respect to assets not actually sold.

6. Rebates should be made available every five years for the amount by which an individual's income-tax payments for the last five years have exceeded, by more than 10 per cent, the total which he would have paid if his taxable income each year had been exactly one-fifth of his total taxable income for the five-year period. (It is very doubtful whether gifts, inheritances, and bequests should be brought into the calculation, on either side, for purposes of determining such rebates.)

We submit that the scheme of personal taxation which these proposals define has many merits and no serious shortcomings which are apparent. It meets the requirement of following a few simple general rules; and it promises to be more nearly fair among persons than any other scheme which would satisfy that requirement. On the administrative side, moreover, it has merits which are likely to be underestimated. The system of rules is as nearly foolproof as possible; it provides an abundance of internal checks; and it exploits rather fully the peculiar virtues of the income-tax form, namely, the possibilities of the automatic cancelling of errors at different points in time. Taxpayers would be obliged to account for every acquisition and every disposition of property; values at time of transfer would enter into the declarations of both taxpayers; and gain and loss calculations will (almost) always proceed from a basis already reported by the previous owner. Thus, declarations will record a substantially unbroken chain of selling prices or appraisals; and falsification or error at one stage can always be compensated or at least detected at the next stage. Finally, the system would tend to alter as little as possible the course which would have been followed, if there had been no such taxes, in commercial and financial practices and in the management and distribution of private wealth; and it would minimize the diseconomies arising from the continuous and disturbing enactment of stopgap expedients for dealing with the inventions of tax-avoidance specialists.

It should be immediately obvious that no such scheme of personal taxation could effectively be employed by the individual American states. The states lack adequate jurisdiction; and effective enforcement not only is unattainable by the states but, if attained, would involve an extravagant duplication of administrative machinery and administrative activities—not to mention the dangers of cutthroat competition to hold and attract persons of wealth. The broad jurisdictional powers of the federal government are indispensable, as is an intergrated national organization for administration and enforcement. The states are reasonably competent to impose real-property taxes, special assessments, highway taxes, and license charges; but it should be evident, even without the eloquent testimony of experience, that they cannot contribute much to the development of equitable personal taxes.

On the other hand, the kind of levies which represent the proper contributions of the state and local bodies to our total system of taxes are inadequate to their expenditure responsibilities. Many of them could not abandon their existing income taxes and death duties without serious disarrangement of their finances; and most states now rely largely upon undesirable revenue devices. The only promising solution thus lies in a generous sharing of federal revenues from personal taxes with the states.

But would this not involve a thoroughly dangerous measure of federal centralization—a dangerous increase in federal powers at the expense of the states? The question may properly give us pause. The maintenance of a vital sort of state and local government, and the reservation of large freedom and large responsibilities to the smaller jurisdictions, are indispensable for the preservation of representative political institutions. Special students of the various kinds of governmental activities are prone to urge, each in the field of his own special study, a measure of centralization which, if achieved in all the special fields, would reduce state and local government almost to sheer ceremony. Everyone seems to want a degree of centralization, in those activities which are objects of his special interest, far larger than a wise economy of centralizing devices could possibly grant. Do we not offend here on this score, losing sight of larger interests in our zeal for equitable personal taxation and mitigation of inequality?

Any judgment on this point by one who confesses to such special interests may properly be received with a presumption of bias—although the study of fiscal policy is perhaps more conducive to balanced views on such matters than are other specialties. There are grave dangers here; but we submit that the scheme *could* be carried out in such manner as to yield only good results. First of all, the federal government must eschew arrangements which would enable it, through the distributions, to influence state and local policies (except perhaps in matters of income and inheritance taxation). Conditional grants-in-aid are unobjectionable so long as they involve only modest contributions to worthy causes. Such devices are totally undesirable, however, in connection with distributions of the magnitude here in question. The revenues from the personal taxes should be shared unconditionally; and the rules determining the relative shares should be designed to prevent both discretionary, administrative manipulation and frequent or substantial alteration by future Congresses. In other words, the initial legislation should serve to settle definitely the basic question of policy.

From this viewpoint, only one basis of distribution seems to merit consideration: every state should receive the same fraction of the revenues collected from tax-payers subject to its jurisdiction. The tax being a purely personal levy, the jurisdictional basis is residence or domicile; and, while the basic principle raises hard questions in some cases, it appears to afford an adequate general rule. Marginal cases may require complicated procedures and awkward compromises of conflicting claims; but they are unlikely to defy tolerable solution or to bulk large enough in total to threaten the stability of the underlying policy. This policy would appear to be the only alternative to chaos; to have Congress struggling indefinitely over the division of, say, three billion dollars annually among the various state treasuries would be dreadful and intolerable. This is a danger of the scheme; but the very magnitude of the danger would probably assure scrupulous and co-operative efforts to avoid it.

The objective should be that of effecting the same relative distribution of revenues as would obtain (except for jurisdictional and administrative difficulties) if every state imposed the tax with the same base, the same personal exemptions, and the same scale of rates. We might thus achieve arrangements which, besides enforcing a necessary uniformity among the states, would involve substantial centralization only as regards the technical administration and enforcement of the tax. And this kind of centralization seems nowise ominous as regards the independence and responsibility of our state and local bodies. They would be left in full control of their spending activities and under the necessity of providing most of their revenues from their own tax levies.

Let us now turn briefly to questions of the rates of tax. Many authors attempt to state a straighforward case for progression and to argue that the optimum degree of progression would involve heavy rates of tax in the upper brackets. It is not inconsistent, however, to suggest that progression has gone to seed rather ludicrously in our federal taxes. We have been so preoccupied with dramatic levies upon fabulous incomes and estates that we have almost forgotten to tax the large ones at all. When one considers the proportion of governmental expenditures to the national income, our income (and estate) taxes, except for a mere handful of taxpayers at the top, are simply trivial. Congressional committees and treasury experts, when proposing revenue measures, should remind themselves of what our income distribution actually is, instead of reflecting on their own conceptions of a modest living. Exemptions appear to be determined on the assumption that rates will be 100 per cent, and rates, in turn, as though there would be no exemptions. The result is a decorative sort of progression, yielding much discussion, much indignation, and very little revenue—and a total revenue system resting largely on taxes borne by persons far below the level of the income-tax exemptions. Moreover, the whole procedure involves a subtle kind of moral and political dishonesty. One senses here a grand scheme of deception, whereby enormous surtaxes are voted in exchange for promises that they will not be made effective. Thus, politicians may point with pride to the rates, while quietly reminding their wealthy constituents of the loopholes. If we had a more moderate sort of progression—a scale of rates which responsible leaders really approved—it would be less difficult to obtain the urgently necessary changes in the basis of levy. It is high time for Congress to quit this ludicrous business of dipping deeply into great incomes with a sieve.

For the future, the main question is whether our taxes shall fall mainly on people with incomes ranging from $3,000 to $20,000 or largely on people below the $2,000 level. What happens to the rates beyond $20,000 is not of major importance. This is not to say that rates are now excessive in the upper brackets (although they may be higher than the opinion of their time will support effectively); only that they are absurdly low in the case of what conventional discussion strangely refers to as the lower and middle-sized incomes.

One hears much talk about the desirability of lowering the personal exemptions. This change would increase the administrative burden enormously; and little moral gain can derive from trivial levies upon millions of persons. We need to realize that exemptions greatly reduce the effective rates for most persons now subject to the tax and to see that large exemptions and low initial rates simply do not belong in the same law. The normal tax alone should provide the great bulk of our income-tax revenues.

To complete the summary of specific proposals, we may now add three to the six already listed:

7. The rates of tax in the lower brackets should be sharply increased, with an initial rate of about 20 per cent, but

without increase of the effective rates at the top of the scale. (The existing exemption for single persons and the existing credits for dependents should be retained, but the joint exemption for married persons should be reduced to $2,000.)

8. Federal revenues from the normal tax (the initial or basic rate) should be shared equally with the states, on the basis of collections, i.e., on the basis of taxpayer residence or domicile.

9. Save for the gasoline taxes and certain levies desirable for regulatory purposes, all excises, tariff duties, license taxes, and other miscellaneous regressive levies should be eliminated from both federal and state tax systems.

These nine proposals define our proximate conception of the taxation millennium.

PRINCIPLES OF DEBT MANAGEMENT

Earl R. Rolph

The offering of gratuitous advice to finance ministers is an
honorable and ancient role of economists. There has been no
shortage of pronouncements about how a national debt should
be managed.[1] Clear statements of principles are not so plentiful.
It is the purpose of this paper to offer a principle appropriate for
national debt management.

National debt management shall be taken to refer to any official action, by central banks as well as treasuries, designed to
alter the quantity and kinds of a national government's debt obligations outstanding in private domestic hands. Foreign-held
national debts and the debts of subsidiary government units are
excluded from the inquiry. No attempt is made to distinguish
sharply monetary and fiscal policy as usually conceived.

Reprinted from *American Economic Review*, XLVI, I (June, 1957),
302-320, by permission of the author. The author acknowledges the help
of his colleagues at the University of California, Berkeley: Howard S.
Ellis and George F. Break.

[1] See, for example, the symposium "How to Manage the National
Debt," by S. E. Harris, L. H. Seltzer, C. C. Abbott, R. A. Musgrave, and
A. H. Hansen, *Rev. Econ. Stat.*, Feb. 1949, XXVI, 15-32, and any text-
book on public finance or money and banking.

The principle to be elucidated is an efficiency rule; it extends an old idea in economics to another area. An outstanding national debt is looked upon as providing a utility to a government. Different debt combinations may provide the same utility but at different costs to the government. The composition and size of an outstanding national debt is optimal when the marginal utility of each kind of debt instrument is made proportional to its marginal cost.

A national debt is said to have a utility (or, alternatively, a social function) when a government has a preference for some pattern of monetary stability and when an outstanding debt affects expenditures for current output. A national debt of any size as given by past financial practices may be reduced to any figure at all by the simple expedient of substituting created money for debt. A national government has the option of purchasing its outstanding liabilities. An experimental reduction of a national debt by official purchase is objectionable provided that the changes thereby induced in private expenditures are objectionable. The utility of an outstanding debt is its effectiveness in preventing as high a level of private expenditures as would occur if the debt were reduced to zero, when such a high level of private expenditures is contrary to official stabilization objectives.

The marginal utility of an outstanding debt is normally positive, but, like that of whiskey, it can on occasion be negative. Its marginal utility is negative when private expenditures are too low judged in terms of a stabilization goal. Then the debt should be reduced (*i.e.*, money should be substituted for debt) until total private expenditures reach a level consistent with official stabilization policies. The utility of an outstanding debt therefore rises during upswings and falls during downswings of business activity.

The concept of cost of a national debt is troublesome. There are the administrative expenses involved in the issuance and reissuance of particular kinds of debt instruments, the honoring of coupons, and the keeping of records. The main expense is, of course, the interest commitment of the government. An efficiency principle calls for making these costs a minimum for any given utility of a debt combination.

In discussions of economy in government, only rarely is attention directed towards means of curtailing these expenses. Yet the interest expense of many national governments is a substantial item in their budgets, and historically it has often been the largest single item.[2] The lack of concern cannot be attributed to the insignificance of the amount of the costs of an outstanding debt. Nor is it explained simply by the fact that the interest expenditures are classified as transfer payments. The interest expense is usually looked upon as a fixed charge, not subject to control by legislative or administrative decision.

Even though the main cost of an outstanding debt is a type of transfer payment, there are reasons to economize on the amount. A transfer program of a government increases the spending potential of private groups. Devices are needed to offset the inflationary effects of transfers as well as those of government expenditures for current output. Of the offset devices available, taxes are easily the most important. As a practical matter, tax devices are subject to diminishing returns since the greater become the revenue requirements of a government the more it must resort to inferior tax devices.[3] Such considerations as fairness, equity, and economic efficiency in taxation are given less weight as the revenue pressure increases. If, somehow, the substantial transfer payments made by national governments could be eliminated, a revised tax program could be an improved one simply because less stress would need to be placed upon the selection of tax devices primarily for their revenue potential. This consideration alone suggests the importance of avoiding unnecessary costs in connection with a national debt.

[2] J. S. Mill observed that the interest on the British national debt amounted to about one-half of the government revenues in his day. See *Principles of Political Economy* (Ashley, ed.), Book V, Ch. 7, par. 3, p. 879.

[3] A similar point is made by Roy Blough, *The Federal Taxing Process* (New York, 1952), p. 234.

Interest costs are subject to the test of economy just as other transfer payments are and for the same reasons.

The precept that a government should attempt to minimize the cost of its outstanding debt in a manner compatible with the social objective of debt management rests then upon two fundamental value judgments: (a) that some level and some changes in the level of private expenditures are from a social point of view superior to others, and (b) that the expense to government for its outstanding debt should be minimized for any given stabilization goal. These value judgments are reasonable in the sense that their denial would conflict with well-entrenched beliefs about the responsibilities of national governments in the contemporary scene.

I. THE CONCEPT OF A NATIONAL DEBT

Certain views about debt management and governmental fiscal operations have already been violated by the suggestion that an outstanding debt has a utility to a government. Anyone whose ideas have been framed by the current textbook literature, and, I am afraid, the technical literature as well, "knows" that government borrowing is a stimulating and debt retirement a deflationary policy. The impression has been created that rising national debts are necessary if government finance is to exert a stimulating influence in growing societies.[4] Just what is meant by statements that government borrowing is inflationary or that debt retirement is deflationary? Taken literally, such statements are patently untrue. Official sales of government debt, for example, induce higher rates of interest. Would anyone claim that official measures that raise rates of interest are inflationary? Nothing so crude as this can be intended. What is presumably meant is that a government deficit of a given size plus government borrowing of an equal amount together raise the level of

[4] See, for example, S. E. Harris, *The National Debt and the New Economics* (New York, 1947).

national income.[5] The validity of this proposition need not for the moment concern us. What does matter is the idea that the change in a government's debt depends rigidly upon the size of its budget surplus or deficit. Those who look forward to persistent increases in public debts presumably do so, not out of love of large public debts, but because they view this development as a necessary by-product of a stimulating tax-expenditure policy.[6]

Yet there is no economic requirement that a national government allow the budget facts to dictate the change in its outstanding debt. Indeed, any budgeting unit has greater freedom than this because deficits or surpluses may be covered by release or absorption of cash. Persistent surpluses can be tolerated indefinitely; anyone is free to hold more cash. A person or a business, however, experiencing persistent deficits runs up against the combined constraints of his dwindling assets and impaired borrowing power. But a national government is not subject to these constraints in dealing with its own people. A sovereign government can obtain whatever amounts of cash it wishes. A central

[5] There are difficulties with this proposition. One is the implicit theory that the combined effects of government expenditures, transfer formulae and tax formulae can somehow be reduced to the effects of a budget deficit and surplus. In some fiscal theories, this view is repudiated. Another is the assumption that the stimulating effect of a deficit, granted that this method of statement makes sense, is greater than the deflationary effect of the sale of an equal amount of debt. Systematic demonstrations of this position are surprisingly rare. William Fellner, who has pursued the question, poses the issue in terms of the comparative effect of a given marginal increase in government expenditures for goods and services and an equal dollar increase in the sale of government securities. His results vary from an increase in gross national product equal to the increase in government expenditures at one limit to a contraction of unspecified amount at the other. See his *Monetary Policies and Full Employment,* 2nd ed. (University of California Press, 1947), pp. 174-85; also Hugo Hegeland, *The Quantity Theory of Money* (Goteborg, Sweden, 1951), pp. 228-40.

[6] This appears to be A. H. Hansen's position. After observing that future expansion of the economy will require large increases in the quantity of money, he writes: "It is not probable that this could happen without a substantial increase in the public debt." *Monetary Theory and Fiscal Policy* (New York, 1949), p. 195.

bank has become the standard instrument to provide national governments with unlimited funds.

To obtain a concept of a national debt that reflects this choice open to debt officials, we need to restrict the definition of a national debt to those obligations of a government that are held outside official agencies including, especially, a central bank. The *net debt* or the *outstanding debt* of a national government may therefore be defined as those contractual obligations of a national government and its agencies.[7] Agencies include all government corporations as well as the central bank. The change in the size of the outstanding net national debt is an independent variable subject to the control of official groups. We are not bound to suppose that a national government must either sell debt or tax in order to finance itself.

II. EFFECT OF DEBT OPERATIONS UPON PRIVATE EXPENDITURES

Our first main proposition is that an increase in the size of the net debt of a national government, given the debt composition, has the effect of *decreasing,* and a decrease in the net debt has the effect of *increasing,* GNP expenditures. It is elementary that the sale of government securities by a central bank is a deflationary policy. We simply generalize this observation to sales of government debt by any official agency.

The defense of this proposition is identical with the defense of monetary policy. It would be inappropriate to attempt a full-dress defense of that position here.[8] Happily skepticism about

[7] This concept of a national debt is, I suggest, the relevant one for economic analysis. An exchange of assets between a Treasury department and a government corporation or between a Treasury department and the central bank is a bookkeeping arrangement. What matters is the increase or decrease in the government's debt in private hands. We have long become accustomed to view the quantity of currency as consisting of currency outside the hands of official agencies. For the same reason, the stacks of national debt held by the government and its central bank should not be counted as debt that matters.

[8] Of the various systems of the determinants of aggregate expenditures,

the efficacy of monetary policy appears to have dwindled in professional circles.[9]

There are, however, a number of ways to explain the effect of government debt operations on private expenditures. One way relates debt change to the rate of interest and the rate of interest to national income through an investment schedule. This method is denied us because it presupposes that the pattern of rates of interest can be reduced to a unique rate, whereas the analysis to follow requires that the pattern of rates be a variable.[10] A related approach, but one that does not require the

---

the neo-Keynesian position, as employed for example to demonstrate the balanced budget theorem, would presumably imply that debt operations are without effect. Government expenditures and private investment are treated as autonomous, *i.e.*, unexplained, and consumption is treated exclusively as a function of current income after taxes. There is nothing left for interest rates and hence for government debt policy to influence. For a clear exposition of this point of view, see P. A. Samuelson, "The Simple Mathematics of Income Determination," in L. A. Metzler *et al.*; *Income, Employment and Public Policy, Essays in honor of Alvin H. Hansen* (New York, 1948), pp. 133-55.

The original Keynesian position, at least as expounded by Keynes, implies that debt sales are deflationary except when "the" rate of interest has reached its floor, since investment is treated as a (negative) function of rates of interest.

The quantity-of-money approach and the cash-balance doctrine give similar results because official debt sales decrease and debt purchases increase the quantity of privately owned money, and expenditures are treated as functionally related to the money supply.

The asset position, which the present writer finds congenial, makes both private consumption and investment expenditures depend upon the capital values of assets and hence upon their yields, and debt operations are functionally related to capital values. See Rolph, *The Theory of Fiscal Economics* (Berkeley, 1954), Ch. 5.

[9] Skepticism does continue to survive; witness the views of W. L. Smith ("On the Effectiveness of Monetary Policy," *Am. Econ. Rev.*, Sept. 1956, XLVI, 588-606). Like others before him, Smith somewhat spoils the purity of his position by allowing that monetary policy may work too well (*ibid.*, p. 599, bottom).

[10] There are other serious difficulties with this approach. A fundamental one is the justification of a negatively sloped investment schedule. In this connection, see A. P. Lerner, "On the Marginal Product of Capital and the Marginal Efficiency of Investment," *Jour. Pol. Econ.*, Feb. 1953, LXI, 1-14; and J. A. Stockfisch, "The Relationships between Money Cost,

assumption of a single rate of interest, examines the effects of debt operations through their influence upon the money demands for goods and services. This approach is used here.

A change in the outstanding debt, say an increase, means that official agencies succeed in persuading people and organizations to hold public debt instead of holding other things. The necessary and sufficient condition for getting any good, including government debt, out of government hands and into private hands through a market mechanism is a reduction in the price of the good as compared to what it would be if the government offer to sell were not made. It is sufficient for this conclusion that the amount demanded of anything be a negative function of price.

If the other things that debt buyers are persuaded not to hold consist entirely of money, the government obtains cash that by definition would not have been used to finance anything else. In this limiting case, the sale of more debt has a zero direct deflationary effect on private expenditures. But the necessary condition for this limiting case is that government debt and money be treated as perfect substitutes by each debt buyer. Ordinary observation suggests however that government debt and cash are not generally so treated. People do not shift altogether out of holding cash and into holding debt as the result of a slight reduction in the prices of debt. Rather they are found to hold both debt and cash in the face of large variations in the prices of debt. Thus an increase in the outstanding debt is accomplished by inducing people to give up the holding of cash and other assets. This behavior means that the money demand schedules for these other assets are pushed downward by a positive debt operation. Similarly a reduction in the outstanding debt increases money demands for other things, except in the limiting case when people and organizations who hold debt treat it as a perfect substitute for money.

Investment, and the Rate of Return," *Quart. Jour. Econ.*, May 1956, LXX, 295-302.

III. EFFECT OF A CHANGING COMPOSITION OF PUBLIC DEBT

The second main proposition is that different kinds of national debt instruments may have different utilities per dollar to a government. In order to show that this is possible, it is first necessary to demonstrate that public debt instruments are not generally treated as perfect substitutes. If they were so treated, some investors should be found holding all of one form; or if found holding more than one, they should be prepared to make all-or-none choices among debt forms. An investor found holding bonds and bills should in the event of a slight rise in the yield of bonds part with all of his bills. We know that holders of government debt commonly hold various public debt forms and continue to do so in the face of variations of yields. Various debt forms are different, although related, commodities.[11]

Granted that various debt forms are not a homogeneous commodity, the hypothesis may be advanced that the utility of various public debt forms is positively correlated with their maturity. A shift in the composition of an outstanding public debt of given size that reduces its average maturity increases private expenditures, and vice versa for increases in its average maturity. Like any empirical generalization, this proposition does not hold for all circumstances.

The conditions necessary for the hypothesis are twofold: (a) of various public debt forms, the shorter their life expectancy, the more they must possess the characteristics here called "moneyness," and (b) the marginal utility of the moneyness of assets must be positive. By the moneyness of an asset we mean that its

[11] This observation should not be interpreted to imply that markets for government securities are necessarily imperfect or, in deference to E. H. Chamberlin, characterized as imbued with monopolistic elements. The market for U. S. Treasury bills may be perfectly competitive and so may the market for 30-year bonds without implying that bills and bonds are the same commodity.

realizable price is predetermined and known for any future date.[12] Thus an asset other than cash—demand deposits and currency —has a maximum of moneyness when it is exactly like cash except in not being spendable as such. Savings deposits ordinarily fill this requirement precisely. So do many demand forms of government debt such as U.S. savings bonds. Short-term government debt does not fulfill this requirement exactly because some variation can occur in the price of the instrument during its life that cannot always be confidently predicted in advance. Yet the description of such holdings as "liquid" or "protective" assets among financial practitioners is based on the fact that the prices of such instruments can vary only within narrow limits during relevant periods. By contrast, the longest maturity conceivable —a perpetuity—exposes its holder to the possibility of large gains or losses; it is unlike money. It was this observation that led Henry Simons to describe government-issued perpetuities as "pure" debt.[13]

For long-term public debt forms to be more effective in curtailing private expenditures per dollar outstanding than short-term, it is also necessary that the marginal utility of the moneyness of assets be positive. For if it were to be zero, investors would look only to the income in holding or acquiring assets, and the perfect substitution assumption, so often found in theoretical discussions, would come back into its own.[14] Since it may

[12] F. Modigliani objects to a similar concept employed by J. R. Hicks on the following grounds: "Whatever one's definition of liquidity, to say that a government bond, a speculative share, a house, are money in different degrees, can at best generate unnecessary confusion. It is true that money and securities are close substitutes, but this connection is to be found elsewhere than in degrees of moneyness . . ." ("Liquidity Preference and the Theory of Interest and Money," *Econometrica*, Jan. 1944, XII, 45-88, reprinted in *Readings in Monetary Theory*, p. 235.) Yet his claim that securities and money are closer substitutes than are money and real assets presupposes that there is something special about securities that makes them substitutes for cash. I suggest that this something needs a name, and "moneyness" seems as good as any.

[13] See Henry Simons, "On Debt Policy," *Jour. Pol. Econ.*, Dec. 1944, LII, 356-61. Simons viewed short-term instruments as partly money.

[14] If the only relevant dimension of debts is the yield, they become

be assumed that the marginal utility of future income is always positive—this is a necessary condition for the functioning of a money-price system—the condition that the marginal utility of the moneyness of assets be positive implies that the subjective or computed yields of securities vary inversely with their degree of moneyness.[15]

The condition that the marginal utility of the moneyness of debts must be positive applies, but in the negative sense, to debtors as well. If yields were positively correlated with maturity, and if debtors were completely indifferent about the maturities of their obligations, they could always gain by concentrating their debt in the shortest form. Consequently only short-term private securities would be left outstanding or the yields of securities of different maturity would become equal. In the latter event, the marginal utility of the extra moneyness of short-term securities would become zero.

If our twin conditions are satisfied, namely that shorter-term obligations possess stronger money characteristics than long-term public debt and that the marginal utility of the moneyness

---

homogeneous commodities because future dollar income is inherently homogeneous.

[15] Subjective yields may differ from market yields to maturity for many reasons, such as tax considerations or anticipations of changes in the capital value of the asset. However, the point of view here adopted is inconsistent with the type of expectation theory to explain differences among market yields to maturity presented, for example, by F. H. Lutz and J. R. Hicks. That position makes the strong requirement that any one investor should select securities only on the basis of income. If he is found holding one-year maturities yielding 4 per cent and two-year maturities yielding 5 per cent, he is assumed to expect that the yield on one-year maturities will a year hence rise to approximately 6 per cent. This requirement means that all debt forms when classified by maturity must be perfect substitutes. See F. H. Lutz, "The Structure of Interest Rates," *Quart. Jour. Econ.*, Nov. 1940, LV, 36-63, reprinted in *Readings on the Theory of Income Distribution*, pp. 512-20; and J. R. Hicks, *Value and Capital* (Oxford, 1939), pp. 144-52. Hicks, unlike Lutz, tries to have it both ways holding that interest is to be explained by the degree of departure of an asset from being like money—degrees of illiquidity—and that income is the only relevant dimension of debts. This inconsistency is alluded to by Lutz, *op. cit.*, p. 528.

of assets is generally positive, an official debt operation designed to shorten the average maturity of the public debt becomes an inflationary measure.

To establish this result, let us examine a case least favorable for it, namely one in which public debts have no moneyness features not shared by private debts. Suppose that private debts are treated, maturity for maturity, as perfect substitutes of public debts. In addition, suppose that borrowers can sell debts of any maturity they please and can do so under competitive conditions. Consider, then, the position of a representative borrower. To satisfy the condition that the marginal utility of the moneyness of assets is positive for him, he will be in equilibrium with respect to a distribution of maturities of his outstanding obligations only when the market yields of his debts increase with the remoteness of their maturity. In the absence of objective constraints, other than differences in yields, on the maturity distribution of his debts, a representative borrower would prefer longer to shorter obligations at the same yields because of the correspondingly reduced necessity for maintaining a liquid position.[16] A central bank or treasury operation designed to shorten the average maturity of public debt calls for the purchase in the market of long-term bonds and the sale of an equal amount of short-term bills, thus lowering the yields of bonds and raising those of bills. This altered pattern of yields induces our representative borrower, granted no change in his preferences, to shift his debts toward the longer maturities. Since he prefers longer-term to shorter-term obligations at the same yields, he now finds that it costs relatively less to satisfy this preference. Thus his adjustment may appear simply to offset the official maneuver.

However, from his point of view his entire position now entails less of something he dislikes, namely risk—the negative of moneyness; and the marginal disutility of risk increases with in-

[16] The assumed conditions rule out credit rationing such that lenders discriminate against particular borrowers. They do not rule out consideration by lenders of the risk position of a borrower.

creasing risk.[17] People will bet small sums when they will not bet large sums at the same odds. Applied to a borrower's asset position, our theory means that he now will be willing to take more risk than he would have before because his liability position entails less risk. But taking more risk is another way of saying that he will be inclined to hold less cash since cash is the safest possible asset to hold. In other words, he is induced to acquire more real assets.

This conclusion is not upset if creditors refuse to regard private debts as providing the moneyness features associated with public debts. In fact, a large segment of private debt contracts are entailed assets. The creditor is expected to hold them for the life of the contract. In such circumstances, short-term private debts are not good substitutes for short-term public debts; they are closer substitutes for those public obligations held mainly for income purposes, that is, public bonds. An official operation designed to shorten the average life-expectancy of the public debt remains stimulating because the addition of bills to the market induces investors to hold less cash while not affecting their inclination to hold short-term private debts, and at the same time the subtraction of long-term debt induces creditors to offer more attractive terms to private borrowers at all maturities.

The above argument may be unnecessary for those to whom it is intuitively obvious that long-term public debt is less like money than short-term. However, our twin conditions do help in making judgments about the circumstances under which the hypothesis will not hold. In countries, for example, where the local population has limited trust in the obligations of their governments, all public debt obligations may be treated as unlike money. The assumption of investors in Western countries that the obligations of their governments are free of default risk is not shared by the people of some of the less developed coun-

[17] For a good defense of this view, see E. D. Domar and R. A. Musgrave, "Proportional Taxation and Risk-Taking," *Quart. Jour. Econ.*, May 1944, LVIII, 388-422.

tries, and often for good reasons. What is more important, however, is the failure of the condition that the marginal utility of the moneyness of assets is generally positive. In many countries, the experience of persistent inflation appears to have undermined a taste for domestic money and moneylike assets.

For Western countries, at least for the period since 1930, the twin conditions appear to have been generally satisfied. Individuals as well as organizations have exhibited a positive liking for assets because of their moneyness features. The success of governments in pouring out huge quantities of demand forms of government debt as well as short-term debts at yields less than, and often much less than, the yields on long-term debts strongly suggests, but of course does not prove, that the marginal utility of the moneyness of assets has generally been positive. People have indicated a willingness to pay something in foregone income to possess securities for their moneylike features. Whether this set of tastes can be expected to endure is of course a speculation.[18]

IV. OPTIMUM SIZE AND COMPOSITION OF PUBLIC DEBT

Our two basic propositions may now be represented graphically. Let government debt be grouped into two classes, say, 90-day bills and 30-year bonds. In Figure 1, along the vertical axis measure the amount of 90-day bills, and along the horizontal axis, units of 30-year bonds. In both cases, the unit is the maturity value in dollars. Suppose that the amounts of debt inherited from the past are those shown by point Q. Then the 45° line VM is a constant-debt line. The curves G_4, G_3, G_2, and G_1, are (private) GNP isoquants. A GNP isoquant shows the combinations of short-term and long-term debt that leave private expend-

---

[18] Prior to 1914, short-term rates were commonly above long-term rates—a fact that seriously damages a liquidity or moneyness approach to explain differences in yields. The authoritative empirical study of this experience is the work of F. R. Macaulay, *Some Theoretical Problems Suggested by the Movement of Interest Rates, Bond Yields and Stock Prices in the United States since 1856* (New York, 1938).

itures upon current output unchanged, given the public debt inherited from the past and given all remaining government financial policies.[19]

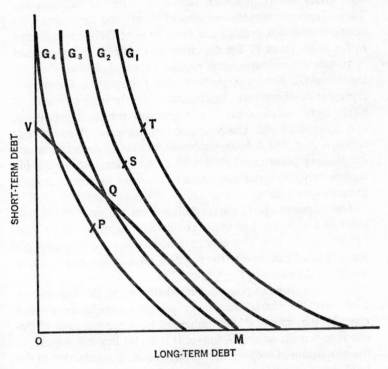

FIGURE I

[19] In the realm of fiscal measures other than debt measures, the conditions mean that government expenditures are treated as given, and its subsidy and tax formulae (not their yields) are also treated as given. In the realm of monetary measures, other than debt measures, the customary or legal reserve requirements of banks are to be treated as invariant, and any access to central bank funds except by open-market operations is excluded. These *ceteris paribus* conditions are necessary to avoid mixing the effects of the debt operations with the effects of other fiscal and monetary policies. Once the effects of each class of policies have been determined, integrated analysis of the combined effects of any combination of official monetary, debt, and fiscal acts becomes possible.

The relations among the isoquants are as follows: Consider the point Q, the quantity of debt inherited from the past. Let official agencies decrease the debt without altering the composition, giving the combination shown as P on the isoquant G_4. Then G_4 shows all combinations of short- and long-term government debt that provide the same level of GNP expenditures as found for point P. The G_4 curve also indicates a higher level of private expenditures upon current output than that given by the curve G_3. Similarly, points S and T on curves G_2 and G_1 represent combinations of outstanding debt resulting in successively more deflation, *i.e.*, lower levels of private expenditures upon current output. The economic justification of this representation is our first fundamental proposition: a decrease in the outstanding government debt with composition unchanged, increases private expenditures and an increase in debt decreases private expenditures.

The slopes of the G curves follow from the proposition that short-term debt has less utility per dollar (maturity value) than has long-term debt. This condition means that the isoquants cut the VM line from above (the negative slope of any one G curve is greater than that of the VM line). Let us suppose, for example, that government policy is intended to make the outstanding debt have the same effect upon private expenditures as that given by the amount of debt inherited from the past; the objective is to remain on the G_3 curve. If it is also desired to increase the proportion of long-term debt there must be a reduction in the total debt; otherwise the objective of leaving private expenditures unchanged would be defeated. To offset the deflationary effect of the increase in the proportion of long-term debt, the government should simultaneously increase the quantity of money.[20]

---

[20] The G curves must be convex to the origin because, as successive substitutions of short-term for long-term debt are made, total debt increases and the money supply decreases. But the successive substitutions of short-term debt, *per unit* of long-term debt withdrawn, must necessarily increase because short-term debt becomes an increasingly poor

The most efficient method of managing the debt is found when the utility of debt, the realization of some level of private expenditures upon current output, is obtained at the minimum expense. The main cost, annual interest expense, depends mainly upon the size of the debt, its composition and the price or yield of the securities.[21]

The interest cost of various debt combinations is shown graphically in Figure 2. Let the axes have the same meaning as in Figure 1, and let *Q* also be the amount of debt inherited from the past. At prevailing interest rates, say 2 per cent on short-term and 4 per cent on long-term, the interest cost to the government of all debt combinations that result in the same interest cost as the *Q* combination is shown by the line *LM*. The selection of a lower rate of interest for short-term securities reflects the condition that moneyness of assets has a positive utility— yields on short-term securities are lower than on long-term. The linear relation shown by *LM* could hold, however, only if variations in the proportion of government debt could be accom-

---

substitute for money as the supply of money decreases. A similar analysis will show that the curves must also be convex for decreases in short-term and increases in long-term debt.

21 Theoretically, since interest on government debt is a form of transfer income, the expense to the government should be measured by the interest paid to private groups minus the tax liability occasioned by the interest. This factor is of importance for our topic only if there is a significant difference between the tax liability per dollar of interest paid on short-term and on long-term government debt. Tax treatment of interest on government debt varies widely among countries; it is still common to exempt such income altogether under income tax laws. Furthermore even in countries that appear to subject interest income from government debt to the same tax treatment as other income, the channeling of this income through financial intermediaries such as insurance companies serves to dissipate the amount that becomes reportable income to individuals, especially when, as in the United States, the accrued interest on life insurance policies is tax exempt. Whether, on balance, these and other considerations result in differences in the effective rate of income taxation of the interest on different classes of federal government securities in the United States is a nice question to which no definite answer can as yet be given.

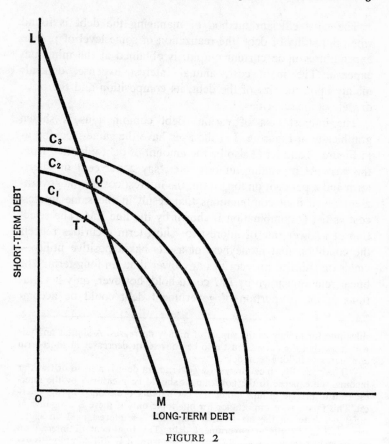

FIGURE 2

plished without any change in rates of interest. But this would be to treat short- and long-term securities as one commodity, and their relative yields as invariant.

A more appropriate way to reflect these facts is by the iso-interest curves C_1, C_2, and C_3. A curve such as C_2 is defined as all combinations of long-term and short-term debt that result in the same interest commitment of the government as the interest cost at point Q. Iso-interest curves may be expected to be concave. For example, at point Q, $1 of bonds carries the same interest expense as $2 of bills. As bills are added and bonds subtracted from the market, the yields on bills will rise and those on bonds will fall. Then, moving from the combination given by Q, increasingly smaller amounts of bills must be substituted for a given amount of bonds if total interest costs are to be held constant. Thus the C curves are concave or linear. They are linear in the limiting case when bills and bonds are generally treated as perfect substitutes. A lower curve such as C_1 is defined as the combination of debt that results in the same expense as the combination shown by T. The interest cost is lower for C_1 than for C_2 because the debt has been reduced and the rates of interest on both short- and long-term securities are lower.

When the C curves of Figure 2 are placed together with the G curves of Figure 1, the optimum solution emerges as shown in Figure 3. With the initial amount of debt at Q, the interest expense is that indicated by the iso-interest curve C_2. If the policy is to obtain the level of private expenditures indicated by G_2, the debt is too large and the proportion of short-term debt is also too great. To obtain the optimum solution, the composition should be changed by increasing the proportion of long-term debt and the entire debt should be reduced. This result is given by the tangency solution shown as point S. There is a saving in interest expense indicated by the difference between the interest cost for C_2 combinations and that for C_1 combinations. This saving will be mainly at the expense of those organizations and persons in the economy who like to hold large amounts of short-term government securities.

Our solution remains subject to two restrictions: The assumptions that a national debt consists of two classes of securities only and that current rates of interest accurately measure the cost to the government of an outstanding debt. Only the former will be considered in detail.[22]

---

[22] The use of current yields to measure the interest cost of an outstanding debt ignores the possible capital gains or losses a government may experience in debt management. Since even an abbreviated analysis of this

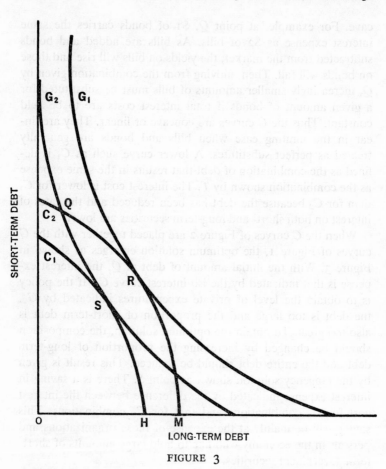

FIGURE 3

Instead of two classes of securities, let the kinds of government debt outstanding vary from some minimum maturity, say one day, to some maximum, say a perpetuity. The market-yield curve Y_m in Figure 4 shows the yield-maturity relation observed at any date. Y_m is positively sloped to reflect the fact that actual

aspect of the topic is rather involved and has not resulted in any important revision of the basic point of view, the question will be passed over.

market-yield curves have exhibited this characteristic for many years.[23] From this market-yield curve, we may construct what may be called an economic-yield curve, shown as Y_e. An economic-yield curve is derived from two functional relations, the market-yield curve as shown and a variable multiplier. The variable multiplier refers to the number of units of government debt measured in par values required to make a given change in private expenditures upon current output. Suppose, for example, that the sale of $1.00 of debt of 25-year maturity or greater would reduce private expenditures by $1.00. Then if the sale of some shorter maturity, say 20 years, reduces private expenditures by less than $1.00, more than $1.00 of 20-year maturity debt is required to have the same GNP effect as $1.00 of 25-year maturity debt. As the maturity approaches zero, government debt approaches being money and the multiplier approaches a maximum. If empirical information on the variable multiplier can be secured, any point on the Y_e curve may be derived. Select, say, point S on curve Y_e. The distance RM is the market yield of a unit of debt of that maturity, say, 3 per cent. Let one and one-half units of debt of this maturity have the same GNP effect as $1.00 of debt of 25-year maturity. Therefore the distance SM is obtained by multiplying the distance RM by one and one-half. The effectiveness of debt—the size of the multiplier—is a decreasing function of the maturity of the debt up to some point.

Economical debt management calls ideally for making the Y_e curve a straight horizontal line. The interest on a national debt is a minimum when the interest cost of each type of debt instrument per dollar of "product" (*i.e.,* change in private expenditures) is equal. Then if at any given time the composition of a government debt is such that its economic-yield curve is negativly sloped, the short-term end of the economic-yield curve should be lowered and the long-term end raised. This result is

[23] Yield-maturity curves for U.S. federal securities have exhibited positive slopes since about 1933. In earlier years, flat curves and even negatively sloped curves are sometimes found.

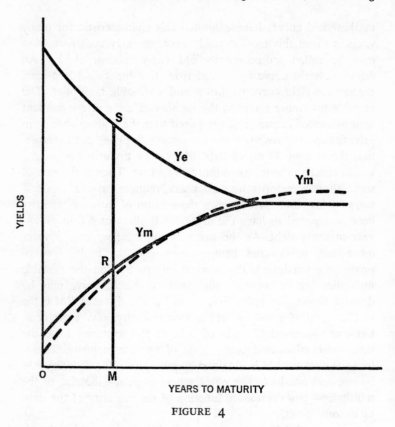

YEARS TO MATURITY

FIGURE 4

accomplished by retiring short-term maturities and selling long-term, and, if an unchanged level of GNP expenditures is desired, by reducing the total debt. In the process of doing this, the market-yield curve will twist, with the lower end shifting down and upper end shifting up, somewhat as shown by the dotted line Y'_m. As this shift occurs, the economic-yield curve tends to flatten out and if the job is done perfectly, it becomes a straight line.[24]

[24] If debts of all maturities have the same effect upon private expenditures, the multiplier is invariant, and the economic-yield curve coincides

V. DEBT POLICY AND COMMERCIAL BANKS

An outstanding public debt will have a utility to a government regardless of the kind of commercial banking system, provided that banks operate under financial constraints. As already observed (see Section II), sale of debt by official agencies is a deflationary operation except in the limiting case when buyers treat government debt as a perfect substitute for cash. A strong government can, for example, decree that government debt of certain types shall constitute legal reserves for banks and make its debt a kind of money for banks. Alternatively, a central bank may announce that the prices of each kind of government debt will be fixed and, provided the announcement is accepted in good faith, make the debt a kind of income-yielding money. The crucial aspect of these and many other schemes is the inducement made to banks to treat government debt as a perfect substitute for cash. To the extent that such schemes are successful, and in recent wartime financing they were successful, the government persuades banks to create money for government account without imposing any restrictions upon their power to create money for private account.

But if banks are subject to effective reserve requirements, whether set by law, custom, or prudent practice, the acquisition of any earning asset including government debt is subject to constraints. If any one bank is induced to hold more government debt, it must forego the acquisition of other assets. The position of a bank in this connection does not differ in principle from that of an individual or an insurance company. All have limited means; all must make competing choices with respect to asset

---

with the market-yield curve. In this event, a government should behave just as if it were a private operator in the market and look only to keeping its interest expense a minimum. The debt should be concentrated in the shortest maturity that is practicable in view of administrative costs, unless the market-yield curve becomes flat before all of the debt can be shifted.

holdings. Thus a government's sale of debt which happens to be purchased by banks reduces the demands of the latter for other assets.

A banking system of money does influence the utility of an outstanding debt and also affects the comparative utility of different debt forms. The peculiarities of a banking system of money arise from the fact that liabilities of a particular kind of private organization are money and that these organizations can change the quantity of this money by their own operations. It is the latter fact that has special relevance for the present topic. If reserve requirements were 100 per cent, a banking system of money would differ only in inconsequential details from a pure government currency system. Banks would have lost their power to create and destroy money—a main reason advocates of a 100 per cent reserve system urge its adoption. We may analyze the role of fractional reserve systems with respect to debt management by comparing such systems with a 100 per cent reserve system.[25]

The lower the reserve requirements of banks, however established, the greater, *ceteris paribus*, is the utility of an outstanding debt to a government. An experimental reduction of an outstanding debt by the substitution of central-bank-created money for debt permits banks as a group to multiply their holdings of earning assets. The multiplier is of course the reciprocal of the reserve ratio. Thus the lower reserve requirements are, the greater will be the inflationary effect of debt reduction and hence the greater is the utility of an outstanding debt to a government. This observation is simply another facet of the well-established theory that fractional reserves provide a more sensitive financial structure than do 100 per cent reserve systems.[26]

Fractional reserve systems also tend to reduce the utility of

[25] There is no intent here to argue in favor of or against the 100 per cent reserve plan.

[26] See J. G. Gurley and E. S. Shaw, "Financial Aspects of Economic Development," *Am. Econ. Rev.*, Sept. 1955, XLV, p. 536.

short-term relative to long-term government debt. With fractional reserves, banks need to hold some of their assets in forms that they regard as similar to cash to provide for contingencies such as large adverse clearing drains. By contrast, with 100 per cent reserves, or more generally, higher as opposed to lower reserve ratios, the needs of banks for cash-like assets are satisfied more by the reserves themselves. The marginal utility of the moneyness of assets may be expected to diminish. In addition, larger as opposed to smaller reserve ratios result in a smaller income from banking, and the marginal utility of income may be expected to be greater on this account. This factor would operate in the direction of inducing banks to sacrifice liquidity to obtain more income and hence hold more of their assets in long-term government bonds. An experimental shift in the composition of an outstanding public debt in the direction of lowering its average maturity may, therefore, be expected to be more expansionary under a lower as compared with a higher set of reserve ratios.[27] The institution of a fractional reserve system of banking does not upset the principle that debt management is conducted most efficiently when the marginal utility of each public debt form is made proportional to its marginal cost.

VI. CONCLUDING REMARKS

There remains untouched the crucial question of how to implement the suggested principle. Such a task would be far from simple; in fact no government could expect to achieve the precise size and composition of debt forms called for by the rule. Yet it is not an objection to a principle that it may be difficult to implement. Its role is to give direction to policy, to permit students and others to agree upon what constitutes relevant information, and to indicate types of financial administration most appropriate for the realization of rational decisions. As such, the

[27] This suggests that the spread in yields of public securities classified by maturity is a function of reserve ratios.

principle is offered as a guide for debt management (including open-market operations) in the same spirit that the principle of marginal cost pricing has been offered as a guide for the regulation of public utility prices, and indeed for analogous reasons.

GOVERNMENT'S ROLE IN A FREE ECONOMY

Gerhard Colm

It is almost a cliché to call the Employment Act of 1946 a milestone in the development of the government's responsibilities in the economic sphere.

The Act, and similar statutes adopted in other democratic countries, was an expression of the people's determination that appropriate government policies would be used to avert depressions and unemployment. It was, in a way, an expression of confidence that a satisfactory economic performance could be accomplished within the framework of a free society; not through a policy of laissez faire, but through deliberate economic and fiscal measures.

The U.S. government—as well as every other government of modern times—was, of necessity, concerned with such matters as agriculture, industry, transportation, foreign trade, finance and labor relations long before there was an Employment Act. But the Act marked a new era in that it proclaimed government concern with the performance of *the economy as a whole*.

Reprinted from *Challenge, The Magazine of Economic Affairs* (November, 1962), pp. 11-14, by permission of the publisher. Published by the Institute of Economic Affairs, New York University.

Since the American government is so organized that regional and local interests find effective expression both in the legislative and executive branches, the Employment Act established machinery in the two branches—the Joint Economic Committee and the Council of Economic Advisers—to articulate the government's concern with the performance of the economy as a whole. The duty of the Executive to submit an annual Economic Report to Congress and the duty of the Joint Economic Committee to evaluate these reports provided the link between the two.

Both the Council of Economic Advisers and the Joint Economic Committee are advisory agencies. The Committee has no responsibility for drafting any specific legislation, and the Council has no operating functions. While the Act did not prescribe any specific policies to accomplish its stated goal of promoting "maximum employment, production and purchasing power," it is clear from the legislative deliberations that preceded its passage that fiscal and monetary policies were regarded as the main instruments for achieving the Act's purpose.

Since 1947 was the economy's first year of operation under the Employment Act, we can now look back on 15 years' experience with it under the aegis of both political parties. Has this performance fulfilled the expectations of the Act's framers? What lessons can we learn from our experience thus far?

The passage of the Employment Act of 1946 was largely motivated by the nation's concern that post-World War II demobilization might cause the economy to revert to the depressed condition which prevailed during the 1930s. While no such depression has taken place during the last 15 years, nobody would claim that the avoidance of a serious depression can be attributed solely to government policy under the Employment Act. As a matter of fact, the United States was faced with economic problems in the postwar years that were quite different from those expected by the Act's framers.

The first problem economic policy makers had to face was

inflation, which abated in 1949 but was resumed with the beginning of the Korean war. This period came to an end in 1952. Government policies certainly mitigated the inflation through a variety of measures recommended by the President in his Annual Economic Reports. In the switch from a proposed tax reduction in 1950 to tax increases in response to the Korean war, the Joint Economic Committee played a decisive role. In general, it is probably fair to say that the machinery of the Employment Act proved helpful in the fight against inflation without claiming anything like a perfect record.

The problem of inflation, however, did not end with the Korean war. It continued in the form of a "creeping" price rise. The Economic Reports of the President and those of the Joint Economic Committee between 1952-62 greatly contributed to a better understanding of the difference between a price rise stemming from excess demand on the one hand and one resulting from the exercise of "market power" by business and unions on the other. However, only in exceptional cases did government action go beyond admonishments to business and labor to exercise self-restraint in price and wage policy. The principal exception was President Kennedy's action last spring to prevent a steel price increase.

The Council of Economic Advisers, for its part, has developed general guidelines for a noninflationary wage policy, but there is no machinery to implement them. Proposals have been made that fact-finding committees should look into the price, productivity and labor cost situation of key industries. Yet even such apparently moderate proposals have been suspected as being steps in the direction of price and wage control. Both business and labor believe they can pursue their own interests better by "free" collective bargaining and "free" price policy than by injection of the "public interest" represented by government as a third party in price and wage determination.

Yet the increasing talk about the public interest in such matters has undoubtedly had some restraining effect on business and union attitudes. Nevertheless, there remains the task of finding an acceptable structure within which prices and wages can be determined without jeopardizing the public interest.

A second characteristic of the postwar period were the frequent—but short-lived—recessions. As far as recessions are concerned, the machinery created under the Employment Act must serve first as a "storm warning system" and secondly as an instrument to formulate countermeasures.

Encouraged by the Council and the Joint Committee, tools for business cycle diagnosis have been greatly improved—first by the monthly publication of *Economic Indicators* and, most recently, by the monthly publication of *Business Cycle Development*. The latter publication organizes statistical data in an attempt to construct a kind of economic barometer.

Spectacular advances have also been made in sample surveys of businessmen's plans to invest as well as the buying intentions of consumers. In addition, electronic computers have been used for quickly processing available statistical information.

Still the record of the Council as a storm warning agency is far from perfect. Failures in diagnosis can be partly explained by the problem of politics. President Truman fought his 1948 campaign on an anti-inflation platform. It took some time until the Council found the indications of an approaching recession in 1949 clear enough to change the advice it was giving the President. Another example is the denial by the Chairman of the Council during the Presidential campaign of 1960 that a recession was in the making when many economists thought that available economic indicators did not permit any other interpretation.

Not all failures in diagnosis, however, can be blamed on politics. In the summer of 1962 some observers of the leading indicators believed that a recession was imminent while others believed that a period of slow expansion might be followed by a new rise in economic activity in 1963. Thus, despite all the technical advancements in the diagnosis of the business cycle, economic forecasts remain statements about *probabilities*. Actions on the basis of forecasts therefore inevitably run the risk that the forecast was in error. Evaluating the possible harm by not acting in time on the one hand, or by acting prematurely on the basis of an uncertain forecast on the other, always requires a mixture of economic and political judgment.

There is no question that the current political debate about the need for antirecession policies is based on a quality of economic intelligence which is far superior to anything available 15 years ago. But this is still no guarantee that the right decisions will be made.

Not only have we improved our ability to *predict* recessions; we are much better at combating them, too. The use of variable financial terms for residential construction and home improvements has been particularly successful. Statistical analyses suggest that deliberate government policies have made at least some contribution to mitigating recessions and promoting recoveries.

During the entire postwar period the desirability of using temporary but substantial tax cuts as an antirecession device was continually discussed. In order to use this device without the delay involved in legislative deliberations, it was proposed that the President be authorized to cut taxes up to a specific amount if the economic indicators demonstrate a need to bolster sagging purchasing power.

While there is no inclination in Congress even to consider such a delegation of authority to the President, the idea that tax reduction and the deliberate creation of deficits should be used as an appropriate antirecession tool is gaining acceptance. In recent discussions before Congressional committees this principle was hardly contested. The questions under debate were rather:

1. Is it certain that a recession is imminent, or is it possible to wait until a tax cut can be worked out in conjunction with tax reform?

2. Should tax reduction be associated with an increase in expenditures or with a reduction in expenditures? Those who believe that government expenditures are too high argued for ex-

penditure reduction without considering that such action would counteract the economic effect of tax reduction.

3. Should the deficit be financed entirely by corporate and individual saving, or should the banking system play its part through action by the Federal Reserve System?

While at the time of this writing no immediate tax reduction has been recommended by the President or adopted by Congress, the debate again shows the advances in thinking about antirecession policies which have been made during the last 15 years. However, it is happening at a time when it is increasingly clear that the frequent recessions are but an expression of a more deeply rooted problem—inadequate economic growth. When President Kennedy appointed Walter Heller as Chairman of the Council of Economic Advisers, he emphasized that growth was his major economic concern. This concern was reflected in some parts of the Economic Report of January, 1962. But, in the final analysis, the available information on the factors which make for growth and the existing obstacles in their path have not been used as a springboard for proposing a comprehensive program of action.

The recent statement by the President that he does not intend to recommend an immediate tax cut probably reflects his opinion that such legislation would be supported by Congress and the public only if adopted in the case of a clearly visible recession. The American public, however, has not yet accepted the idea of a tax cut as one element in a comprehensive program designed to stimulate economic growth and combat chronic unemployment.

In any case, a policy of domestic economic expansion is complicated by our balance of payments deficit. Many people feel that the fiscal and monetary measures needed to insure full employment and a high rate of growth would at the same time aggravate the balance of payments problem. My personal view is that a policy of domestic economic expansion would not in the long run hurt our payments position.

Here, then, is a major unresolved problem which is one of the reasons why the Administration's economic policies sometimes seem hesitant and wavering. Under the Employment Act, it is the job of the Council of Economic Advisers and of the Joint Economic Committee to help resolve such policy dilemmas. In this regard the machinery created under the Act has not fulfilled its purpose.

Proposals have repeatedly been made to add to the Employment Act the objectives of price stability, economic growth and a balanced payments position. Actually, however, the Act has always been interpreted to include these objectives which are completely compatible with its language and spirit. Therefore, I cannot see any particular reason to specifically add them. The main difficulty is that the government has not been able to work out a policy which would place these various goals in proper perspective. Such a policy would integrate programs to promote price stability, full employment and an international payments balance with an all-embracing approach to balanced economic growth.

The Council of Economic Advisers has given advice in this direction, and I am sure that the President has recognized its soundness. There is, however, no unanimity within the Administration on the relative importance of the various goals and of the monetary and fiscal policies needed to accomplish them. The Council can only advise the President on its own views and inform him of the conflicting views which exist. The Council cannot be expected to coordinate its own ideas with those of the Treasury, the Federal Reserve System and private interest groups unless the President adopts a particular policy.

It appears to be the President's judgment that the time is not ripe for obtaining needed political support for such a comprehensive policy of balanced economic growth in his own official family (including the Chairman of the Federal Reserve Board), in Congress and in the various interest groups in the private sector. On the other hand, the political forces which might support such a policy cannot be mobilized unless the President provides determined leadership.

Consequently, hesitation in formulating and adopting a comprehensive program for economic growth cannot be regarded as a failure in the machinery established by the Employment Act. Nevertheless, improvements in institutional and statistical devices could be used to highlight the need for such a program.

Under the Employment Act the President in his Economic Report must present estimates of the levels of employment, production and purchasing power necessary to achieve the Act's goals. President Eisenhower and his Council have been criticized inside and outside Congress for their failure to live up to this provision. The Report of January, 1962—President Kennedy's first—was a big step forward, but further progress is still needed.

I believe that national economic projections, both long-term and intermediate, would help to demonstrate the potential levels that could be attained in key sectors of the economy if we attain full employment and utilize all the available technological possibilities. These projections would also indicate the investment required for technological advances and additional productive capacity. Such national economic budgets require coordinated projections of economic data and projections of federal, state and local transactions. These budgets would provide useful tools for the economic evaluation of various long-term government programs. They could also serve as guides for tax and debt management policy. They would help businessmen to determine potential markets for their products and the feasibility of expanding capacity. Projections of this kind are now provided by private research organizations. But their usefulness for long-term business planning would be greatly enhanced if the business community could rely on the government to contribute to a program of balanced economic growth through appropriate fiscal and monetary policies.

Congress recently appropriated funds for a study of the problem of economic growth under the direction of the Council of Economic Advisers. Thus the proposed development of a medium and long-range national economic budget requires no radical innovation but only a further development of programs which have already been initiated. There is no doubt, however, that a great educational effort is needed before national economic budgets are accepted as the tool for the formulation of long-range economic policies.

On the legislative side, a substantial improvement is needed if the Joint Economic Committee is to live up to the role which was envisaged for it under the Employment Act. It was created (a) to appraise the Economic Reports of the President, (b) to conduct economic studies of its own, and (c) to advise the Congress on legislation needed to accomplish the purposes of the Employment Act.

The Committee has regularly issued appraisals of the President's Economic Reports and has conducted very valuable studies of relevant topics. It has held hearings which gave academic and research economists, and representatives of business and labor, an opportunity to discuss current economic issues. Some of the reports have become valuable material for teaching and have helped to bridge the gap between an academic and a more practical approach to economic policy. In all these respects the Joint Committee has made valuable contributions which have probably exceeded the expectations of the framers of the 1946 Act. The Joint Committee has, however, been much less successful in giving legislative advice to its Congressional colleagues.

At present, the Joint Committee has an impact on legislation mainly through the fact that its members are also members of other committees which consider legislation related to the economy. Actually, the Joint Committee has been most successful as a kind of postgraduate training ground for legislators. Some of the outstanding speeches on economic matters in the Senate and House have been made by members of the Committee, and there is no doubt that its existence has raised the level of economic sophistication in Congress.

I believe, however, that a more regular channel should be provided to bring the Joint Committee's advice to the attention of the Congress as a whole. The fact that reports by the Joint Committee are made available to other members of Congress hardly assures that much attention is paid to them. It would be desirable if other committees which are considering legislation affecting the economy would hear representatives of the Joint Economic Committee to obtain their views (if necessary, majority and minority views) before legislation is framed. If a committee's proposal is not in accord with the views expressed by the Joint Economic Committee, this conflict should be officially reported to the Congress. As far as I know, the Joint Committee has presented its views only in exceptional cases, such as the Korean war tax program, or in relatively minor problems, such as those involving appropriations for certain statistical programs.

It is significant that the House Committee on Ways and Means held its own hearings before those of the Joint Economic Committee on the economic outlook in July/August, 1962 when the question of an immediate tax reduction was being considered. It is obvious that the Joint Committee has not yet been successful in obtaining recognition from the other committees as the source of advice on legislation affecting the economy.

The interest of busy legislators can only be assured if they know that the Committee's work has a tangible impact on legislation. Consequently, if the Joint Committee were required to present its views on all legislation and appropriations affecting the economy, it would be more nearly playing the role assigned to it under the Employment Act.

Our 15 years' experience with the Employment Act has definitely proven the importance of this basic legislation, particularly as a means for dramatizing national concern with the economy as a whole. The machinery created under the Act has assisted the President in policy formulation and has made him less dependent on cabinet members who naturally tend to give advice from the point of view of their respective departments. The Joint Economic Committee has been most effective as an educational enterprise in the broadest definition of the term. It has been less effective in directly giving advice on economic and fiscal legislation.

The United States is engaged in a great venture to prove that an economy with free institutions can be adapted to the needs of the space age. But success in this venture requires deliberate government policies. While the experience of the past 15 years has been encouraging, improvements in the machinery and more boldness in policy formulation and implementation are needed if we are to meet the great economic and social challenge of our time.

SECTION V

💥 *Local Government Finances*

State and local governments in the United States are currently spending more than $70 billion to provide public services. These governments require tax revenues to support projects and programs for education, highways, public welfare, sanitation, police protection, parks and other programs. The primary sources of tax support for state government functions are sales and gross receipts taxes. Local governments rely almost exclusively on the property tax source of revenue.

The property tax in its broadest sense is a wealth tax or a tax on tangible or intangible wealth that has exchange value, which is often difficult to ascertain. Property taxes and death taxes on wealth rest heavily on human value judgments—judgments that are unprotected by built-in effects or market bargaining about the property involved. Although much of the criticism of property taxation is realistic and justified, the tax remains because of the difficulties inherent in finding and initiating alternative taxes. On the positive side, the criticism itself has sparked attempts to improve administration.

The poor administration of the property tax has permitted widespread assessment inequalities to persist among and within taxing districts. Poor administration and assessment has resulted in property tax evasion.

The most difficult problem in improving property tax administration is how to make sure that all taxable property in a given district is uniformly appraised in terms of market value. Although two-thirds of the states require full value assessment, the assessment practices in most of these states do not resemble legal requirements. In the other states, where fractional assessment is permitted, assessment inequity is a persistent problem.

Since the future points to the need for more, not less, active state and local governments, and since reliance on the property tax is not likely to diminish, problems with property taxation will probably continue to dominate local government revenue complications. If this type of tax is to meet the needs of modernity, action must be directed toward existing assessment problems. In the following reading, Dr. Harriss provides insight and perspective into this problem area of property tax administration. His appraisal introduces a singularly comprehensive structure for discussion of assessment problems. Not only would he give tax officials access to the records of property owners, but he also proposes thorough investigation of typical cases, including on the spot physical surveys.

VALUATIONS OF PROPERTY FOR TAXATION

C. Lowell Harriss

Valuation is done by people, human beings with all their strengths and limitations. The quality of valuations will depend to great degree upon the quality of the persons making them, the tools and assistance available, and the conditions under which valuers must work.

These points are so obvious that I hesitate to raise them, especially since they are by no means new. Yet they apply to problems that to a considerable degree remain unsolved, at least in America. More important, they take on *new seriousness as tax rates seem destined to stay at high levels*. An error in valuation is not minor if the tax rate is 30, 50 or 80 per cent! [1]

Moreover, in a world that seems unlikely to "settle down"

Reprinted from *Public Finance*, IX, 1 (1954), 24-40, by permission of the author and the publisher. This article is a development of comments made at the Seventh Congress of the International Fiscal Association, Paris, September, 1953. Some of the study underlying this report was done under a grant from the Columbia University Council for Research in the Social Sciences. Work done for the Finance Study of the Mayor's (New York City) Committee on Management Survey also contributed directly.

[1] The owner suffers if the valuation is too high. Other taxpayers, making up the revenue loss, suffer if valuation is too low.

soon, *relative* values of different properties are certain to change. A set of property value figures which are good at one time may contain serious discrepancies a year later not only in listed securities.[2] The whole process of investment will likely be distorted, perhaps significantly, if some kinds of investment are more accurately valued for heavy taxation than the others.

INTRODUCTION

I have worked in some detail on two types of American taxes requiring property valuations. The property tax, an annual tax levied almost exclusively by localities, is imposed at rates generally from 1.5 to 3 per cent of current market price; even when business is good, the annual tax will often be 50 per cent, sometimes very much more, of the net amount remaining as income to the owner. The tax is based on a value estimate made ordinarily by a local official at intervals from one to 10 years, generally from 2 to 4 years; in fact, the tax in most localities applies primarily to land and buildings.[3] Property owners have varying amounts of opportunity to protest valuations made by the Government appraisers.[4] Death and gift taxes are imposed by the national and state governments at progressive rates ranging to around 80 per cent. The tax applies to values of gratuitous transfers, the values being estimated first by the taxpayer or his

[2] The proposal that values for tax purposes be set "once for all," or even for long periods, seems to me completely unacceptable for any taxes except those at very low rates indeed. In some cases, the possibilities of tax capitalization might induce me to modify my conclusion; I have not yet analyzed this phase of the problem. Obviously, however, if tax rates are high and the tax value fixed, new kinds of risks enter into investment and capital formation. In the United States "once for all" valuation would not be permissible under our constitution.

[3] Furniture, jewelry, inventory of businesses, securities, cash, and other types of non-real-estate property are taxed to varying degree in some localities. In most cases, the tax on such property is administered very poorly, and the law is often almost a dead letter.

[4] The appeal system means that valuations too high will tend to be protested by the taxpayer while those too low will remain unchallenged. A downward bias in values used in computing tax is certain to result.

representatives and then reviewed by government officials and sometimes by the courts.

Both of these taxes present valuation problems different from those of most of the valuation problems of income, sales, turnover, or customs taxes. Valuations for these latter taxes can usually rest upon a price determined in a market by parties with opposing interests. For the great bulk of cases, the tax officials can properly assume that the value resulting from the market's dealings is as good as any and accept it. For the income tax there is often an additional assurance that an error in valuation —one year's depreciation, for example—will be largely offset by an opposite error later. Property and death taxes, however, rest heavily on judgments of value by human beings, judgments that are unprotected by built-in offsets or by market bargaining about the particular properties involved.[5]

In America we have tolerated valuations of very poor quality. Some familiarity with British experience leads me to believe the valuations there are far from uniformly good. Continental tax valuations are also apparently somewhat less than perfect. The consequences are bad—and to a considerable degree unnecessary.

When tax rates are high, discrepancies in valuation can produce indefensible irregularities in tax burdens, and decisions on broader investment and economic matters may be distorted. Moreover, the evil effects of law evasion and the wide latitude for administrative discretion seem certain to grow when the foundation of a tax is haphazard and not firmly grounded on clear, objective fact.

Today there is a new reason to deplore bad tax valuation: The economic integration of Europe may be impeded by the practical inability to rely upon tax valuations of widely varying quality;[6] death and property (capital or wealth), taxes, for ex-

[5] Some of the more troublesome problems of tariff valuation arise when Government officials will not accept the reported market value of the transaction or of the currency involved.

[6] If values in one area are generally low, higher rates can offset to some extent the general effect of undervaluation. When many areas are

ample, could hardly form an important part of a unified tax system if the very bases of the taxes, value estimates, inspired no general confidence.

SOME PROBLEMS OF PROPERTY VALUATION

Brief comment on some of the actual issues of property valuation may help the person who is not in working contact with the problems to understand them better. The illustrations here, selected largely from my own experience, are examples only.

What is the value goal? "Value" is a term somewhat like "beauty" or "humor." We use it successfully for many purposes without precise definition. However, when we attempt careful definition, we may find wide differences of view about what "value" does mean in fact, just as we have different ideas about what is funny, witty, or beautiful.

Partly because of the many meanings and nuances of meanings of the term "value," it is hard to select one concept and then hold to it. As one after another hard problem arises, we humanly attempt solution by slipping into the use of other value concepts. The result, however, is not only inequality but also loss of firm guides and bases for judging results. Yet defining a goal which in fact can be applied consistently seems at times impossible.[7]

What are the physical characteristics of the thing to be valued? Assuming that the items to be valued have been disclosed[8] there remains the job of finding precisely what each is

---

part of the same economic system, however, it becomes extremely difficult in practice to get uniformity in total tax loads. American States have tried "to equalize" property taxes among localities but without great success.

[7] Some formulation of current market price seems generally acceptable as the value norm. Yet it can fail when applied to things that are not being sold—a railway road bed—or that cannot be sold—contingent interests in a personal trust.

[8] Discovery of property is itself a major problem of taxation, but one excluded from discussion here. Value may in fact depend partially upon the extent to which a type of property lends itself to concealment.

physically. The valuer must know more than that there is a "small farm" or "large office building" or "used truck" or "diamond necklace." For real estate, for example, he needs to know dimensions of land and buildings, the number and type of improvements, the quality of the land, the state of repair of buildings (as well as the original details of construction), the degree of physical deterioration of furnaces, elevators, etc. Maps and up-to-date surveys are essential. Pictures of buildings, descriptions from original construction plans, and permits for building changes are also needed to learn what are the physical aspects. Yet more is needed, an on-the-spot examination by a person (or staff) qualified to judge technical conditions, generally an architect or engineer. Obviously, there are limits to the thoroughness of skilled engineering investigation possible and needed, but when tax rates are high, poor physical inspection of properties is bound to lead to significantly bad values. Jewelry, art objects, furniture, business inventory, and other such property must also be examined physically to learn what of the things affecting value exist. (Note that such intangible property as listed securities can as a rule be described in words, fully and simply.) Adequate physical examination can be made, of course, but it requires time and highly developed skill.

What legal or economic factors reduce or enhance the worth of the property? Knowing complete physical features is still not enough for valuing properties, especially real estate. Two properties as physically identical as possible may differ in value because one is subject to easements or has special rights the other does not; mortgages, rent controls, zoning, adverse occupancy, defects in title, and other such factors influence value, sometimes greatly. Not infrequently, their very existence is hard to discover, and more often their significance is difficult to measure.[9] The skills needed to handle valuation problems of this type

[9] By their very nature assessments as such can seldom have a market, but they can at times materially affect the value of a property, up or down. The effects of rent controls today will depend upon estimates of their future life and significance.

well are distinctly different from those needed to determine physical characteristics, and much rarer.

What income does the property yield?   A central factor in valuation, of course, is the actual, and expected, income from the property. Adequate income data will sometimes be readily available (for property other than securities). More often, however, much careful study is needed. For example, in the case of real estate, finding all elements of gross income, including non-money benefits to the owner, may be easy, but for many types of properties, including farms, it is often hard.[10] Still harder, as a rule, is to learn what expenses, made or accrued, are properly chargeable against the year's operations. Study of the accounting records applicable to the property is needed. Moreover, the scrutiny of accounts must be by a person with a knowledge of accountancy and in addition with a knowledge of the practices that may be expected from the type of business and owner involved.

Some of the most perplexing valuation problems arise when properties and the businesses conducted in them are so closely intertwined that separation of the net results into that attributable to the property and that attributable to the management becomes necessary. Yet management certainly makes a big difference, and one is wrong to attach to the property any values which the management as such creates. When one firm owns several properties and pools the results, the amount yielded by any one property may be indeterminable. The mere mention of depreciation and obsolescence will bring to mind familiar problems of computing annual net income.

What are market prices of property?   Tax values will ordinarily be related to market prices, actual or modified in some way. Yet in any period of a year or two, or even more, only a small fraction of real estate, and to lesser extent most other properties (except some securities, inventory, and small items of machinery, etc.) will be sold. The market bears little resemblance to highly organized and active markets which economists think of when they use the term. Yet there may be enough trans-

[10] Has the user paid some of the taxes?

actions to provide a good sample. When supplemented by data on bids and offers, the sales figures must suffice.[11]

For real estate, especially, getting data on selling prices is far from easy, at least in the United States. There is no assurance that the figures reported for public records are accurate. Even when they are, the public records do not necessarily show precisely what was sold. The crops on the land, the fixtures in the store, the air conditioning equipment in the office building, the outstanding leases of the apartment building, and untold other things that effect value need not be reported to comply fully with the law. Hence significant facts of sales will sometimes be known only to the persons involved. Others can learn a great deal by diligent and intelligent effort, but both skill and energy are needed. If valuation is based on capitalization of earnings, there is a tremendous task of learning the rates at which buyers and sellers are capitalizing different kinds of income streams from tenements, office buildings, patents, etc. Moreover, one always faces the possibility that some sales were not representative of general conditions because one party or the other got an exceptionally good bargain.

How should interests in trusts and subject to other fiduciary limits be valued? [12] In the United States, only partly for tax reasons, increasing amounts of property are being put in trust and hedged by various legal restrictions. Investment in life insurance and annuities is growing and commonly with settlement options that "mix" the ownership. Even when there is no question about the value of the trust or life insurance as a whole, there may be grave doubt about *who* owns *how much*.

For death and gift tax purposes, however, it is important to know the value of specific parts of a whole. Actuarial skill can

---

[11] Is there not a substitute in the form of original cost minus depreciation? Hardly! The estimates of depreciation cannot be accurate for determining value unless they are what the market sets.

[12] This aspect of valuation has been seriously neglected in the literature of public finance with which I am acquainted. One consequence of inadequate valuation of such wealth is that some property owners will take deliberate advantage of any biases in valuation to escape tax.

provide some answers—good answers if the right actuarial data and procedures are used. Yet for some situations actuarial data are neither available nor appropriate—the future costs of medical care for a widow or the prospects of her remarriage or the trustee's judgment about the maturity of a beneficiary.

The interest rate appropriate in valuing trust interests, annuities, etc., may also be far from clear; an error of half a percentage point can be far from trivial. No fixed rate can be correct for all cases; careful discrimination, however, is itself a huge job. Somewhat similar are problems of valuing contingencies, such as the right to cancel a twenty-year lease in ten years. How figure the value of such an option today? What if both parties have a right to reopen a contract?

Interests in closely-owned businesses. In the United States, and perhaps elsewhere, the shares of businesses owned by a few persons can present extremely difficult valuation problems. Much has been written on the subject, and although in one sense the problems may seem hopelessly difficult, there are general guides which can help yield better, rather than poorer, answers. Skill and effort are essential.

Owners of a closely-owned business can sometimes count upon liquidating to get at least the value of the underlying assets, a total of values which may at least set a minimum of worth. Comparison with the values of shares of firms whose securities are actively traded is helpful. Yet for many years the shares of some leading corporations have sold for much more than book value. Moreover, rates at which earnings of major corporations have been capitalized in the market on any given day have varied widely. Then, too, size itself makes a difference in value. Thus the record of listed securities may provide no clear guide for valuing closely held firms. Moreover, closeness of control is an important value factor in itself—worth a good deal to those who have it, perhaps, and of negative value to those on the outside without it. (Among the values attaching to closeness of control in the modern world are some resulting from opportunities at tax avoidance or evasion.) The firmness of patent position, the role of particular persons, the vulnerability to competition, and a host of factors may affect the worth of businesses in ways very hard to measure. Good results require intensive study of the business, the control group, the industry, and often the region. Not a small assignment!

These seven examples of problems of valuation have been noted to indicate something of the challenges that must be faced. Others, and there are many, may at times be more important. This brief discussion, however, should suggest that tax valuation can make widely varied, as well as extremely complex, demands on the valuer.

METHODS OF IMPROVING THE QUALITY OF VALUATION

In some respects, at least, the problems are growing more complex, as well as more important money-wise. Yet, while men have made their problems more difficult, they have also improved methods of solving them. Today's needs call for two somewhat related actions. (1) Vigorous, rational effort should be made to use more fully the best techniques so far developed, and (2) continuing efforts should be devoted to developing still better techniques. Whatever the second holds is unknown, but the first certainly offers basis for hope and constructive action.

Familiarity with American conditions convinces me that in my country far more could be done than has yet been tried to extend the use of the best methods already devised. I suspect that in other countries comparable opportunities remain.[13]

Obstacles. Of course, there are obstacles. (1) Not unimportant is *public reluctance to have better methods used*. Some of the reluctance is irrational and might be removed by an educational program, in itself not easy. Deeper, however, is a widespread belief that taxpayers can use bad methods to their own

---

[13] Appraising in the United States has become far more systematic and rational in the last twenty years. The improvement has occurred in some government staffs as well as privately, but only a small fraction of government or private appraisals are made with top quality methods.

advantage. Many can and do, and more probably hope to; yet others suffer.[14] Those who suffer probably do not realize the fact, and if they do come to understand it may feel that their time is better spent fighting for more favorable valuations in their own case than for general reform. Fortunately, a small amount of determined leadership championing a meritorious cause can sometimes accomplish a great deal. One test of fiscal statesmanship may be evidence of leadership in improvement of this form of tax administration.

(2) *Bureaucracies have been alleged to be reluctant to change their ways.* Although the charges may often be exaggerated, there is some underlying basis.

The routine of established ways is useful. Things do get done, even if not always well. Upsetting the going procedure not only involves doubts about the success to be realized but will certainly bring many inconveniences to the civil servants who must make the change. Sticking to the old methods is more comfortable than working out new ones. Moreover, if new ways require new skills, difficult staffing and personnel problems may result, especially where seniority is well established and where job security is firmly entrenched. Thus there may be validity to the inclination of bureaucrats to oppose change. Yet progress requires change, and the public may have to expend a little energy to overcome the opposition of some civil servants.

(3) Some types of reform would require *legislative action,* a matter whose difficulty will vary from one place to another. (4) Moreover, existing *judicial decisions* on valuation will sometimes present almost insurmountable obstacles to quick improvement—in the United States certainly. New actions by legislatures, clear and forceful regulations and administration by the civil service, and careful, persuasive argument before the judges

[14] The groups who benefit from poor valuation have an incentive to foster and finance opposition to improvement. Where different governmental units use the same tax valuations, some will probably have stronger reasons than others to obstruct improvement. In the United States underassessment for property tax purposes became virtually competitive within some states.

can eventually bring change, especially if the basic objective rests on sound logic.

(5) *Lack of resources* will always obstruct improvement in this poverty-haunted world. The more important skills for valuation are scarce in relation to the total demand. Governments must bid against the private economy for available service, and with the general standards of salaries they pay will simply not be able to attract enough skill to meet their own needs for complete, first-class accomplishment. Training, too, is expensive in money and time. The typical government is likely to find that taxpayers will not support the increase in staff numbers apparently required. Moreoever, the equipment needed to put some improvements into effect may seem too costly. Although careful studies might show the clear profitability of additional outlays for equipment as well as for personnel, the persons controlling the purse strings may refuse to acquiesce. At best shortage of resources must be expected as a retarding factor; more likely it will be a serious obstacle. Obviously, therefore, plans must seek deliberately to make the most of what becomes available.

Clarification of standard of value. In some cases the value standard may have been formulated about as clearly as humans can do. However, in other cases, perhaps the majority, avoidable ambiguities and inconsistencies remain, perhaps not recognized as such. In such cases the *will* to recognize defects in the existing order is an essential first step. The next step, getting agreement on what is better, is likely to be much harder.

My own feeling is that the standard should be precise, and precise in a way that minimizes the area of discretion left to the valuers. For example, "market value as of a certain day" is more definite than "normal market value." The former (which is widely used in valuing listed securities) limits the person making the valuation much more than the latter, and provides a clearer standard. Yet for other reasons we may prefer some "normal." After all, the accidents of day-to-day fluctuations may be great enough to produce unwelcome variations in taxes (at high rates). Rather than seeking relief in a vague value standard, such as "normal," explicit averaging seems better. The tax value of one period might be the average of values of three or more years. The practical problems of using average values need thorough examination. To the extent that they can be overcome, the possibilities of getting a clearer valuation standard and better valuation are enhanced.[15]

Even when the top policymakers have agreed upon a standard, it will not become effective unless the men on the job understand it and accept it. Here education and supervision offer the chief hope.

Personnel. Major problems center around personnel.

Today every staff is probably too small in sheer number of people, too small, that is, to do a first-rate valuation job. Every staff is more certainly short of some or many of the skills needed, either regularly or occasionally. And every staff likely uses its most skilled manpower with less than optimum effectiveness. Some possibilities of improvement will be apparent to every supervisor and man on the job. Opportunity and incentive can bring improvement internally. Yet the inside view is not enough, if only because some insiders will not be really able to develop and express their views except to outsiders.

How, then, get outside help? There are probably several ways. Special studies made by management engineers or others chosen for their specific competence have proved helpful in the United States. A second method is for wide exchange of ideas among staffs of different jurisdictions. What recruitment and training practices are followed? What seem to be the results of each? Why? Similarly, supervision, promotion, morale, salary, working conditions, and other relevant elements of personnel policies

---

[15] The Haig-Shoup study of New York City finances proposed the use of a four-year moving average as the basis of property tax valuations. One purpose of the recommendation was to remove some of the room for discretion by assessors in fixing tax values. This discretion was the source of some of the apparent irregularities in valuations. The experts noted that an average would virtually eliminate the apparent justification for allowing assessors some discretion to make implicit adjustments for price fluctuations.

can be examined, not only in other government offices, in the same country and abroad, but also in businesses and wherever people work. A big order of course! Yet so much work has already been done that a wealth of information is available for use.[16]

Two partial approaches to the problem of skill probably need wider application (1) development of skill within any organization by *specialization* and *intensive training* and (2) *concentration of the efforts* of persons with each skill on work requiring it as much as possible. Both are aspects of good management, generally obvious but too generally neglected. Division of labor designed to spur specialization will serve here as elsewhere in making scarce resources produce more effectively by developing skills. The existence of skills is not enough, however; when a skilled person works on routine matters, some of that skill is being wasted. Thus one way to get more skilled effort in not a few organizations is to provide more of the less skilled personnel and equipment. Clerks to do the clerical work so valuers can have more hours to work on valuation!

(3) A third approach lies in *supervision*. The quality of supervision vitally influences the effectiveness with which any given staff works. While we sometimes think that supervision is wasteful overhead, we know that it can also be the keystone for success. It can be especially important in transmitting to a large group the special qualities of skill which only one or a few members can have.[17]

(4) Governments might wisely make greater use of another method of getting skill, *use of outside experts*. Until valuation cases get to court, American governments rarely seek the judg-

[16] In the United States, personnel management is developing rapidly and, I believe, with much success. Governments have been participating.
[17] The supervisor himself need not have the skills. His greatest, in fact, may be in dealing with people. Thus he may know little about valuing interests in personal trusts, but he may be highly effective in getting the members of his staff with such problems to work together effectively and to see that the specialist in farm valuation does not try to value trust interests when they appear in an inheritance.

ments of nonofficial appraisers. There are good reasons. Experts may charge high fees. Not all persons who claim to be experts are in fact more competent, or better situated, than their government counterparts. Selection of outsiders is not easy and may rest on little more than political favoritism. Control of outsiders may be hard to exercise. Perhaps most important, the work of experts is likely to range them against the government on many occasions. Reliance on the outsider in one case will show that you believe him to be qualified; when he is your opponent in the next case, you must expect difficulty in off-setting his influence.

Finally, public confidence in the ethical standards of appraisers has in America not yet reached the point where full confidence can always be placed in their objectivity. Despite the difficulties, however, governments would probably do well to try to find ways of using the skills of outside specialists in valuation. For some types of problems, certainly, there can be no other way to get high expertness, for the Government will have too few cases to develop its own experts. Even when it may not seem wise to rely finally upon an outsider's value figure, his assembly of facts and their interpretation can be useful.

Outside experts may also be used in another important way— *training* the government staff. In formal training programs, or informally, nongovernment specialists may contribute to the improvement of the competence of the civil service. The outsiders that can help will be not only appraisers but also architects, economists, accountants, engineers, attorneys, businessmen, and probably others whose specialized work involves valuation. A possible difficulty is that such outsiders may feel an interest in low tax valuations and thus try to "slant" their teaching. At least a partial corrective can be to distinguish between the kind and nature of facts affecting values and the amount of the effects. More fundamentally, however, is the professional integrity and sense of public responsibility of the persons chosen.

Another way to improve skills is to *stimulate exchange of ideas among officials*. Meetings, congresses, and personal visits bring people together, stimulating enquiry and interchange of views. Even the official who believes strongly that his way of doing things is about as good as possible under the circumstances may see new possibilities. He may be asked questions that force him to think more critically or recognize, perhaps subtly and unconsciously, that different procedures of others may have some merit. Conferences may seem to be costly in terms of time and money, to bring a good deal of waste motion. Yet the communication they permit, and in fact require, offers one way to develop and transmit ideas that make for more highly trained officials.

Better information. Good valuation requires data, an answer to the question "What are the facts?" The discussion has already suggested some of the kinds of information needed for valuation. Valuers may occasionally give the impression that they somehow go into a trance to get answers, that intuition is their mainstay. Nonetheless, they must ultimately base their answers on facts of some sort. The more complete and relevant the facts, the better anyone can do the job. (One of the beauties of valuing listed securities is the ease of getting relatively complete facts). Extensive facts help not only in making valuations but also in defending them when they are challenged. The valuer who can point to little else than his own judgment in defending his figure to a supervisor, owner, or court, is in much less firm position than if he could point to a few, or many, pertinent and supporting facts.

For some valuation problems the official agency will need extensive facts, kept up to date. Real estate valuation, for example, requires thorough land surveys. The original job may be very costly; adequate maintenance will also require some expensive effort, but much maintenance can be done by relatively routine operations. Some of the routine will properly consist of checking with other government records. Although "the government" may have information about property in one set of records, that information will not be useful for tax evaluations unless it is in fact available to the valuer. In America, for example, building permit records will often show any substantial change in the construction of a building, but the small clerical effort needed to get this information on to the records of the tax appraisers is too often lacking.

Facts on market prices are central to any valuation system. Yet dealings in some important markets are not open and recorded.[18] Sometimes the buyers and sellers may want deliberately to conceal facts, to hide them from business competitors, inquisitive neighbors, or tax officials. In other cases there may be no reason to disclose facts even when there is no strong reason to withhold them. Laws on what must be disclosed undoubtedly vary widely. So must practice. I suspect that in many cases the actual amounts paid for rental property where rent controls exist would be extremely difficult to determine. It is a help if the mere fact of sale (or lease) must be recorded openly, such as a public record of transfer of title. If the selling price (or rental rate) must be disclosed, the tax valuer gets a bigger help. In America, the public records of real estate sales are more helpful than before 1932 because a federal tax on the papers of transfer is based on the selling consideration, and stamps thus indicate the price. Assuming that the stamps are correct—an assumption not always accurate—the official who wants to use the figures for tax valuations can get a good idea of the price.[19] He may check it by asking confirmation by buyer and seller. Yet he may face a big task in learning whether the thing transferred is precisely what is to be taxed or whether, as is very common, it includes more or less.

[18] In my study of New York City property tax valuation procedures I was much impressed by the fundamental importance of land surveys and by the ease with which maintenance of essential survey records can be neglected without serious repercussions for perhaps ten or fifteen years. Eventually, however, such neglect will prove extremely serious.

[19] In New York and other large cities private firms collect and publish recorded data on real estate transfers, leases, mortgages, subdivisions, etc. Tax officials by subscribing to these services can get the facts without the laborious job of examining the public records. When real estate markets are as active as they have been since 1945, however, the organization and filing of the data obtained so easily constitute a clerical job easily underestimated.

To find this latter, may call for some intensive inquiry. It is here that outsiders who help arrange the transactions have an advantage over the more remote public official. The experienced official, however, with time to investigate can often find out significantly more about transactions than is reported publicly. One or both parties or their agents may be willing to give information, but to get it the government official must spend some time.[20] To evaluate it, he must spend more time.

In any one year only a small fraction of real estate parcels are sold. The whole set of real estate valuations, then, must rest on a small base of actual market transactions. Obviously, therefore, the importance of determining the base as exactly as possible is great. Data on closely owned businesses require even more detailed scrutiny to learn what the sale of each may reveal about values more broadly. For each kind of property that may present valuation problems—interests in trusts, jewelry, inventory, machinery, objects of art, furniture—there will be need for facts, some certainly of a kind that can be obtained. (The concern here, we may repeat, is not with discovering the existence of property, another difficult job). Each type of property presents its own problems of factgathering, but all will yield at least somewhat to persistent, intelligent effort. For example, scrutiny of newspapers and trade publications can reveal useful information. At what prices are things being offered? Are there sales at those prices? How much insurance is carried? What values are being estimated by banks and insurance companies for lending purposes?

Getting data is not enough, of course. They must be assembled and recorded, analyzed and interpreted. Business methods, as well as the methods of leading government agencies, can chart the way to improvement in this part of the problem. Simple matters of housekeeping, such as light and space, as well

---

[20] Some American property tax assessors have had considerable success in getting buyers or sellers to provide voluntarily additional information about transfers. Often an inquiry by mail will suffice to clear doubtful points.

as the condition of filing equipment play a part. The vast progress in adapting and using mechanical equipment offers opportunity for improvement in the efficiency of government tax offices, as some of them have proved for parts of their operations. The public can still aid its officials materially by providing more and better equipment. The orderly recording of facts is a means to the end of analysis and use, for which time and skill are essential.

Responsibility for getting and keeping facts cannot rest entirely on government. Some facts can come only from the taxpayer, and others, as a practical matter, must come from him. In America, taxpayer complaints about the amount of recordkeeping and reporting now required are vociferous and often well justified. Yet some taxpayers keep very poor records, and for some taxes public officials have inadequate access to whatever records the owner may have. A hard fact of life in the modern world is that many persons not equipped or inclined to keep financial records are required to pay taxes at fairly high rates. Perhaps a bit more original recordkeeping might be required. This is a subject on which we need further study, giving special attention to different kinds of taxes and different conditions.

At least two partial solutions can be suggested. (1) One is to give tax officials *access to the records* that are kept. In the United States, property tax assessors do not generally have legal right to examine the books of a property owner before making the original assessment. Bank, trustee, and insurance company records are given a large degree of immunity from tax scrutiny, especially for the property tax. For the income and estate taxes there is legal power to demand to look at the records, but there is generally lack of time to do so, a part of the personnel problem. To make full use of facts now collected, therefore, officials need more time per case and legal right to study the financial records pertaining to the property.

(2) The second is to make *intensive studies* of apparently typical cases. Although many taxpayers will not have records or may refuse to make them available, a few owners will have ex-

tensive data and be willing to cooperate (or under legal compulsion to do so). A completely thorough examination of such cases, including on-the-spot physical surveys (of inventory, crops, condition of repair, etc.), can provide guides for intelligent dealing with other cases. The details and even the relationship of cost and income items will be expected to vary, but thorough knowledge about a few cases will help greatly in judging others and sometimes to the advantage of property owners.

The number and intensity of detailed reviews must obviously depend upon the uniformity found in the cases studied, the availability of staff and records, the amount of outside assistance, and the need. In a large city, for example, studies of apartment buildings would properly get more time than studies of theaters because of the relative importance. And if private experts are available to help value theaters, the limited resources for intensive case studies should hardly be devoted to theaters.

Procedure for appealing disputed valuations. The inherent uncertainties about value, plus the opportunities for error and the incentives toward bias, assure that many disputes about value will arise if tax valuations are anywhere near market prices and if tax rates are high. An essential of good tax valuation is a good system of review and appeal. But what are the requirements of a "good" system? [21] One is that the system be *accessible* in the sense that both the taxpayer and the government can take cases to appeal promptly, conveniently, and inexpensively and get impartial consideration. There is hardly any need to indicate why each is important. There is, however, considerable opportunity for governments to offer better facilities on each score. They can hold review hearings nearer the time the facts apply, get hearings at times and places and in other ways meeting the needs of taxpayers, and try always to keep costs low.

[21] As used here, the term "review" does not include the examination of cases as a part of supervision but only those cases the taxpayer has challenged. I think it is correct to say that in the United States the absence of disputes over property and death tax valuations in a locality indicates substantial undervaluation.

The latter objective may run into another requirement of a "good" system competence. Good review of valuations, even more than making them originally, requires *skill*. The mere fact that a dispute has developed suggests that something more than ordinary issues are involved, so that more than ordinary ability is desirable for solving them. Moreover—and in the United States, at least, this reason is especially important—decisions in cases that go to review tend to set precedents that guide the masses of routine, noncontested cases. *Effort focused on settling disputed cases well, therefore, indirectly helps raise the quality of results in many more cases.*

The reviewing authorities, of course, should be *impartial*. For this reason, they should be removed from the agency originally making the assessment, although the first stage of review will appropriately be in the same department at least if the review is made under conditions which free the reviewer from any pressure to support the original official and if taxpayers are made to feel confident of this impartiality. While progress has been made toward this goal in some parts of the American tax administration, we have not yet achieved it fully. The reviewer should also be immune to political or other taxpayer pressures, other than the weight of fact, to influence valuations, a requirement not easily met in some parts of my country and perhaps in others.

Generally, officials in the administrative organization who have review functions are more highly trained than those who make the original valuations. One exception will arise when specialized property—utility equipment or hotels or art masterpieces—is involved. As a rule, however, positions with review responsibilities are senior and tend to get experienced personnel.

These officials may be overworked; like all of us they will need training to keep abreast of developments. But they are generally men who have worked up the ladder and thus can claim above average training. In America, a great break comes when cases go to court. Then the decision is made by a person trained in the law, not in valuation. Some judges, of course, may have gotten enough specialized training to qualify as highly competent appraisers. Such men are rare, however. The utmost good-will plus extensive training in the law plus the highest integrity in a judge are not enough for the job of valuation. Special skill is also essential. Of course, the judge can get help from the testimony of experts hired by the disputants. Where the experts are pleading a case, however, where they are engaged to help litigants as such, their answers are likely to be influenced by the interests of their employers. The judge does not then get the very best—fully objective—professional judgment.

In my view, the best approach toward solution would be to establish courts or boards composed of men or women chosen on the basis of competence in valuation (plus the other qualities of a good judge). While legal training would be helpful, the presumption would be that the persons were not lawyers. A host of difficulties would arise. I have discussed them elsewhere and believe that in America they are not great enough to make the proposal hopeless. Whatever the specific form of any change, the substance should be to *place more of the decisionmaking on persons especially trained in valuation who are not representing the disputants.*

✣ Bibliography

SECTION I: BUDGETING

Bird, Richard M., "The 1964 Budget: Closing the Gap," *Quarterly Review of Economics and Business* (Spring, 1963).

Blough, Roy, *The Federal Taxing Process,* Englewood Cliffs: Prentice-Hall, 1952, Chapter 4.

Breckner, Norman V., "The Search for an Appropriations Basis," *National Tax Journal* (September, 1960).

Buchanan, James M., *The Public Finances,* New York: Richard D. Irwin, 1965, Chapter 17.

Burkhead, Jesse, *Government Budgeting,* New York: John Wiley & Sons, 1956, Chapter 6.

Howard, William W., "Aren't We Looking at the Wrong Budget?," *The Reporter* (May 23, 1963).

Law, Warren A., "Federal Credit Programs and the Federal Budget," *National Tax Journal,* XV, 4 (December, 1962), 438-41.

Smith, Harold, *The Management of Your Government,* New York: McGraw-Hill, 1965.

Smithies, Arthur, "Federal Budgeting and Fiscal Policy," in *A Survey of Contemporary Economics,* ed. Howard Ellis, Philadelphia: Blakiston and Co., 1949.

United Nations, Department of Economic Affairs, *Government Accounting and Budget Execution,* New York, 1952.

Wallace, R. A., *Congressional Control of Government Spending,* Detroit: Wayne State University Press, 1960.

Wildavsky, Aaron, *The Politics of the Budgetary Process,* Boston: Little, Brown and Company, 1964.

SECTION II: FISCAL POLICY

Brown, E. Cary, "Fiscal Policy in the Thirties," *American Economic Review* (December, 1956).

Colm, G., *Essays in Public Finance and Fiscal Policy,* New York: Oxford University Press, 1955.

Due, John F., "Federal Tax Reform, A Review," *Quarterly Review of Economics and Business* (November, 1961).

Goode, Richard, "Anti-Inflationary Implication of Alternate Forms of Taxation," *American Economic Review*, XLII, 3 (May, 1952), 147.

Hall, Challis, *Fiscal Policy for Stable Growth*, New York: Holt, Rinehart and Winston, 1960.

Hansen, Alvin H., *Economic Issues of the 1960's*, New York: McGraw-Hill, 1960, Chapter 8, pp. 93-118.

Heller, Walter W., "C.E.D.'s Stabilizing Policy after Ten Years," *American Economic Review* (September, 1957).

Jacoby, Neil H., "Guidelines of Income Tax Reform for the 1960's," *Tax Revision Compendium, Ways and Means Committee*, I (November, 1959).

Jones, Donald P., "Can We Make the Right Decision on Tax Reform?," *Financial Analysts Journal* (January-February, 1963).

Keith, M. Gordon, "How Should Wealth Transfers Be Taxed?," *American Economic Review* (May, 1960).

Lutz, Harley L., "Federal Depression Financing and Its Consequences," *Harvard Business Review*, XVI, 2 (Winter, 1938).

Maxwell, J. W., *Fiscal Policy*, New York: Henry Holt & Co., 1955.

Robinson, Warren C., "Benefits Received Financing in the Federal Fiscal System," *National Tax Journal*, XVII, 3 (September, 1964).

Siegel, Barry N., "Expansion of the Simple Model—the Government Added," *Aggregate Economics—Public Policy*, New York: Richard D. Irwin, 1959.

Smith, Dan Throop, "Capital Formation—the Use of Capital," *American Economic Review* (May, 1963).

Sweezy, Alan, "Comparisons of Government Expenditures with National Income," *American Economic Review* (December, 1952).

Ways, Max, "The Real Case for a Tax Cut," *Fortune Magazine* (January, 1963).

Weckstein, Richard S., "Fiscal Reform and Economic Growth," *National Tax Journal*, XVII, 4 (December, 1964).

Wilcox, Clair, "Relations Between Economic Theory and Economic Policy," *American Economic Association Papers and Proceedings* (May, 1960).

Wiseman, Jack, "Public Policy and the Investment Tax Credit," *National Tax Journal*, XVI, 1 (March, 1963).

SECTION III: GOVERNMENT EXPENDITURES

Bahl, R. W. and R. J. Saunders, "Determinants of Changes in State and Local Government Expenditures," *National Tax Journal*, XVIII, 1 (March, 1965).

Bator, Francis M., *The Question of Government Spending* (Introduction), New York: Harper & Row, 1960.

Bator, Francis M., "Money and the Government," *The Atlantic Magazine* (April, 1962).

Blitz, Rudolph, "The Nation's Educational Outlay," *Economics of Higher Education*, U.S. Dept. of Health, Education and Welfare, 1962.

Eckstein, Otto, "Government Expenditures and Budget Estimates," *National Tax Journal* (September, 1957).

Eckstein, Otto, *Trends in Public Expenditures in the Next Decade*, New York: Committee on Economic Development, 1959.

Fisher, Glenn W., "Interstate Variation in State and Local Government Expenditure," *National Tax Journal*, XVII, 1 (March, 1964).

Groves, Harold M., *Financing Government*, 6th ed., New York: Holt, Rinehart, and Winston, 1964, Chapter 24.

Harriss, C. Lowell, "Government Expenditures: Significant Issues of Definition," *Journal of Finance* (December, 1954).

Hirsch, Werner Z., "Analysis of the Rising Costs of Public Education," *Economic Report of the President*, 1962.

Hitch, Charles J., "The Developing Defence Needs—Their Impact on the Federal Budget," *Tax Review* (November, 1961).

Sacks, Seymour and Robert Harris, "The Determinants of State and Local Government Expenditures and Intergovernmental Flows of Funds," *National Tax Journal*, XVII, 1 (March, 1964).

Weidenbaum, M. L., "The Timing of the Economic Impact of Government Spending," *National Tax Journal* (March, 1959).

SECTION IV: CRITERIA FOR EVALUATING GOVERNMENT FINANCING

Beard, T. R., "Progressive Income Taxation, Income Redistribution and the Consumption Function," *National Tax Journal* (June, 1960).

Bird, Richard, "A Note on Tax Sacrifice Comparisons," *National Tax Journal*, XVII, 3 (September, 1964).

Black, Duncan, "On the Rationale of Group Decision-Making," *Journal of Political Economy* (February, 1948).

Blum, W. J. and H. Kalven, *The Uneasy Case for Progressive Taxation,* Phoenix ed., Chicago: University of Chicago Press, 1963.

Chapman, S. J., "The Utility of Income in Progressive Taxation," *Economic Journal* (March, 1913).

Chase, Sam, Jr., "Tax Credits for Investment Spending," *National Tax Journal,* XV, 1 (March, 1962).

Fagan, Elmer D., "Recent and Contemporary Theories of Progressive Taxation," *Journal of Political Economy* (August, 1938).

Fisher, John E., "Efficiency in Business and Government," *Quarterly Review of Economics and Business,* Urbana: University of Illinois (August, 1962).

Gray, Horace M., "Private Affluence and Public Poverty," *Illinois Business Review,* Bureau of Economics and Research, University of Illinois, XVI (September, 1951).

Groves, Harold M., "Neutrality in Taxation," *National Tax Journal* (March, 1948).

Henderson, W. L., "A Progress Report on Post-War Tax Policy," *Business Topics* (Summer, 1964).

Holt, Charles and John P. Shelton, "The Lock-in Effect of the Capital Gains Tax," *National Tax Journal* (December, 1962).

Hugh-Jones, E. M., "The Voluntary Exchange Theory of Public Economy," *Quarterly Journal of Economics* (February, 1939).

Krutilla, J. V., "Welfare Aspects of Cost Benefit Analysis," *Journal of Political Economy* (June, 1961).

Mildner, Erwin and Ira Scott, "An Innovation in Fiscal Policy: The Swedish Investment Reserve System," *National Tax Journal,* XV, 3 (September, 1962).

Musgrave, R. A. and A. T. Peacock, *Classics in the Theory of Public Finance Introduction,* New York: Macmillan Co., 1958.

Saville, Lloyd, "Regional Contrasts in the Development of Local Public Finance," *National Tax Journal,* XV, 2 (June, 1962).

Simpson, Herbert D., "The Problem of Expanding Governmental Activities," *American Economic Review* (March, 1934).

SECTION V: LOCAL GOVERNMENT FINANCE

Bridges, Benjamin, Jr., "State and Local Inducements for Industry," *National Tax Journal,* XVIII, 1 (March, 1965).

Buchanan, James M., *The Public Finances,* New York: Richard D. Irwin, 1965.

Davies, David G., "An Empirical Test of Sales Tax Regressivity," *Journal of Political Economy* (February, 1959).

Ecker-Racz, L. Laszlo, "A Foreign Student Ponders the 1957 Census of Governments," *National Tax Journal* (June, 1959).

Elison, Larry M., *The Finances of Metropolitan Areas,* Ann Arbor: Michigan Legal Publications, The University of Michigan Law School, 1964.

Gardner, Wayland D., "Studies of the Tax System," *National Tax Journal* (December, 1961).

Hady, Thomas F., "The Incidence of the Personal Property Tax," *National Tax Journal* (December, 1962).

Howards, Irving, "Property Tax Limits in Illinois and Their Effect Upon Local Government," *National Tax Journal,* XVI, 3 (September, 1963).

Lubar, Robert and Charles E. Silberman, "The Taxes Closest to Home," *Fortune Magazine* (June, 1959).

Maxwell, J. A., *The Fiscal Aspects of Federalism in the United States,* Cambridge: Harvard University Press, 1946.

Maynes, E. Scott and James N. Morgan, "The Effective Rate of Real Estate Taxation: An Empirical Investigation," *Review of Economics and Statistics* (February, 1957).

Oster, C. V., "State Retail Sales Taxation in the United States," *Retail Sales Taxation,* Columbus: Ohio State University Press, 1957.

Quindry, Kenneth E. and Don M. Soule, "Adaptability of Local Governments Revenue to Economic Differentials in Kentucky," *National Tax Journal,* XVI, 3 (September, 1963).

Schaller, H. G., ed., *Public Expenditure Decisions in the Urban Community,* Washington: Resources of the Future, 1962.

Sigafoos, R. A., "Appraisal of the Municipal Income Tax, Its History and Problems," Public Administration Service, Chicago, Illinois, 1959.

Stephens, G. Ross and Henry J. Schmandt, "Revenue Patterns of Local Governments," *National Tax Journal,* XV, 4 (December, 1962).

Stewart, Charles T., Jr., "Migration Effects of Sales Tax Disparity," *Southern Economic Journal* (April, 1959).

Taylor, Milton C., "Local Income Taxes After Twenty-One Years," *National Tax Journal* (June, 1962).

℀ *Index*

CONTRIBUTORS

BUCHANAN, JAMES — Professor and Chairman of Department of Economics, University of Virginia

BURCK, GILBERT — Chief Business Staff Writer, *Fortune Magazine*, Chicago, Illinois

COLM, GERHARD — Chief Economist, National Planning Association, Washington, D.C.

DILLON, CONLEY H. — Professor of Government and Politics, University of Maryland

ENTHOVEN, ALAIN C. — Deputy Assistant Secretary of Defense, Washington, D.C.

HARRISS, C. LOWELL — Professor of Economics, Columbia University

JACOBY, NEIL — Professor of Business Economics and Policy, Dean of the Graduate School of Business Administration, University of California, Los Angeles

KENDRICK, JOHN W. — Professor of Economics, George Washington University, Washington, D.C.

KRUTILLA, JOHN V. — Economist, "Resources for the Future," Washington, D.C.

MARGOLIS, JULIUS — Professor of Business Administration, University of California, Stanford

MOOR, ROY EDWARD — Joint Economic Committee, Professor of Economics, George Washington University, Washington, D.C., Brookings Resident Professor of Economics

MUSGRAVE, RICHARD A. — Professor of Economics and Public Affairs, Princeton University

MUSHKIN, SELMA A. — Economist, U. S. Office of Education. Senior Analyst, Advisory Committee on Intergovernmental Relations, Washington, D.C.

ROLPH, EARL R. — Professor of Economics, University of California, Berkeley

SAMUELSON, PAUL A. — Professor of Economics, Massachusetts Institute of Technology

SIMONS, HENRY — Deceased, formerly Professor of Economics, University of Chicago